BLINDED BY THE LIGHT

By the same author

Better Than Working

BLINDED
by the
LIGHT

2001:
A Sunderland
Football Odyssey

RICHARD HAKIN

MAINSTREAM
PUBLISHING

EDINBURGH AND LONDON

First published in Great Britain in 2001 by
MAINSTREAM PUBLISHING COMPANY (EDINBURGH) LTD
7 Albany Street
Edinburgh EH1 3UG

ISBN 1 84018 508 2

A catalogue record for this book is available from the British Library

Typeset in Berkeley Book and Helvetica
Printed and bound in Great Britain
by Mackays of Chatham.

Acknowledgements

Ian Todd, Dave Errington, Richie Cockton and especially Tracey Hawkins of the Sunderland AFC Supporters' Association (London & Southern England Branch) for arranging trips to games despite everything that fate, flood and Railtrack could throw at them.

Tracey Hawkins of the London Branch for match tickets.

Dr Joan Beal, Director, The National Centre for English Cultural Tradition, University of Sheffield, for advice on the Wearside dialect.

Graeme Anderson of the *Sunderland Echo*, Rob Mason at Sunderland AFC and Alan Brett for help with the history of 'Mackem'.

Ann Round MA, BLitt for advice on the English Civil War.

Andy Sprott for Mission Impossible.

Deep Stottie for match tickets.

Mark and Jill Scrimshaw for bed and board.

Anna for editing, support, tea and sympathy.

TO ANNA

Contents

2000–01 Dramatis Personae

PETER REID
Sunderland manager, Scouser and inspiration for *The Dictionary of Modern Slang*.

KEVIN PHILLIPS
Aka 'Super Kev': Sunderland striker and legend. Ex-supermarket shelf-stacker who progressed to leading Premiership scorer for 1999–2000. But then how successful a shelf-stacker can you be when you're five foot seven?

NIALL QUINN
Sunderland strike partner to Phillips. Long-time servant of Arsenal, Man City and Ireland. One-time *Guardian* columnist and reportedly responsible for luxurious lifestyle of several bookies.

THOMAS SORENSON
Sunderland goalkeeper destined to become World's Number One. Danish hunk, whose appearance invariably prompts mass swooning on the terraces.

MICHAEL GRAY
Sunderland full-back and captain. Local lad. Hero.

ALEX RAE
Sunderland Scottish midfield terrier. Not a good combination with 'dark alley' and 'meeting'.

BOB MURRAY
Sunderland Chairman, visionary and saviour. Dragged the club up from the Second Division and personally responsible for Sunderland's move to the Stadium of Light. Knighthood pending.

BOBBY SAXTON
Sunderland assistant manager and scariest man on Wearside.

MACKEMS
Sunderland AFC (aka 'the Lads') and their supporters.
Colours: Red-and-white stripes.
Home ground: Stadium of Light (SOL).

GEORDIES/MAGS/THE TOON/THE SCUM/THE SKUNKS
Newcastle United FC and their supporters.
Colours: Black-and-white stripes.
Home ground: St James' Park/Sid James' Park/St Hotch Potch Park/ Skunk Park.

ALAN SHEARER
Newcastle striker and captain/wit and raconteur/ sparkling conversationalist.

BOBBY ROBSON
Newcastle manager and ex-manager of Fulham, Ipswich Town, England, PSV Eindhoven, Sporting Lisbon, Porto and Barcelona. Decent bloke – even for a Mag (although he does have an alarming propensity for wearing white ankle socks).

KEVIN KEEGAN
England Manager. Ex-manager of Newcastle and Fulham who somehow managed to walk away from both posts at crucial times with little public opprobrium. PR genius.

Travelling Light

*And her father was a Sunderland supporter, so there
was never much joy in that household*
– TERRY COLLIER, WHATEVER HAPPENED TO THE LIKELY LADS

Nnggghhhhaarrgghhiissssssyyarrrrrrrr!!!!!!

It's not a word you can say nor a sound you can make, but an emotion, raw, pure and visceral. An explosion of primal gut feeling, like the best sex, or the worst heartbreak, or the moment when you finally realise that a deceased loved one is never, ever coming back.

But for a goal?

Saturday, 5 May 1973. FA Cup final, Wembley Stadium. 3.31.31 p.m. Or thereabouts. The corner from Billy Hughes, the leap by Watson, then Halom chests it down to Ian Porterfield. He cushions the ball with his left thigh, spins and volleys in one blinding blur and . . .

Sunderland 1, Leeds United 0. Ha'way the Lads. Ee-i-adio, we've won the Cup.

That moment, that strike of a ball defined my eighteen years of life to that point and, to be honest, has continued to do so, as the greatest single instant of my existence. Yes, yes, I know it's sad, but such flashes are catalysts for the football fan – by which I mean the genuine fan, the kind who travels the country following Plymouth Argyle, as opposed to London stockbrokers who support Manchester United.

If the above event means absolutely nothing to you, then simply consider the facts. Leeds United were one of the best club sides in Europe, the defending Cup holders and the strongest favourites for decades to retain the trophy. Three months prior, Sunderland had been languishing near the bottom of the old Second Division. The last time they'd won the Cup, hell, won anything, had been 1937. If you wanted to waste a few quid the bookies would gladly oblige, quoting meaningless odds of 200–1. It could have been 2,000,000–1. I mean, come on – when, in any kind of contest, have you ever known a 200–1 outsider romp home?

It was a day of impossible romance, what one paper indeed called 'The Impossible Dream'. A team of no-hope Jacks felling the ultimate giant. Yet when Sunderland skipper Bobby Kerr, all five foot five of him, with a career twice blighted by broken legs, finally lifted the cup, I knew my days of following Sunderland were over. Not in the sense that I'd never support them again, despairing at their inadequacies, railing at their failures. I'd been doing that since I was twelve, six years of watching them play some of the worst football known to mankind, each season a frantic struggle against relegation that they finally lost in 1970. No, there was no way I was giving up on them.

But in that instant of euphoric celebration I recognised the zenith, realised that whatever they achieved from there on could never match this peak. They could win the World Club Championship while providing every player in a triumphant England World Cup side and it wouldn't be as good as this. God, what a relief. No longer to live in the desperate hope that some day my team would win something, a trophy to boast about, to make me proud. Done, dusted immortality assured. From now on I could relax, secure in the knowledge that they could no longer hurt me.

Which, oddly enough, coincided neatly with my leaving the North-east. While not exactly turning my back on my team, my life began to go down other avenues. I moved to Sheffield to attend university, student finances limiting trips home for games. On graduating with a degree in accountancy, I went into theatre stage management, defying logic, common sense and a lucrative career. Working six days and evenings a week left little time for anything, never mind a football team. Then into the film industry as a camera assistant, living in London but travelling the world making documentaries. Twelve years on, watching Sunderland had become a fond but distant memory. And then the final act, emigration to New Zealand – hell of a trek for a home game.

1997, back in England. What on earth's a Premiership? And Division One is now Division Two? Except that Two is Three. The game has not only moved on while I've been away but transmogrified into a totally alien being, of foreign players, all-seater stadiums and money, money, money. Twenty-five quid to get in? Players on forty grand a week? Hmm, Toto, I've a feeling we're not in Kansas any more.

Ah, but Sunderland have just been relegated, so some things haven't changed.

The Stadium of What?!!

The club have just bid farewell to their (and my) home at Roker Park, and are now entrenched in the outrageously named Stadium Of Light. Pretentious? Moi? The original 'Estadio Da Luz' is the long-time abode of Benfica FC in Lisbon. Flashy Latinos can get away with names like that, but a bunch of Geordies? (Or, to be accurate, as I later discover, 'Mackems' – since when was I a Mackem?) Apparently Sunderland Chairman Bob Murray justified the name as a tribute to the miners of Wearmouth Colliery, on whose abandoned site the stadium was built, the moniker supposedly embodying the spirit of the Davy lamp. Really? Nothing whatsoever to do with Monty Python? In a sketch from the 1970s, an archetypal television football reporter, all sheepskin jacket and ice-cream microphone, earnestly addresses the camera. 'I'm speaking to you from the Stadium of Light, Jarrow.' So there you have it. But Bob Murray will deny it to his grave.

I have to go.

BLOODY HELL!!!

This is not a football ground, it's a spaceship. A blaze of brilliant red, forty-two thousand seats, defiant in their vibrancy, encompass the world's biggest and greenest snooker baize. Above the soaring terraces an unbroken white canopy sweeps round in a perfect oval. In a region where football has often been described as religion, this is a cathedral of staggering impact. I take my seat, or rather I'm shown to my seat by a uniformed steward. At Roker Park you chose your spot from your very first visit and stayed there ever after. Everyone knew and respected everyone else's little patch of concrete. I half expect the steward to take my drinks order. It's football, Jim, but not as we know it.

Yet as three o'clock approaches the old tingle starts. I'd forgotten it was like this. Nerves growing, stomach tightening. It's like meeting an old lover, a passionate relationship that has peaked and dimmed but still burns bright.

Five to three. Suddenly Prokofiev's 'Romeo and Juliet' blasts from the PA, then a surging rock track, then fireworks, then the entrance of the gladiators. Oh my God, what is this? A roar, no, a scream erupts around the ground. Yes, yes, I remember now. My team, my Lads. Ha'way the Lads!! Ha'way y'buggers!!

It's hopeless. I'm hooked. The world's greatest game, the world's greatest drug.

That year we miss promotion by a whisker in the most dramatic play-off final ever, but in '99 we cruise it, champions supreme with a record tally of points.

Back in Division One – sorry, the Premiership. Phillips and Quinn on the rampage, third in the table by Christmas, tickets impossible to get. Legendary home games against Man United, Newcastle and especially Chelsea, where the crowd reaction to Phillips' second goal in a 4–1 rout is described by *The Guardian* as 'a collective scream verging on the sexual'.

The Millennium season beckons. I've had seasons where I've attended every home game but never every game, league and cup, home and away. It seems the perfect Millennium project, cheaper than the Dome (just) but a lot more enjoyable. But the logistics are daunting. I'm living in London and each of the nineteen home games (not including cup matches) will involve a round trip of 564 miles. That's . . . 10,716 miles! Then the away games, a breeze at a mere . . . 4,971. Total: 15,687 miles. Auckland was only 12,000.

And there's the problem of tickets. A season ticket will guarantee me all the home games, but tickets for away matches are strictly limited. Sunderland has always boasted a passionate away support (must be all that Viking heritage and a genetic drive to conquer new lands) and tickets are allocated on the strict basis of loyalty points. Available only to season ticket holders, a point is granted for every away game attended in the previous two seasons. There are thirty-six thousand season ticket holders, yet the allocation of tickets never exceeds three thousand. Some hardcore supporters will have amassed around forty points over the previous two seasons. By comparison, I'm Norway in the Eurovision Song Contest. I need a cunning plan.

I discover the London and Southern England Branch of the Sunderland AFC Supporters' Association. A fraternal organisation for ex-pat Mackems (don't worry, I'll explain 'Mackem' later on), the Branch organises trips to all Sunderland matches but, more importantly, is also awarded a small number of tickets for each away game to distribute among its members. With some seven hundred faithful in the Branch, the odds still seem pretty long, but better than me versus thirty-six thousand. But I'll need to raise my profile pretty quickly if I'm to have any shot at the tickets.

The Branch has a football team. You can judge how seriously they take the game from the fact that they call themselves 'The Pink Flamingos'. When I ask the origin of the name, I'm greeted with a variety of knowing but secretive looks among team members. They make the Masons look like the Brownies. I can only await the first match, but I'm in.

The first game of the season approaches. A home match against Arsenal. I've got my season ticket, my rail ticket, my replica shirt. Cry God for Harry, England and Kevin Phillips.

Sunderland – the final frontier.

Arsenal (home) – Premier League

Mr Wenger is a very intelligent man and entitled
to his opinion. I just think it's a load of crap
– SUNDERLAND MANAGER, PETER REID

6.00 a.m., Saturday, 18 August. London – and it's pouring. Well of course it is, it's August. Ahead of me is a seventeen-hour day, five hundred and sixty-four miles of travel and an outlay of about sixty pounds – and all for ninety minutes of football, the highlights of which will probably be featured on *Match of the Day*. The enormity of what I am about to undertake is suddenly overwhelming, an expensive and exhausting slog to the far-flung corners of the Premiership. Now that I've pledged to this crusade, now that I have to do it, there's a definite fall-off in the joy factor.

At King's Cross I meet up with the London Supporters' Branch for the eight o'clock train. For a collection of supposed ex-pat north-easterners there's a distinct mixture of accents, with more than a few strains of London and Essex. I shouldn't begrudge a southerner the right to exercise their good judgement by supporting my team, but I grew up in the simple and touching belief that you backed your local team, good or bad, through fair wind and foul. Then some bugger invented the wheel and now the whole of Asia supports Man United.

My sense of self-grandeur in my own quest is quickly deflated on realising that several here attend every Sunderland game as a matter of course, often taking in reserve matches as well. Humph. The founder of the Branch, Ian Todd, seems as near as dammit a full-time football fan, going not only to every Sunderland game but also to every England match, home and away, and, just to prevent the onset of boredom, visiting every League ground in the country. I hastily revise my plan of casually hinting my intent in the hope of eliciting gasps of admiration. The most likely reaction would be a bemused 'Aye, and . . .?'

On-board we settle down for the three-hour journey to Newcastle. It's business as usual among the regulars, albeit infused with the frisson of a new schedule. For the football fan, hope springs eternal on the first day of every season. No matter how disastrous the previous year, whatever humiliations were endured, that was then and this is now, a new dawn where all is possible. For most, of course, such hopes will end in the agony of a narrowly missed championship or promotion, the tears of relegation or, worse, finishing mid-table, the damning indictment of a dull team. Winning can evoke admiration, relegation genuine sympathy, but mid-table safety is boring. Sunderland generally engage in desperate encounters with promotion or relegation, invariably determined by the last game of the season, a yo-yo phenomenon that has bred a hardy fatalism among the supporters. But then following Sunderland and common sense have never had much in common.

Most fans accept the cyclical nature of football – there's always next week, next month, next season, when losses can be reversed and pride restored. Unless, of course, you happen to be Man United, whose supporters' stupor is regularly maintained by the tedium of winning.

There are several Arsenal fans in the carriage. Back in the '70s, having rival supporters in the same vicinity was a cue to light the blue touchpaper, but alongside the gentrification of football there seems to have been a general condemnation of past excesses. Sure the Neanderthals still exist, but with greater match security even the knuckleheads realise that they have to keep their rumbles discreet, now bizarrely arranging fights away from the grounds by cellphone and internet. Beats me how they use either without an opposable thumb.

Personally I don't mind people supporting other teams (be a bit boring if the entire nation followed Scunthorpe – and just think of the ticket hassle) but I genuinely don't understand it. How can they possibly feel the same passion for their club as I do for mine?

Several opposing fans greet each other as old mates. There's the inevitable rival banter and catching up on tales since previous encounters. Perversely there's a degree of one-upmanship in how dismissive you can be of your own team's prospects, an acknowledged courtesy that involves you ridiculing your lot and indulging in bouts of self-mockery if the opposition will do likewise. This allows a healthy critique of both sides while avoiding any unpleasantness. Nobody believes it, of course, all are secretly passionate about their respective heroes, but it evokes a gallant charm with an entertaining degree of self-deprecation. The Gunners bemoan the recent loss of stars Petit and Overmars while Sunderland fans point to a disastrous pre-season tour of

France and Holland, where the team managed to lose every match except an epic tie against Dutch amateur part-timers ASV Apeldoornse Boys. Quite. An Arsenal fan mentions that their new foreign imports have been taking lessons in English as a foreign language. 'Not much use in Sunderland.'

Privately I fear we're going to get 'well turned over', as the saying goes. Arsenal have an embarrassment of riches in all departments, while Sunderland are hampered by several pre-season injuries. One of the more bizarre casualties concerns midfielder Alex Rae. A 'robust' player, he'd been suspended for three games the previous season for elbowing a player in the face. On his first match back, Sunderland's final game of the season, he did exactly the same, this time earning the four-match ban which was officially preventing him from playing today. Yet his suspension had been made irrelevant when, in pre-season training, he was injured in what manager Peter Reid described as 'a bit of a freak accident'. From which I can only deduce that he'd finally managed to elbow himself in the face.

Even with a full team we'd be struggling, the memory of last season's 4–1 drubbing at Highbury all too fresh. As ever, our hopes lie with strike pair Niall Quinn and Kevin Phillips, Sunderland's answer to Batman and Robin. Phillips was one of few English players to emerge with any credit from Euro 2000, largely on the basis that he never played. But then why would Kevin Keegan want to pick the Premiership's leading scorer? That would be just plain stupid.

Keegan is supposed to be attending today's game to open the new extension to the North Stand. I'm sure he'll be warmly received, particularly given his strong past links with Newcastle United and an unswerving devotion bordering on boy-band girly fan worship of Geordie striker Alan Shearer. But to be fair, Shearer was absolutely magnificent in Euro 2000 and will be sorely missed from the England line-up . . . One Sunderland fan relates how he recently caught Shearer and several Newcastle players trapped inside a pre-season training ground with apparently no key to the locked enclosure, forcing Big Al et al. to yell for help while vainly trying to pull the fence down. 'And Brenda didn't have the bloody camera! I was saying, "Where's the bloody camera?" I could have got that! Been worth a fortune! But she didn't have the bloody camera!'

Oh Brenda, why didn't you have the bloody camera?

We arrive in Newcastle and board the local service for the twelve-mile journey to Sunderland. The regional train company has obviously bought a job lot of those funicular trains that wind their way up the mountains of South America. Most of the crowded, rattling journey is spent contemplating a neighbour's elbow or armpit, while trying not to dwell on what might laughingly be referred to as 'emergency procedures'.

Around the stadium a market has sprung up for the sale of child footballers. Several large green plastic cages contain kids displaying their soccer skills. What a brilliant idea, tackling both juvenile crime and potential unemployment. But no, it's a Nike Skills Day, a cheap way for Sunderland to spot any promising talent and for Nike to sell more plimsolls. I see a couple of kids with potential but you'd have to feed them and take them out for walks 'n' stuff, so I head off into the stadium.

Inside the new North Stand extension it's the first day at school. Slightly bewildered fans clutching shiny new season tickets wander aimlessly around the stark grey concrete passages, as if looking for a prefect to tell them in which class Miss Hope is teaching Form 4B. Meanwhile equally bewildered stewards make a pretence at holding important conversations with each other to avoid admitting that they haven't a clue either. All I know is that my seat's somewhere up high.

After several base camps, the sherpas start whinging (you can't get the staff) and I tackle the final stretch alone. Removing my oxygen mask, I take in the full glory of the stadium. I can just see the pitch through the clouds below. My seat's a touch higher than I expected. And steep! Fortunately I'll only be sitting here for every game this season.

I eagerly await the arrival of brave Sir Kevin to officially open the new stand. But Heavens to Betsy, Kevin doesn't show! Shurely shome mishtake. I only hope nothing unfortunate has befallen him. Otherwise he would certainly be here, enjoying ribald banter with the good-natured crowd while he explains his reasons for not picking local hero Phillips in an otherwise abject England team.

Five to three. The Prokofiev blasts out and the packed stadium breaks into a roar of hope and expectation. The fireworks explode and through the smoke come the teams, bright shirt colours clashing sharply with the impossibly green pitch.

For Sunderland the only new face is central defender Stanislav Varga, a Slovakian international whose Byronic profile and dark flowing hair make him look like a refugee from the Gypsy Kings. The Arsenal thoroughbreds stroll through the pre-match kickabout with an air of confident mastery, impatient to get on with the task of winning the Premiership. Christ, they've left Bergkamp on the bench! Yet they still boast Henry, Vieira, Kanu, Parlour, Grimandi. Love may be blind but we could get slaughtered here.

The game starts and with his first touch Varga delivers one of the best Sunderland passes I've ever seen, a laser-guided fifty-five-yard effort that splits the Arsenal defence in two. Then a brilliant tackle. Then another. The crowd is ecstatic; Reidy's got another bloody bargain.

Arsenal surge forward, Vieira cutting a swathe through the Sunderland midfield with runs that have the home players scampering back, snapping at his heels like demented Jack Russells. Vieira's interpassing with Silvinho and Henry threatens to tear the Sunderland defence apart but Varga stands firm, keeping Arsenal at bay almost single-handed.

Finally an Arsenal chance. Parlour's in open space with an open net, but he elects instead to pass to his own supporters behind the goal. Then he muffs another. Perhaps the gods are smiling on us today.

Sunderland full-back Makin keeps Kanu under wraps with marking so tight that he must have seen the washing instructions inside his shorts. And Varga keeps performing miracles. We survive to half-time but home keeper Sorenson is injured and the impressively named substitute Jurgen Macho will be making a deep-end debut.

Arsenal continue pressing in the second half. Then after fifty-three minutes there's a Sunderland breakaway, a cross to Quinn, Seaman flounders and YES YES YES!!! One–nil.

Arsenal bring on Bergkamp to join Henry and Kanu up front. What a line-up. Twice Kanu goes close, Parlour blasts the side netting while Macho foils Henry with a late dive.

The final fifteen minutes, and it's all Arsenal and it's all agony. Sunderland players dive in with last-ditch tackles. It's not pretty, it's not skilful, but it's gutsy, effective and exhilarating. The crowd are screaming for the final whistle and then, in the last minute, Vieira is sent off for elbowing Sunderland's Williams. All hell breaks loose, the Arsenal players crowding the referee with snarling faces, but all for naught. We hold on. We've done it, we've done it. Arsenal manager Wenger accuses Williams of shamming the injury that got Vieira sent off, to which Reid replies with his customary candour.

The statistics confirm Arsenal's dominance, nine shots on goal to Sunderland's one. We should have lost about 5–1. We've lucked it and we know it – which makes the triumph even sweeter. True fans don't go in for that bollocks about wanting a good victory well won. Winning is all that matters, three points is three points and We Don't Care.

Saturday, 18 August 2000
SUNDERLAND 1   ARSENAL 0
(Quinn 53)

PLAYED	TRAVELLED	SPENT	POSITION	STATE OF MIND
1	564 miles	£60.60	What, after one game?!	Sheer relief

Manchester City (away) – Premier League

Peter Reid – the only man to spell 'tea' with two 'f's
– LEFT-LUGGAGE ATTENDANT, NEWCASTLE STATION

'And God saw everything that He had made, and behold, it was very good.'

And then He spotted Manchester.

Oh well, we all make mistakes.

Despite years of urban regeneration programmes, Manchester continues to resemble a bad hangover. A defiantly dull landscape of wasteland, old factories and council estates screams out like a belligerent teenager: 'I'll take your dosh, pal, but I'm not fookin' changin'.' I'm sure there are pleasant parts of the city, but the local council must scurry them away whenever I visit, like Auntie Ethel hiding the china when the kids come round. Moss Side in particular is the devil spawn of the brood. You can spot the attempts to brighten the place up in the odd patch of green, its newly planted grass and saplings, laughably incongruous, the posh kid on his first day at comprehensive. But you just know that in about six months he'll be skiving off and mugging old ladies and Manchester will have won again.

It's a mid-week away game so I've managed to get a ticket, but Sunderland still sell out their allocation for a trip that will see no one get home before the small hours. The match will finish after the last train back to London, so the Supporters' Branch hire a coach for the four hundred-mile round trip. We all meet at Ye Olde Swiss Cottage pub, the unofficial headquarters of the Branch, mine host being a lifelong ex-pat supporter. I recognise a few faces from Saturday's game and am gradually welcomed into the fold. Mid-week away matches are always a true test of faith and my appearance speaks well of my allegiance.

Outside the pub, our driver mooches around, waiting for the off. He's about fifty going on miserable, his face the definition of 'lugubrious'. British comedies of the '60s always seemed to feature the archetypal long-faced character as the put-upon, hen-pecked husband. And here he was, in glorious monochrome.

The journey descends into the minutiae of common lore from which I am at present excluded. Unfamiliar nicknames, in-jokes and references to past trips emphasise my new status, and I can only sit quietly and acquire my own stock of knowledge. There's already talk of the first game in November against Newcastle, arch-enemies and our nemesis since 1898. The rivalry between the two sets of supporters could never be described as healthy or friendly. Only recently have away supporters been allowed to attend the games once more, because of past troubles. Last year Sunderland bussed 700 fans into Newcastle under police escort. I start to have mixed feelings about going, even if I can get a ticket. I think I may need a Plan B – and probably C.

One aspect of travelling with the Branch soon becomes evident: the obligatory pre-match visit to the pub. It's a ritual prevalent throughout football but particularly in the North-east, so our schedule has to incorporate a fuel stop. But rather than risk the dubious hospitality of the Man City fans by drinking around the ground itself, we opt for stopping off at Macclesfield and then going straight to the match. Except that our driver misses Macclesfield. Twice. To miss it once might be regarded as a misfortune, to miss it twice . . .

We arrive at Lancashire Aero Club. To be honest, no one on the coach seems particularly bothered that our schedule has just flown away. Far more pressing is the need for a pint at the nearby pub. It's at this point that I have to confess the innermost shame of my Northern soul: I . . . I . . . I'm not much of a drinker. There, I've said it, I've finally come out of the lounge bar. Alcohol tends to have a bizarre effect on me – I become witty and interesting. So naturally I avoid it wherever possible.

Of greater interest is the action on the airfield. It is a small aerodrome, the kind that featured in British films about the RAF during World War II, where chaps would lounge around on deckchairs waiting for scramble and brag about recent sorties. 'Pranged a one-oh-nine then tallied home to Blighty in time for cha. How about you, Bertie, old boy?' The derring-do descendants of those former warriors are still battling the skies, but now in craft laughably devoid of all but the most basic essentials. Microlights buzz the gathering dusk like gnats on steroids, completing practice circuits before descending to land, then at the last second hitting the throttle and soaring off for another lap. The appeal of trusting my life to a lawnmower slung beneath a kite has always eluded me, so I suppose I wouldn't have been much of a Spitfire pilot. Probably more the cheery Geordie batman, amusing the officer chaps with his quirky tones.

By now it's about half-six and nobody has emerged from the pub. With the game starting at half-seven we seemed to be cutting it a bit fine, given the likely heavy match traffic. I wander over to the driver.

'What time do we need to leave?'

'Well, whenever they tell me, sir.'

I hate it when people call me 'sir'. Apart from the fact that it makes me feel ancient, I'm also uncomfortable at the forced obsequiousness. And I had been hoping for a more decisive reply, given that the driver is supposed to be getting us there on time.

I wander into the bar and find everyone in relaxed mid-pint mode. Obviously I was panicking unnecessarily and after about ten minutes we all troop back to the bus.

We hit the traffic.

Then the driver doesn't know the way to the ground. Now call me old-fashioned, but having hired a coach for the specific and sole purpose of going to a football match, you'd think the driver would have checked how to get there. Fortunately one of the group can remember the route from past visits and guides the driver as we inch our way through the traffic and the complex one-way system. We arrive at five minutes to kick-off. And there was me thinking we weren't going to make it in time.

As we rush towards the ground, a shiny-headed, wild-eyed Sunderland skinhead is ranting at whoever will listen. 'Who wants a fight then? Come on, who wants a fuckin' fight?' Obviously his idea of the pre-match kickabout. Bemused City fans walk by but noticeably avoid eye contact and my brother-in-arms, whom I'd prefer to keep at arm's length, is left frustrated at the lack of challengers. He clearly just wants to fight for the sheer fun, bravado and excitement of it, something past administrators and authorities failed to grasp when trying to tackle violence at games. They'd blame unemployment or social deprivation, or make pleas for restraint and responsibility, all completely useless for a bunch of lads fuelled by beer and testosterone and itching for a scrap. It was only when the psychologists were booted out and replaced by more police, more stewards, all-seater stadiums and CCTV that some sanity was established.

Two seasons ago City were in Division Two and I'm afraid the ground still looks it. We're sitting on a temporary stand made of scaffolding and planks and exposed to the elements. A vigorous goal celebration would probably send it tumbling, so if we score we'll have to just clap politely. Welcome to the Premiership, City. A guy in front of me takes it all in with ironic disdain. 'Top seat, top stand.'

After Saturday's win we're brashly confident about beating a City side that got tonked 4–0 by fellow newcomers Charlton. And with the other promotion team, Ipswich, for our next match, we could be looking at full points after three games. So being 1–0 down after three minutes is not part of the plan.

Sunderland, frankly, are bloody awful. Where on Saturday our defence was organised and solid, now it creaks and groans like a wedding-night bedpost. Twice City come close before scoring again after twenty minutes. The young guy next to me calls out in despair, 'This is the worst I've ever seen them.' He obviously wasn't at last season's game against Coventry, 3–0 down after eighteen minutes. I still wake up at nights, sweating.

City's star player is Paulo Wanchope, a tall, awkward, gangling Costa Rican who regularly seems to stumble over the ball, yet still manages to beat his opponent. At times you think he'd struggle to get into a pub team, at others he's scoring goals for fun. And wouldn't you know it, tonight he's on fire.

Another Wanchope near miss but we hang on until half-time. Several Sunderland players look like they'd rather stay on the pitch than face their manager's team-talk. For those of you unfamiliar with Peter Reid's – oh, how can I put it – 'idiosyncratic phraseology', I'll digress at this point. An unashamedly fast-talking, blunt-speaking Scouser, Reid first came to wider public notice – or notoriety – during the television programme *Premier Passions*. A fly-on-the-wall documentary series, it followed Sunderland throughout their 1996–97 campaign which ended, typically, in last-day-of-the-season relegation. But the lingering image was that of Reid repeatedly lambasting his players during half-time. I think he entered the *Guinness Book of Records* for the most obscenities uttered during conversational speech. He peaked at thirteen 'fooks' a minute. That's one every four-and-a-half seconds. Do not try this at home.

And then there's Bobby Saxton.

I think the only time I caught Reid blushing on the programme was when his Yorkshire assistant manager decided to weigh in with his own opinions on how to deal with the opposition: 'Just get up their fuckin' arses, man.'

If the pair ever wanted to quit football, I'm sure they could make a comfortable living as motivational speakers on the corporate sales circuit.

'Just break their fookin' doors in and get their fookin' signatures on the fookin' contract.'

'Aye, brek their fuckin' arms if you have to, but if yer fuckin' figures aren't up by 10 per cent, y' know where I'll be stickin' yer fuckin' Mondeo.'

The second half starts and as if we don't have enough problems in defence, Varga, our man of the match against Arsenal, is taken off injured after just two minutes. It looks like it's going to be a long trip back. But whatever Reidy said seems to have worked and we start playing. We've got more of the ball, Phillips goes close then finally Quinny heads one in after twenty minutes. Like flicking a switch, the confidence is back and now we're knocking it about like Brazil. Three minutes later Phillips takes a cross on his chest and volleys into the top corner. The temporary stand shudders in an explosion of relief. We're back, we can win this bastard.

Then, typical Sunderland, we stop playing, as if the players feel they've done all they need to for tonight. From having the game in our grasp we let it go, City come back and Wanchope scores two late goals for a comfortable 4–2 win.

If you do something often enough, you're supposed to get used to it. God knows how many times I've seen Sunderland lose and, fook, it still hurts.

We slope out of the ground. I nip into the toilet where a guy is relieving himself while recounting the match to someone on his cellphone. I think the concept of the videophone has some way to go.

Back on the coach all is quiet as we drive along anonymous streets. We stop in traffic, some fifty yards back from a junction. I look out to my left and suddenly a young kid, maybe sixteen and whippet-thin, sprints by. And I mean sprints. He'd be looking back at Greene, Lewis, the lot of them. Then another guy, older, runs by. The scene has the feel of two mates larking around until a third runner appears. He's wielding a bottle. Then two more guys. The kid is black, the others white. The white guys are wearing Sunderland shirts.

There's a racism league table that lists football clubs according to the proportion of non-white fans among their supporters. Sunderland are invariably top or near the top. It is possible to look around a packed stadium and not see a single non-white face. That in itself doesn't imply that the supporters are racist and it can partially be explained by the lack of significant immigration in the North-east. But while older attitudes have certainly changed, probably helped by Sunderland's several black players over the years, there is still an undercurrent fuelled by a small hardcore of morons. The club has instigated various anti-racism measures and campaigns to tackle the problem but still it lingers, like an obnoxious party guest that no one knows how to eject.

If I'd had a cellphone I could have called the police, but I have no idea where we are. At the junction the kid turns left, his pursuers follow. The coach moves off but when we reach the junction all have disappeared. It's over in seconds.

I don't know why they were chasing him. Maybe he was a naive City fan who'd unwisely taunted a Sunderland crowd drowning their sorrows. Maybe he accidentally bumped into them while passing. Or maybe it was just a case of wrong place, wrong time. It often doesn't take much. But as they sped off into the darkness, the abiding impression was of a bunch of rednecks chasing a young black kid into the Alabama night.

Wednesday, 23 August 2000

MANCHESTER CITY 4   SUNDERLAND 2
(Haaland 22, Wanchope 3, 78, 89)   (Quinn 64, Phillips 67)

PLAYED	TRAVELLED	SPENT	POSITION	STATE OF MIND
2	937 miles	£105.20	Still meaningless	Depressed

Ipswich Town (away) – Premier League

Ipswich are shite, man – it's just that we're shiter
– SUNDERLAND FAN

Going to a game at Ipswich is a bit like visiting your granny's for tea: it's pleasant, relaxed and unlikely to end in a punch-up. Going to a derby match at Newcastle is more like a day trip to Hades. But Ipswich is easy – well, easy if you can fathom the complexities of the new privatised rail system. When people ask me what changes I've noticed about Britain since returning from New Zealand, it's the mundane, everyday aspects that catch the eye rather than the broader issues. While the desperate hopelessness of the Thatcher years has gone, there's still the same weary cynicism that pervaded life in Britain before I left. But all these new rail, phone and power companies! Now, trying to work out the cheapest way to make a call, buy a train ticket or turn the oven on has become a Byzantine exercise of comparisons. Stephen Hawking may have mastered the mysteries of time and the universe but I bet he's paying too much for his electricity.

So a simple day return to Ipswich offers a choice between two companies, each with a baffling array of fare options that vary according to day of travel, time of travel and whether I want to go via Edinburgh. I choose blindly, knowing with irritating certainty that I've picked the most expensive.

On the train I'm sitting near a group of Sunderland fans that includes one teenage girl, her father and his mate. It seems that the girl has broken the North-east's most sacred code: going out with someone from 'that other lot'. The father's friend is at a loss to understand. 'Y'knaa you're your dad's pride and joy, yet you're gannin oot with a Scum?'

At which point Dad feels obliged to intervene with fatherly understanding. 'Aye, she hates Newcastle but she luvs her Darren.'

You know, I think there could be a nice little story in that. Though I'm not too sure about calling the hero 'Darren'. Robbie, perhaps. And the girl . . . Julia? Hmm, two clubs, both alike in dignity . . .

Ipswich has a clean, friendly, if rather dull persona. The ground is an easy walk from the station, as opposed to places like Coventry which involve a half-hour hike through some decidedly dodgy backstreets. Portman Road is a classic pre-Premiership Division One ground, OK in itself, but the sight-obscuring stanchions and corrugated roofing are light years away from Sunderland's own Light Fantastic. Since acquiring their new home, Sunderland fans have developed a confident superiority. Dismissive of all other stadiums, they now greet every ground with a ditty to the tune of 'When The Saints Go Marching In':

> My garden shed
> Is bigger than this
> My garden shed is bigger than this.
> It's got a door and a window
> My garden shed is bigger than this.

OK, so it ain't Cole Porter, but it usually raises a smile. And while the Blues' stadium may be nothing special, at least the pitch is in good nick – but then you'd expect that with a farming community.

Since their glory days under Bobby Robson in the '70s and early '80s, Ipswich are one of a number of sides that have flirted with the top division without being able to establish a firm foothold. The formation of the Premiership in 1992 caught them napping, the big money passed them by and they were relegated in 1995. Only now, after several near-misses, have they finally managed to scramble their way back into the top flight. Even despite our abysmal display against Man City, we're pretty confident about taking today's game.

There's a good atmosphere around the ground. Unlike Leeds or Newcastle, there's no history of trouble between the two clubs. Both sets of fans accept that while they won't be challenging for the title, at least they can enjoy the glow of being back in the Premiership after too many years scrabbling around in the lower division. The Sunderland fans are, as ever, numerous, loud and boisterous, enjoying the day out. Quite often away fans can make more noise than the home contingent, given the concentration of the more committed travelling supporters compared to the disparate array of locals of varying degrees of passion. Hence when the Mackems fail to get a response from the Ipswich crowd to a bout of challenging taunts, they follow up with their own chants of 'Ipswich' – in high-pitched falsetto.

With Sunderland yet to hit their straps and Ipswich the new boys from Division One, you know the football's not going to be top drawer, but perversely there should be enough mistakes to make it interesting. And as soon as Sunderland start playing I'm proved horribly right.

Our passing is terrible and if in doubt, bang the long ball to Quinn, a tactic perhaps still unknown among one or two tribes in the rainforest but blindingly obvious to everyone else. Our midfield is doing nothing and Don Hutchison, our new signing hailed as the classy creator we need, is failing to make an impression. Sunderland supporters are quick to criticise all but the most favoured of players and Hutchison is anything but, having committed the cardinal sin of being born in Gateshead, i.e. as near as dammit a Mag. Furthermore, his languid style gives an impression of laziness, one quality that North-east fans can never accept in a player, however talented. With us playing so badly, Hutch gets the worst of the abuse. 'He's Scum, he's a cheat, he does nowt, man!'

And when yet another pass goes astray: 'Who was that to? Me?'

Not that Ipswich are much better, but having managed a good draw against Man United and with the Premiership still a novelty, they're being spared by the crowd. Also their fans lack the bigoted passion of the Mackems, who are either adoring or venomous. Sunderland are only ever magic or shite. And today we're shite, sparking the fierce rage of a love betrayed.

The first half is a mess of bad passes and squandered chances. Quinn is kept under wraps by the wonderfully named Titus Bramble, a nineteen-year-old defender presumably signed from Thomas Hardy United. Meanwhile Phillips' game is summed up by his chipping the ball over the bar with only the goalkeeper to beat.

The second half is little better, but Ipswich start to threaten more. After seven minutes they score, which is not entirely unpredictable, but the manner certainly is. Bramble robs Phillips of the ball in his own half, runs seventy yards unopposed and slots home from ten yards. It's one of those goal-of-the-month strikes you can do little about.

With their heads up, Ipswich surge forward, hit the bar among several near-misses and have a goal disallowed. We're just praying for the end. When the announcement is made of an additional two minutes to be played, a Sunderland fan sums up our performance: 'You could add another fuckin' ninety and we still wouldn't score.'

So instead of three wins out of three, it's now just one from three, and that we only managed by the skin of our teeth. But Peter Reid says there's no panic.

He said much the same last year as we entered a twelve-match run without a win.

Saturday, 26 august 2000

IPSWICH TOWN 1   SUNDERLAND 0

(Bramble 52)

PLAYED	TRAVELLED	SPENT	POSITION	STATE OF MIND
3	1,100 miles	£151.30	15th	Weary acceptance of reality

West Ham United (home) – Premier League

And they all lived happily ever after in
Goalmouth Close . . .

It's the first evening home game of the season. The last train back to London leaves at eight o'clock so I'm going to have to stay overnight at a guest house. The traditional area for B&B in Sunderland is down on the sea-front at Roker, Sunderland's answer to the Côte d'Azure. Seaside resorts out of season can be depressing, but Roker manages a homely charm. About a mile from the anonymous city centre, the promenade displays an array of cheerful if faded small hotels and guesthouses. The accommodation list provided by the Tourist Office has the usual plethora of indecipherable hieroglyphics to indicate the facilities provided by each establishment. Scanning it brings home to me what a shallow and meaningless existence I lead. To fully appreciate some of these places, I need to acquire a wrinkled shirt, three children and an Airedale Terrier. And what in a Roker guesthouse passes for 'Leisure Facilities'?

I take pot luck and ring a name at random. The proprietor couldn't be more helpful and is soon telling me about taxis, directions and the free bus service to the match. I ask about breakfast: 'Fruit juice, cereal, toast and marmalade with full English breakfast of eggs, bacon, sausage, beans, tomato, fried bread, mushrooms, hash browns and black puddin'.'

I can feel my arteries breaking out in a cold sweat. 'Er, do you cater for vegetarians?'

'Oh aye – we leave off the black puddin'.'

At Newcastle, I take the afternoon train to Sunderland but get off at Seaburn. It's about a mile from Roker but the sun's out and it's a pleasant walk to the seafront. Away from the promenade, Roker has the appearance of a small Scottish town, with tidy rows of neat, low cottages and immaculate gardens. The odd large house with a dovecote and crenellated walls adds eccentricity and all in all, it's a real charmer. I mean, how could you not like a place that boasts a pet-grooming shop called 'Millionhairs' and a 'foundation garments emporium' named 'Sadie The Bra Lady'?

The seafront is clean and fresh with a long, wide and pristine beach. Even with autumn approaching, the sands and shoreline are busy with swimmers, canoeists and the inevitable kids in red-and-white shirts kicking a ball around. Along the promenade is a monument to local lad and eighth-century historian Abbot 'The Venerable' Bede (' . . . and in the blue corner, Friar "Say Your Prayers" Cuthbert'). In his *Ecclesiastical History of England*, Bede wrote of the key roles played by the early Danish settlers, thereby paving the way for the eventual transfer of Tommy Sorenson.

At the guesthouse the owner is whippet-thin and wiry. He must skip breakfast. The bedroom is spacious and bright, and the large bay window looks out on to the seafront. Given the en suite bathroom and the included breakfast, the room rate is ridiculously cheap, and I have to check the calendar to see if I've time-warped back to the '70s.

The bedside table offers the usual collection of leaflets and brochures promoting local attractions. And what attractions! 'Visit Hartlepool Power Station! It's Fun! It's Exciting! It's Radioactive!' Then there's 'Sunderland – City For The New Millennium!', extolling plans for a new arts complex, shopping centre and transport system. It's all very commendable but phrases such as 'a dynamic city with a thriving centre' make it sound a bit like 'Sheffield – City On The Move!' at the start of *The Full Monty*.

Being in Roker I have to visit Roker Park, Sunderland's old ground. I know the stadium's been demolished and replaced by a housing estate, but I can't believe there's nothing left at all of the old place. I start walking up from the seafront and realise that, without thinking, I'm choosing the same route I used to take twenty years earlier. It's a common trait among home supporters at any ground. There may be many ways to approach a stadium but the first one you experience tends to be the one you stick with. Gradually you become aware of shorter or quicker alternatives but you stay faithful to that first true path. My road ran parallel to another lane separated by just twenty yards of wasteground, but never once did I consider going that way. You'd see the same faces across the divide at every game, but no one ever crossed over. And nor do I today.

I turn the final corner and . . . it's a genuinely shocking moment, a stomach punch to the senses. When you've turned the same corner and seen the same scene for years on end, to be suddenly confronted by an entirely different picture is unnerving and disturbing. The newsagent, pie shop and pub are still there, but the towering wall of the Roker End is now an array of modern houses, the Main Stand a spread of tended gardens. It's all gone, vanished without trace.

I walk around the estate. It's remarkably compact; impossible to imagine a fifty-thousand-capacity stadium being crammed into such a small area. Ah, but the spirit of Roker is not entirely dead. Within the estate there's Midfield Drive, Clock Stand Close, Turnstile Mews, Goalmouth Close and, my favourite, Promotion Close (as it invariably was). All very moving, but for a truly evocative memory of what going to matches was all about, I would have preferred to see Pie Parade, Crush Close and Bovril Boulevard.

West Ham are currently bottom of the table (although 'bottom' after just three matches is a bit meaningless, a full five points behind the leaders). But while they've never been a team to challenge for the title, to see them lying last is a bit of a shock. They've a reputation for playing attractive football rather than grinding out victories, but you certainly don't think of them as relegation fodder.

Following his injury at Man City, our star defender Varga is out for several weeks. His spectacular debut against Arsenal has already granted him heroic status and he's now known as 'Stan Viagra' – because he's dead hard and never stops (don't blame me, I didn't make it up). With his absence we've had to acquire a new centre-back, Emerson Thome, a Brazilian signed from Chelsea (where else?) for a club record fee of four and a half million pounds. I can remember when George Best was valued at an outrageous three hundred thousand pounds. With only three clean sheets in the last twenty-four games, our defence has been leaking like a sieve and we need to plug the gaps if the season is going to be anything but a struggle. Apparently Thome's imposing build has earned him the nickname of 'The Wall'. I just hope he's a bit more mobile.

The other new signing to make his debut tonight is Julio Arca, a nineteen-year-old left wing-back from Argentina. Nobody's ever heard of him but at three-and-a-half million pounds for such a young kid, he must be a bit special. Along with other transfers our squad numbers thirty-six, huge by past standards but now considered a healthy size for a full season's competitions. My only concern with our foreign signings is how well they'll be able to understand Reid's team talks (although I suppose a teacup hurled across a dressing-room is the same in any language).

Before the game Kevin Phillips, following his thirty goals last season, is awarded with The Golden Boot which, although sounding like a consolation prize from Jeux Sans Frontières, is actually a prestigious award given to Europe's leading striker. Having started off stacking shelves in a supermarket, followed by two years as an apprentice at Southampton cleaning Alan Shearer's boots, only to be rejected and end up playing full-back for Baldock Town, you could say the lad done brilliant.

We almost have a dream start when Kevin Kilbane, our left-footed right-winger (I know, it doesn't make sense to me either), cuts inside two West Ham defenders and curls a powerful drive against the post. Minutes later he almost scores with a similar effort that whizzes over the bar. Meanwhile on the left wing, the diminutive Arca is tying West Ham in knots with a display of speed and skill. For a team whose sole tactic for the previous two seasons has been to launch the high ball to Quinny, this is staggering stuff. From my position high in the North Stand, I can even see patterns emerging, clever intricate moves down the wings linked with flowing midfield passes. Who are these guys?

West Ham respond with their usual quick accurate passing, orchestrated by the majestic Paolo Di Canio. George Best believes that the great players all have superb balance and Di Canio is a prime example. He looks as if he was born with a ball at his feet. He even looks good without the ball. Hell, I could watch the guy run for a bus. And with his protégé Joe Cole in similar form, the two of them form a constant threat to our defence.

Yet it's Sunderland who strike first after twenty-five minutes when Kilbane whips over a cross for Arca to head in at the near post. Compared to our display against Ipswich, Reid's obviously done a swap with some passing aliens.

But seven minutes later normal service is resumed when we clumsily fail to clear a Di Canio corner and Suker scores from close range. For the rest of the first half, West Ham turn on the style, with one particular move that even has the home crowd applauding. And Di Canio's up to his tricks, even trying to nick a corner from a blatant throw-in.

We last out till half-time. Reid obviously decides to throw invention to the winds and we resort to form with the high ball to Quinn. With the fancy stuff out the window, Sunderland dominate the second half, as West Ham's quality play has perhaps never been matched with the kind of steel required when things get basic. But they defend well and nearly snatch it twice in the closing minutes. First Mickey Gray gives the ball away to, of all people, Di Canio, but luckily he shoots wide. Then in the last minute their sub produces a brilliant save by our reserve keeper Macho Man. We've survived – just – but our defence at times looked its shaky old self and we need Varga back as soon as possible.

Next morning and the dining room awaits. I bid a fond farewell to my feet, as given the looming banquet it's unlikely I'll see them again for weeks. The proprietor bids me a cheery 'Good morning' as he arrives with my breakfast on a fork-lift truck. On a side table he's amassed the EU Toast Mountain. I can't see me eating lunch. Or ever again.

The morning paper makes grim reading. We're still stuck uncomfortably near the bottom of the table but, worse still, Newcastle are top. For many supporters, the respective position of each side matters far more than trophies or actually where you are in the table. To be above the enemy, even by just one place, is to give you the edge in workplace ragging and one-upmanship for at least the coming week. So for the moment the Mags are undeniably Top Dog. And next week we play Man United.

Away.

Tuesday, 5 September 2000

SUNDERLAND 1   WEST HAM UNITED 1

(Arca 25)   (Suker 32)

PLAYED	TRAVELLED	SPENT	POSITION	STATE OF MIND
4	1,664 miles	£213.60	15th	Sense of Impending Doom

Manchester United (away) – Premier League

Stand up if you're from the North
– CHANT BY SUNDERLAND FANS

'Good morning, Richard, it's Tracey here. You're a very, very lucky boy. I've got you a ticket for Man United.'

There are certainly worse ways to start the week. And it's been years since anyone's called me a 'boy'. Tracey is 'Ticket-And-Travel-Tracey' from the London Supporters' Branch. She somehow manages to combine running a young family with organising the trips and match tickets for the Branch's seven hundred members. Chuck her the Middle Eastern crisis and she'd probably sort it out in her coffee break. On hearing that I've got a ticket, I quell the urge to express my gratitude in such gushing terms as the blessing of her little cotton socks, the desire that she be sprinkled with angel dust and the pledging of my soul and undying devotion. I mean, I wouldn't want to embarrass her. So I've saved it for the book.

I have a confession to make. Now it's nothing horrendous, like ever having voted for Thatcher, supported Newcastle or sung along to 'Lady In Red'. And in claiming *mea culpa* there are extenuating circumstances. But when I was seven years old and growing up in Whitley Bay on the North-east coast . . . I supported Manchester United. Now quiet, come on, settle down. Bear in mind this was the early '60s, pre-replica shirts, pre-*Match Of The Day*, pre-Sky Multi-Global Inter-Planetary Satellite Sport. I didn't follow football, I'd never seen a match and I didn't even know about Sunderland. But I knew about Man United. Heck, everyone knew about Man United. With the Munich tragedy still fresh in the memory, the country had taken them to their hearts and the Red Devils were the nation's favourite team. It's probably analogous today to a kid in a small town in China or India supporting Man United because they know nothing else.

Anyway, I pestered my mum to save the tokens from seven thousand packs of Typhoo tea and sent off for the official team photo – in full colour! Two years later I saw the light, switched my allegiance to Sunderland and the rest is history. But I wish I'd kept that photo. By now it must be worth at least fifty pence.

For most teams, 'The Theatre of Dreams' is more the stuff of nightmares. United haven't lost at Old Trafford since December 1998 and Sunderland haven't won there since 1968, on the last day of the season which, ironically, saw Manchester City snatch the championship from United's grasp with a win at Newcastle. Nowadays the prospect of playing United at home has become so daunting that a draw is a stunning victory and losing by only a couple of goals quite respectable. In fact, you probably don't want to win at Old Trafford because it might upset Sir Alex, a man so scary he could probably persuade Hannibal Lecter to go veggie.

As soon as you walk out of Old Trafford station you're subjected to a deluge of stalls and shops selling merchandise, official and otherwise. In addition to the stuff lionising United, there are several items disparaging Liverpool, surprising given that City would be the most obvious main rivals. But it's the other reds who come in for abuse, with T-shirts showing a crowd of Harry Enfield's 'Calm down' Scousers and the slogan 'Stand up if you've got a job. Or ever had a job. Or ever seen a job'.

On the worship side, it is United's past heroes who catch the eye rather than their current successors. Dominant is Bestie, his image deified in quasi-religious paintings. There's also Law and Cantona but little of Charlton, who for all his footballing perfection seems not to have grabbed the imagination to the same degree. I guess that's what happens when you're just a great footballer.

I steel myself to buy a programme. Given United's apparent ambition to establish their own currency, I've filled out a mortgage application for this necessary match-day souvenir, but I'm pleasantly surprised. It's just the usual two quid but bulges at a hefty seventy-six pages and Sunderland are given a decent amount of coverage. There's no swathe of corporate adverts and I'm beginning to think that United's links to big business have been exaggerated, until I spot the back page. It lists all of their official sponsors. All twelve of them. And more than a few seem unlikely partners for an elite squad of highly tuned athletes.

'Jaffa Cakes – Official Favourite Half-time Snack of Manchester United'.

'Pepsi – Official Soft Drinks Supplier to Manchester United'.

'Carling – Official Suppliers of Beers and Lagers to Manchester United'.

'Eurobet – Official Betting Partner of Manchester United'.

'Woolmark – Official Proud Partner of Manchester United'.

Somehow I couldn't see these gelling with Sir Alex's half-time team talk:

'Right lads, who wants a Pepsi with their Jaffa? Or there's lagers in the corner. Now I've had a tip for the four o'clock at Kempton and . . . who let those bloody sheep in here?'

For all the hype of Man United being a 'big' club, the reality is even more impressive. Everything is on a huge scale. The stadium walls dwarf the surrounding area while the official store (you couldn't just call it a shop) is a football version of Macy's, Selfridges and GUM rolled into one. Even at 1.00 p.m. it's packed like the January sales. Again it's Best who grabs the attention, the monitors replaying his scampering run past Chopper Harris and his Merry Men to score his favourite goal against Chelsea in the League Cup.

Outside the store, an imposing statue of Sir Matt Busby looks down on the empire he created. I sit on the car park wall opposite the five-storey glass frontage of the North Stand. For all my own allegiance, the impression is undeniably that of being at football's Mecca. And there's a good feeling about the place, unlike the '70s when the Stretford End prided themselves on being masters of the morons. Now it's face painting and wearing your colours and chats with the opposition. I get talking to a United fan (from Yorkshire). He's about my age and we swap reminiscences about Sunderland's Slim Jim Baxter, our genius wing-half from the '60s who tragically became Not-So-Slim Jim-And-Tonic in a long battle with alcohol. We also compare notes on visiting supporters: he rates Sunderland the best and Middlesbrough the worst. I just don't understand this carping criticism of United fans being undiscerning.

I start the long climb up the enclosed stairwell of the stand. Emerging into the stadium, it looks like someone's given God a Meccano set. With nearly seventy thousand seats the place is obviously huge but not particularly attractive, a mishmash of disjointed stands that compares poorly to the unbroken sweep of the Stadium of Light. On the far side, the North Stand reaches up into the clouds. There's actually a vertigo warning on the back of the tickets.

The Sunderland crowd are already in their seats and in good voice, taunting the United supporters for their claim to be from the North. For most away fans this is arguably the biggest game of the season, a cup final that you know you're probably going to lose, hopefully in not too humiliating a manner. But come what may, it's a day out and you're there to give a good account of yourselves.

One ray of hope for us is that United are without Keane, so that just leaves a pitiful midfield of Beckham, Butt, Scholes and Giggs. One certainty about playing at Old Trafford is that you know you're going to have to score, 'cos as sure as hell they will. So a lot will depend on Quinn and

Phillips. When Sunderland run out I see Quinn has his hand in plaster, an injury from the West Ham game.

The match starts but you'd never know it by the crowd. It's like playing in front of sixty-four thousand librarians. I start looking for the sign saying 'Quiet please'. For all our taunts, the United fans refuse to sing: 'We're not going to sing or even shout, because we know we don't have to in order for Manchester to win. Our vocal support is surplus to requirements, so we shall maintain a dignified silence.'

Meanwhile on the pitch the onslaught has started and in the first minute Sheringham heads just over the bar. The speed and accuracy of United's passing is breathtaking. We're playing well (for us), but any attack is quickly snuffed out. The ball zings out to Giggs or Beckham and suddenly a flood of red shirts is bearing down on our penalty area.

So it doesn't take long for United's first goal, a classic cross from Beckham and a clinical header by Scholes. The library finally stirs and I swear I can hear applause. Watching United must be like living on a diet of cream cakes. Watching Sunderland is strictly a Hovis affair. We're down but not downhearted and do our best to rally the cause. An inflammatory chorus of 'You'll Never Walk Alone' finally stirs the home crowd, it being the anthem of the hated Liverpool.

To their credit Sunderland steady themselves and begin to stem the red flow, but upfront we're getting nowhere. Admittedly Quinn is hampered by the cast on his hand, but last season's telepathy with Phillips has yet to resume, so the flick-ons and headers go frustratingly astray. United have no such problems, the attacks inevitable and relentless. They hit the post then Cole just misses with a delicate lob. We hang on till half-time without further loss but we haven't managed so much as a corner.

Into the second half and we give away a free kick just outside our penalty area. Don Hutchison makes his most significant contribution of the afternoon by disputing the award, thus not only getting himself booked but, under the new ruling, having the kick advanced by ten yards. It's now just nine yards from our goal. Sunderland bodies block the goalmouth like a troupe of Russian acrobats, Beckham blasts, but the pyramid stands firm.

Revived by the close escape, we surge forward and start to press. From our first corner Thome heads on to Quinn who flicks on for a certain equaliser. Yes! No! Somehow Barthez scrambles the ball away, launches it upfield, Sheringham's unmarked and we're two down. A typical United goal: you've got them on the ropes then *snap*, they strike out of nothing.

It's game over and with eight minutes left, Scholes blasts a second from long range to make it 3–0. For United it's another step towards another title, another day at the office. We lost well, if one can do so, but we're slipping ominously towards the sludge at the foot of the table and once stuck there it can be hellish tricky to get out. Still, one glimmer of light from the afternoon: our last three matches at Old Trafford have gone 5–0, 4–0 and 3–0. So come 2004 we're due for a win.

Saturday, 9 September 2000

MANCHESTER UNITED 3   SUNDERLAND 0

(Scholes 13, 82 Sheringham 75)

PLAYED	TRAVELLED	SPENT	POSITION	STATE OF MIND
5	2,074 miles	£276.60	17th	Grudging acceptance of the inevitable

Derby County (home) – Premier League

Where'd you park the minibus?
– TAUNT TO SMALL CONTINGENT OF DERBY SUPPORTERS

It's the week of the petrol protest. In just a few days, a small, disparate group of farmers and truckers have managed to instigate a fuel crisis that thousands of miners failed to achieve throughout the 1984 strike. Then again, the miners didn't experience quite the same 'softly softly' approach from the police that has been adopted towards the fuel protesters.

In expectation of travel delays I catch the early train and typically arrive bang on time with hours to spare. I decide to have a look around Sunderland. In all the years I went to Roker Park, I never once ventured over Wearmouth Bridge into the town centre. I'd simply get off the matchday bus from Blyth with the eleven or so other die-hards (the coach company needed at least twelve people to put on a trip and in the dire early '70s even raising a dozen was sometimes a fan too far), walk the five minutes to the ground and afterwards return straight to the bus. The idea of exploring further afield never entered my head, but why would it? I was there for one reason only, and the town seemingly offered little else.

Now, many years later, I realise how little I missed. The centre is a bland pedestrian precinct of brand-name shops, an anonymous scene that could be any mid-sized town in England. But before long you realise that actually you could only be in the North-east. The give-away is the young women. For a region not exactly renowned for sunshine, there's a healthy display of bronzed flesh. Faces glow with Mediterranean tones but the shades are not quite right, suggesting a nearby mine with a rich seam of orange foundation. Then you spot them. Golden branches of Tan-Fastic fast-tan tanning salons (now say that again quickly) beam at you from every corner, Burger Kings for the burnished. And there's the clothes. Shop windows parade spangled creations that are invariably tight, tiny or short, offering body coverage in inverse proportion to the prevailing climate. The intention is clear: party, party, party! Go into Sunderland or Newcastle on a Saturday night and you'll see packs of girls on the prowl, brashly defying the elements in pursuit of a good time. This is an area where respectable department stores sell T-shirts proclaiming 'Ibiza 2000 – Fat Lasses On The Pull'.

With time to kill I visit a fish and chip shop. Inside it's warm and welcoming, a trait common to most places in the North-east. The cliché of people up here being friendlier than down south is well-founded when it comes to shops and cafes. You find yourself instantly engaging in chatty conversations with helpful waitresses and shop assistants that in London would indicate some faddish staff training initiative. But the real McCoy is impossible to reproduce, emotional light years beyond 'Have a nice day'.

I once spent several months doing research for a documentary about the history of fish and chips. The meal arose in the mid-nineteenth century from two separate dishes: 'French' potatoes, and fish that was initially fried and then sold cold from trays by street vendors, perhaps one of the earliest fast foods. The exact time and location of first fusion, where the two elements were combined to such devastating effect, and who did so, was never fully determined. The main contenders were two old family firms, one from Mossley near Oldham, the other in East London. In the 1960s the Fish Fryers' Association celebrated the supposed centenary of the dish, awarding the accolade of origin to the London family, which caused an instant uproar of protest from the attending Lancashire claimants.

Anyway, the point of all this is that I ended up eating an awful lot of fish and chips and concluded that while it's a meal that's not difficult to do well, it's incredibly easy to do badly. And today I've discovered the masters of disaster. I never knew batter could be grey – and not just grey but lumpy, tasteless and flecked with black specks. Whatever poor fish lay beneath the impenetrable crust had long since lost its flavour. But I long ago took the British Hypocritic Oath of Never Complain (just whinge a lot afterwards).

I head for the train station, where I've arranged to meet my 'contact'. In addition to the official channels, I've now discovered an alternative source of away match tickets and the upcoming Liverpool game is completely sold out. My supplier is not a tout, just a fellow supporter with the occasional spare. Strictly speaking it's illegal, but the legislation was developed to curtail the excesses of the black market, rather than prevent mates passing on the odd ticket at face value. We arrange a discreet meeting. It's not exactly Deep Throat in a basement car park, more Deep Stottie in the snug of a dimly lit pub. (Just in case you live in Islington, stottie, or stottie cake, is sort of Geordie focaccia.) Over a pint, envelopes are surreptitiously exchanged. 'OK, that's five thousand pounds now and the other five thousand when I read Shearer's obituary.'

After the poor start to the season we badly need a victory and today seems our best chance. Derby have yet to win a game and are stuck with us near the bottom of the table on the same miserly four points. It's a classic 'must-win six-pointer', in which the victors not only gain three points for themselves but also deny three for their nearest rivals. And from the kick-off it's clear that Derby are going for the jackpot.

Rams' strikers Burton and Christie, who sound like a couple of Victorian grave robbers, are threatening to leave us for dead. After just ten minutes Burton screams a drive over the bar, then Christie forces a one-handed save from Sorenson, finally back from his injury against Arsenal. Their neat, surgical passing slices through our defence at will, and eventually strikes a vein. Burton shoots, the net bulges and the Derby fans yell in triumph. The scoreboard flashes 0–1. Oh terrific. But hang on, it's just a goalkick. Burton's shot has blasted the side netting in a sufficiently convincing manner to fool both crowd and scoreboard operator.

As wake-up calls go, it's both a cold shower and a kick up the bum. Reid is off the bench, yelling from the touchline and (gulp) so is Bobby Saxton. The Sunderland players know fear when they see it and finally start to play. Quinn nods a flick-on to Phillips whose rasping shot is only inches high, then Hutchison goes even closer with a long-range free kick that thuds against the bar.

Eventually the pressure tells. Just on half-time Kilbane races in from the right and guides a long-range peach of a curler into Derby's top corner. There's as much relief as jubilation among the home fans, who finally rouse themselves to vocal support. A Sunderland crowd is rarely this quiet, but Derby are not traditionally inspiring opponents. It's oddly analogous to Old Trafford the previous week, but now we're the ones who can't be arsed to sing against such lowly opposition.

In the second half, Sunderland are much sharper. Hutchison hits the bar again from an identical free kick and we have a couple of penalty shots denied. With barely fifteen minutes left, Phillips finally bustles his way through a packed defence to slot home the apparent winner. But several Derby comebacks this season have proved them as difficult to kill off as a graveyard of vampires. With just eight minutes remaining, a defensive slip by Kilbane allows Christie to lob over Sorenson and this one's going down to the wire. Home nerves start to fray, the Derby fans roar them on to an equaliser, but we hang on for a fraught victory. It's not been pretty – such bottom-of-the-table clashes rarely are – but we've got the win and naught else matters.

Saturday, 16 September 2000

SUNDERLAND 2   DERBY COUNTY 1
(Kilbane 40, Phillips 73)   (Christie 82)

PLAYED	TRAVELLED	SPENT	POSITION	STATE OF MIND
6	2,638 miles	£351.80	13th	Faint glimmer of hope

Luton Town (home) – Worthington Cup
Second Round, First Leg

It's wet, it's miserable, it's . . . Luton Town!

My God, this really is a test of faith. A six-hundred-mile round trip in lousy weather with an overnight stay for an early round, first-leg tie against a lowly team in a much derided, almost meaningless competition. If I don't get a ticket for the Newcastle match after this, there's no justice in the world.

Other than the faint possibility of getting into the UEFA Cup, the Worthington Cup (or League Cup as I stubbornly insist on calling it) has little value or credibility in today's currency of Premiership, FA Cup, UEFA Cup and European Champions League. Although it's been around since 1961, the League Cup is still the Johnny-come-lately gatecrasher to the party of 'proper' tournaments. Which is a pity, as it certainly had promising beginnings and after some memorable matches began to capture the imagination. But then sponsorship raised its ugly head and a succession of ridiculous titles started its decline. First it became the Milk Cup, then the Littlewoods Cup, then Rumbelows Cup, Coca-Cola Cup (ye gods) and probably at some point the B&Q-Do-It-All-DIY Cup, before settling with its current moniker. Imagine trying to work any of that lot into a triumphant song. Meanwhile the FA Cup, until AXA got their hands on it, was only ever 'the Cup'; no more needed to be said.

The real death knell for the League Cup was the formation of the European Champions League. In its original format of a simple knock-out competition, the European Cup only involved about eight games even to get to the final and was easily absorbed into the domestic fixtures list. The Champions League has become a many-headed beast with a voracious appetite. There seem to be games every fortnight, involving not just one domestic team but three (the Champions League now being open to also-rans). Chuck in the demands of the UEFA Cup, which can swallow up to as many as five other English teams, and you have almost half the Premiership trying to fit regular European matches into their season.

Something had to give and it was the domestic cups. The FA Cup has remained largely intact, save for limiting replays to just one match, but the League Cup is now the runt of the litter. Any team involved in Europe now doesn't enter until the third round and most of the top clubs treat it purely as match experience for their reserves. The final is invariably won by a mid-table side and even when a top team does triumph, it's of little value to them as their interest lies in the Champions League. So, all in all, it's a Mickey Mouse Cup in both name and content.

I'm staying overnight with Mark and Jill, old friends who live in Newcastle. They've just celebrated their twentieth wedding anniversary, for which they seem to hold me directly responsible, as I gave Mark a lift to their first date. He's a staunch Nottingham Forest fan who has enjoyed their glory days but is now having to slum it in the Nationwide. I resist the urge to lord it over him with Sunderland's Premiership status, though God knows he deserves it with his brutally honest opinions of my team in lesser times ('They're a poor, poor side, Rich'). But I figure he's suffering enough without my twisting the knife. And I don't particularly want to spend the night on a park bench.

I set off for the match and wait in the rain for a number 36 bus to take me to the station for the Sunderland train. After forty minutes a bingo card of buses have turned up, but not a single 36. One helpful driver points out that it's due, which is a bit like saying the sun's going to rise. I eventually give up and trudge the two miles to the station. So for a fast, efficient local bus service, always choose Nexus Transport.

At the station, I buy an awful cup of coffee and pick the wrong queue of three for the ticket office. God has obviously allotted today as Crap Day: crap weather, crap buses, crap queues, crap coffee and a crap competition. What on earth am I doing here?

For all my criticism of the tournament, it still offers a chance of glory for the lower division clubs, and a creditable number of Luton fans have made the journey up for a wet Tuesday night in Sunderland. The romance, the glamour. They're in good voice and all power to them, it's their big day out and we can afford to be sniffily silent. It's a reasonable crowd for such a minor game, twenty-five thousand, and the cheaper ticket prices have attracted lots of kids, so the prevailing tone of any home cheering is oddly high-pitched.

True to fashion, Sunderland field only three players from Saturday's game (Phillips, Sorenson and Williams), the rest being familiar only to those die-hards who attend reserve matches. The reserve team are actually flying high, unbeaten and top of their league. They always manage to draw good crowds, partially because it's cheap, but I suspect also for the satisfaction of spotting potential talent and then being able to brag about it to one's mates when the player matures.

In the first half it rains and . . . well, not much else really. It's like watching a training game, lacking the passion and pressure of a league match, and the home crowd are correspondingly quiet. I'm surprised to see Phillips playing, but he's still lacking match fitness following a pre-season injury and tonight is an ideal opportunity. However unfit he may be, though, his talent immediately draws the eye when surrounded by the pedestrian. His darting runs and clever passes have the Luton defence struggling, but they hang on grimly and, thanks to some good goalkeeping and spurned Sunderland chances, there's no score in the first half.

In the second half, the rain stops. Phillips picks up a gear and makes the first goal after ten minutes. From then on it's only a question of how many. Phillips dashes on to a through pass to score a typical goal after an hour and, with just five minutes left, his rebound shot is tucked home by a team-mate. He could have had a hat-trick but, more importantly he's come through uninjured and looks to be getting back to his old sharpness. And against Liverpool he'll need it.

Tuesday, 19 September 2000
SUNDERLAND 3   LUTON TOWN 0
(Oster 51, Phillips 60, Thirlwell 85)

PLAYED	TRAVELLED	SPENT	POSITION	STATE OF MIND
7	3,202 miles	£403.40	WC 2nd Round	Why am I here?

Liverpool (away) – Premier League

More important than that

I don't know how Smithy got the tickets. He supported Liverpool, but being sixteen and stuck in the North-east, he didn't get to many games. But somehow we were going to Anfield for a sixth-round cup tie against Tottenham, on the sixth of March, 1971.

Obviously Sunderland weren't playing that day (in the sixth round? We hadn't got beyond the third round for four years), so it was a chance not only to see a big FA Cup game but to stand on the Kop, *the* place to watch a football match. They sang the best songs, made the most noise and were said to be worth a goal start for Liverpool. I'd seen them on *Match of the Day*, a swaying sea of red and white, breakers rolling down the terraces whenever the Reds attacked. With regular crowds at Anfield of nearly sixty thousand, the Kop alone could hold thirty thousand. At that time Sunderland were getting less than half that.

We arrived early and, accustomed to the wide open prairies of Sunderland's terraces, I casually picked a spot behind one of the barriers. Yes, I was that naive. By the time I became aware of the crowd building up behind me, it was too late. The teams came out and I experienced the first crushing shock of pressure as I was pinned up against the barrier by the welcoming hordes tumbling down behind me. For the next forty-five minutes, my only memory is of bracing myself as each wave came crashing down. I glanced across to Smithy, his arms similarly outstretched against the barrier. He tried a smile, but he was scared, I could see it. I wasn't. I was terrified. Another crush came, a bad one. I began to see stars and knew I was blacking out. Then, at the vital moment, the pressure eased. At half-time the crowd thinned slightly and I slipped in front of the barrier. I watched the second half in relative safety, but too shaken to take any of it in.

Eighteen years later and I was in New Zealand when the World Service broke the news about Hillsborough. Instantly I was back on the Kop, gasping, struggling; frightening enough, but only the merest glimpse of how it must have been for the Hillsborough victims. First unease, then fear, then panic, then terror. A helpless, horrible death. And only yards away, some guys are kicking a ball about.

Hillsborough should never have happened, but then neither should Birmingham (1985, one dead, twenty injured), Middlesbrough (1981, two dead), Orient (1978, thirty injured), Sunderland (1964, two dead, over ninety injured), Ibrox (1961, two dead, thirty-five injured; 1967, eight injured; 1969, twenty-four injured) or Bolton (1946, thirty-three dead, over four hundred injured). While everyone knows about Heysel and Bradford and Ibrox (1971), people have been dying or getting hurt at football matches throughout the twentieth century. In 1902 twenty-six fans died and over five hundred were injured at Ibrox when a stand collapsed. In 1914 seventy-five were injured when a wall collapsed at – care to hazard a guess? Hillsborough.

The Ibrox tragedy in 1971 had happened just two months prior to my day on the Kop, but you wouldn't have known it. With no police and no stewards, the Kop was a disaster waiting to happen which luckily never did. While Rangers finally tore down their old stands and built anew, the English clubs did little. Reduced capacities, a few more barriers and meaningless signs above exits stating: 'Please don't push – remember Ibrox'. Hardly watershed stuff.

To put it bluntly, until Hillsborough not enough people had died. Or rather, not enough to stop the English authorities ignoring the blindingly obvious dangers of cramming large numbers of people into crumbling ancient grounds. While you can dismiss ten or twenty or even thirty-odd deaths as a bit of a one-off, once you start pushing a hundred, well, I guess you really do have to do something. Bit of a bore though and the unwashed masses won't thank you for it, but better commission a report. But for God's sake don't blame anyone, except perhaps the fans. Bill Shankly was lucky that he never lived to see his quip about football being more important than life and death come horribly true.

The Bolton disaster in 1946 is especially important because it bears out Santayana's comment that those who ignore history are condemned to repeat it. If the lessons of Bolton had been truly learned then Hillsborough would never have happened, it's as simple as that. The incidents were virtually identical, not just in the events and circumstances of the day, but also in the subsequent attitudes of officialdom and the media. The match was a quarter-final FA Cup tie between Bolton and Stoke, two top division teams and sixty-three thousand had packed into Burnden Park with thousands more locked outside. When an exit gate was opened from the inside, hundreds swept into an already packed enclosure. Two crush barriers gave way and the crowd fell forward, creating a pile of bodies. Thirty-three people suffocated to death and several hundred were injured.

In the aftermath, while the authorities initially engaged in appropriate displays of hand-wringing and sympathy, the prevailing opinion was that it was the fans themselves who were to blame. Indeed, Justice Hughes who led the Inquiry referred to the incident as 'the first example in the history of football following of serious casualties inflicted by a crowd upon itself'. Nothing to do, then, with insufficient police or stewards, inadequate crowd control, a failure to make the match all ticket, a delay in closing the turnstiles or an old ground filled to excess. Just the fans.

In many ways the similarities with Hillsborough are extraordinary. On both days the fans were herded through a narrow access channel, while the police were unable to control or clear the crowd outside the turnstiles. The overfull enclosures were not seen as a problem, despite warnings from spectators already inside; in 1989 this was expressed as 'let them find their own level'; in 1946 one senior officer commented that 'a swaying crowd usually righted itself'. Neither match was adequately policed: in 1989 police numbers were down ten per cent from the previous year's match; in 1946 there were more police on traffic duty than crowd control. When both crises broke, they were exacerbated by poor communication between police on the ground and senior officers in control. And, most importantly, the crucial factor that sparked each tragedy was the opening of an exit gate that let in the additional supporters.

After Bolton, the Hughes Inquiry did put forward several suggestions to make grounds 'reasonably safe', but amid the politicking neither the government, nor the Football Association, nor the Football League, nor the clubs were prepared to take the necessary steps to enact them. Burnden Park was seen as an unfortunate isolated incident, the blame for which was placed squarely on 'the mob' against whom 'merely improving safety' would be ineffective. For the general good of the game it was seen as best to move on and distance the sport from the tragedy. (Twenty-six years later this attitude was still prevalent among the clubs. When a loose barrier collapsed amid a capacity crowd at Arsenal in 1972, the Club Secretary dismissed it as 'one of those "once in a blue moon" things'.)

Hence all that emerged was a collection of recommendations that required only voluntary compliance, and which the clubs by and large ignored. This was partially out of reluctance to spend the necessary money, but more cynically reflected a fundamental class prejudice towards those who attended matches. Football was primarily a sport for the working class, for whom a certain harshness of fate and life was deemed their unfortunate lot. Imagine the response if it had been a balcony collapsing at Covent Garden Opera House. And if you want to dismiss that as just a bit of left-wing liberalism, then consider this: when the crush occurred at Bolton, the game was halted and the players sent back to the dressing-room. Half an hour later, when the injured had been treated, the players were brought back and the match played out to the end. With the dead lying in body bags next to the touchline.

Now could you really see that happening at La Bohéme?

Of course, Hillsborough or Bolton could never occur now. The changes brought about by the Taylor Report have ensured that at any Premiership ground, you'd be pushed to so much as sprain an ankle. The stage has finally been reached where 'it will never happen again'. Until you look at the lower divisions. At most Second and Third Division grounds you'll still see the same pre-Hillsborough standing terraces and barriers. Of course, there's little risk because they don't attract large crowds – except at, say, an important FA Cup tie.

November, 1999. FA Cup second round, Exeter v Aldershot. Hardly a tie to warrant foreboding, but a huge game for Aldershot who bring fifteen hundred supporters, far more than Exeter would normally expect from a visiting side. When the match kicks off there are still many Aldershot fans outside the ground. In the ensuing chaos, the exit gates burst inwards and those outside try to enter the already packed terraces. The overfill forces people to spill onto the pitch and the game is held up for half an hour.

Never again?

When any disaster occurs, you get swamped with statistics that ultimately hide what they are trying to convey. Ibrox was bad, but it wasn't as bad as Hillsborough. Of course it was. The death of the young boy killed at Birmingham in 1985 was as bad as Hillsborough for the family involved. But when you actually see the Memorial at Anfield it suddenly hits hard. The numbers become names, people with friends, families and lives; ninety-six names engraved into brown marble on either side of an eternal flame. The youngest was Jon-Paul Gilhooley, aged ten. Thirty-eight of those killed were under twenty. Numbers again. That day on the Kop I was fifteen.

At the base of the plaque lie flowers, scarves, hats and cards, some faded, some newly placed that day. Several people are just standing quietly, reading the names. Then someone walks by and, without stopping, touches the marble. Then another, pausing only slightly to pick out a particular name. And again, fingers to lips, then to the marble, then away. It is done quickly but without embarrassment, the living re-uniting briefly with the dead. Although the Memorial was erected in 1990, this is apparently a fairly recent practice. It is a simple but potent gesture and its emotional impact is too much for me. I head off towards the turnstiles.

Fortress Anfield used to reign over English soccer with an imperious might. Eight Championships in twelve years from 1979 to 1990 and unbeaten at home from 1978 to 1981. Even given Manchester United's subsequent dominance, Old Trafford has never quite matched the intimidating aura of Anfield in the '80s. But then in 1991 Graeme Souness became manager, bringing in new staff and new ideas. While it didn't exactly all go horribly wrong, his break with the traditions of the Boot Room derailed them somewhat. Throw in the trauma of Hillsborough and you had a club with a major crisis of confidence from which they've never really recovered. One FA Cup win and one League Cup victory since 1990 is not what Liverpool are about.

With the Kop finally tamed by rows of seating, the old ground now looks rather jaded and bedraggled, an ageing tiger losing his teeth. For Heaven's sake, one stand even has stanchions! Lacking the size and grandeur of Old Trafford, St James' Park and the SOL, Anfield is currently serving out its notice before the club move to a new super-stadium just a hundred yards away, but it's all rather a sad end to one of the great homes of English football.

In a rare burst of blinding Liverpool sunshine, the teams come out to an impressive chorus of 'You'll Never Walk Alone', a still potent remnant of past glories. I go to check the sides in the programme and realise I've inadvertently bought the first instalment of War and Peace. It's huge, like a modern high-fashion glossy, but noticeably many features concentrate on the glory days of the past. They've even got the interview where Shankly came out with his phrase about football, life and death.

Although Liverpool may not be the force they once were, playing them at Anfield is still no walk in the park and they've won all three home games so far. Apart from Michael Owen, up front they've got Emile 'Which-Wall-Do-You-Want-Me-To-Run-Through-Boss?' Heskey, who tormented us last season by scoring for Leicester in a 5–2 rout and then promptly transferred to Liverpool in time for us to face him again the following week. It's something of a sadistic relief to see him limp off after just eleven minutes. Given his transfer fee that works out at exactly one million pounds per minute.

Two minutes later it gets even better when Phillips picks up the ball on the halfway line. Normally you'd expect him to lay it off for a colleague but he just turns and runs full pelt towards the Liverpool goal. Hamann and the other defenders are backtracking wildly, but Phillips is off. He's now thirty yards out, feints left, goes right then smashes a low curling drive into the bottom corner of the net. It's a brilliant goal, up there with Owen's against Argentina, and a superb two fingers to Keegan for not using him during Euro 2000.

Any trepidation Sunderland had before the match goes in that instant. Phillips and Quinn are causing problems, little Arca's working his magic on the left and at the back Jody Craddock is having yet another solid match alongside Thome.

We continue to hold them, then on the half-hour they are awarded a dubious free kick about thirty yards out. The cross swings over and somehow Michael Owen nips in to head home. How can someone who's five foot seven win a high ball? For the rest of the first half it's full-blooded, end-to-end English Premiership football. Kilbane goes close for us, then just before half-time Liverpool's French midfielder Diomede executes a brilliant overhead kick from just five yards out. The ball's on the goal-line and going in when Sorenson dives full-length to scoop it up into the air and then bring it down safely. It's a jaw-dropping save, like Monty's in '73 and Banks in Mexico, an image that sears itself onto the brain.

The second half is a contest between the two England strikers as both teams continue the high-speed battle. Sorenson produces more miracles in goal, saving first from Owen then Carragher, while Phillips and Quinn test Westerweld at the other end. Then Phillips goes down holding his knee and doesn't get up. Shit, this could be serious. Half the cast of ER race onto the pitch and after a couple of minutes Phillips gets up, limping painfully but presumably OK.

With twenty minutes left, local hero/bad-boy Fowler comes on for his first match this season. You'd think a combination of him and Owen would be irresistible, but they've never really clicked. I half suspect Michael's mum doesn't like him getting too close to that rough boy from Toxteth.

In the last fifteen minutes we actually take the game to Liverpool. Phillips goes close again, Quinny has a good shot saved and Arca shoots high, but for the dying minutes Liverpool pile on the pressure. Our back four are superb, particularly Thome and Craddock, and we hang on for an excellent draw. The scoreline is a repeat of last year's match when we finally turned the corner from an agonising post-Christmas slump. Hopefully it'll have the same effect this time.

Saturday, 23 September 2000
LIVERPOOL 1   SUNDERLAND 1
(Owen 33)   (Phillips 13)

PLAYED	TRAVELLED	SPENT	POSITION	STATE OF MIND
8	3,639 miles	£464.90	14th	Thank God for Kevin Phillips

Luton Town (away) – Worthington Cup Second Round, Second Leg

We were awful . . . for most of the game we couldn't
pass water
– PETER REID

Never having been a London commuter, I've remained blissfully ignorant of its complexities and inherent challenges. I'd hear warnings on local radio about chaos at Watford Junction, but assumed that there was always chaos at Watford Junction. That's why it's there. So having turned up at King's Cross for the train to Luton, I'm not immediately fazed by the complete absence of the place on any destination board. I just assume, 'Watford Junction'. King's Cross is a big station, dominated by its glamour role as a major terminus for inter-city routes, but there's also a smaller section for local trains, scurried away to one side, like the failed son who has caused so much embarrassment. No joy there either.

I know it is possible to travel to Luton. Thousands do it every day. National Rail Enquiries have assured me it is so. If I know nothing else, I know that Luton does exist. But perhaps there is some secret portal through which I have to pass, some initiation ceremony by which I will become 'a commuter' and thus discover this secret land, this Other Eden, this Shangri-Luton. Eventually I throw pride to the winds and ask 'a man in a uniform'. He could have been a Scout master from Nuneaton, but people in uniforms know everything, or at least something, however irrelevant. And lo, behold the Promised Land of Thameslink, yet another bit of King's Cross some seventy yards away from the main station.

I wasn't aware that the Russian authorities were still running trains to the Gulags. At least, not via St Albans. Yet the general demeanour within the carriage is consistent with the prospect of twelve hours at the salt mines. Or perhaps they've also got tickets for the match. With Sunderland 3–0 up after the first leg, this second game has become almost academic, yet duty demands another evening of indifference.

After an hour we arrive at Luton station: the guards, the dogs, the shouting. Either I'm experiencing a bit of overkill by the local constabulary or I'm facing twenty years with a bunkhouse buddy called Sergei. Luton's pretty innocuous, neither unpleasant nor inspiring, and the road to the stadium has the usual collection of burger bars and fast-food joints. If you dropped me here blindfolded, I couldn't exactly say where we were, but I'd sure as hell know we were near a football ground; that sickly-sweet smell of greasy fried onions and burnt meat products of dubious origin gives it away every time.

The entrance to Luton's ground is football's equivalent of Alice's rabbit hole. In the middle of an otherwise perfectly standard row of terraced houses, there's suddenly an archway. Normally this would be the passageway leading to the back lane behind the buildings, but instead there are a couple of turnstiles. Once through, you're walking up a stairway that rises between the houses. It's impossible not to wave to those indoors. And just a few yards ahead of you is a large football stand. The houses must have originally overlooked an old playing field that has since expanded into a football ground which now encroaches right to the very limits of the dwellings. It's like the cartoon about the estate agent showing a couple round a house that overlooks a stadium. 'Don't worry about the noise – they haven't scored in years.'

Once inside, it's an oddball mixture of the traditional and the bizarre. There are the old stands with their dilapidated wooden refreshment huts selling orange-coloured tea and lukewarm pies. Yes, I remember those. And there's the toilets that pickle the nose, standard enough, although they seem to be in the back kitchen of one of the houses. But it's the 'Corporate Stand' that grabs the eye. To the exclusion of any other seating or terracing, a collection of glorified portacabins stretches down one side of the pitch. The overriding impression is of a long row of shower cabinets. It's like a trade show at Bath and Bedroom. They've got more executive boxes than Man United. And strung above the boxes is a high wall of netting to catch any wayward clearances. It's all a bit strange, all a bit . . . *Alice Through The Luton Glass*.

One aspect of older grounds is the proximity to the pitch. At most modern stadiums you're several yards from the touchline but at Luton you're almost in the team. You can see the players, put names to faces, identify far more closely with what's going on. And there's also the novel threat of being hit by the ball. Most amateur footballers can't actually kick a ball that hard, but any half-decent pro can whack it like a thunderbolt. If you're next to the goal, you need the same reactions as the keeper. Even during the warm-up, one of the Sunderland players screams a shot into the crowd, belting a young girl on the head. It obviously hurts, but the offer of keeper Macho's gloves seems adequate consolation.

I'm just about getting used to the ground when the Sunderland team come out and renew my disorientation. There are ten changes from Saturday's side against Liverpool, mostly reserve players getting a run-out. The only senior-team regular is Darren Williams, although Alex Rae is also back for his first match of the season. And if I don't know who all the players are, they don't seem very sure themselves either. They start the game playing like a bunch of strangers, unsure whether to pass to each other. And although we may know that the tie is effectively over, no one's told Luton.

From the outset they threaten our goal: a close shot, a near header and a penalty appeal all in the first fifteen minutes. Then their young striker Liam George waltzes past three of our players. He's close now, only the keeper to beat, but Macho tips his shot over the bar.

All right, that's enough, let's settle this. Rae starts to buzz around in midfield without actually decking anyone and his pass to Michael Reddy nearly lets in the young striker. Reddy's been described by Reid as the best young talent he's worked with, but despite several promising appearances as sub last season, he's yet to break into the first team. Frankly, I can't see why not – he's tall, fast and skilful and just what we need on the right side of midfield to complement Arca on the left. But as Read has said, 'If I listened to the supporters, I'd be making forty thousand different decisions a day.'

One minute later, though, and Reddy comes good. Fellow striker Danny Dichio dummies a pass (well I assume it was a dummy but with Dichio you're never quite sure) and Reddy shoots home from close range. Nine minutes later centre-back Paul Butler scores a rare goal to make it 5–0 on aggregate and finally bury the tie.

While the match ambles meaninglessly on, one Sunderland fan amuses himself by taunting Luton's unfortunately named keeper, Mark Ovendale.

'What's in the Ovendale?'

Which sparks off the rest of the bored Mackem crowd:

'Oven-chips!'

'Oven-proof!'

'Oven-ready!'

'Oven-cleaner!'

In the second half Luton keep pushing but their poor finishing shows why they're near the bottom of the Second Division. However it doesn't seem to deter their fans, who, as the match grinds on, become increasingly ecstatic. What are these guys on? It's probably the same degree of self-delusion prevalent in religious cults. There has to be something wrong to be that happy when you're 5–0 down, struggling in the League and about to get knocked out of an inferior competition. But in the last minute of the game their faith is rewarded with a consolation goal to end a generally dire match.

I head for the exit, musing on this Alice-in-Wonderland ground and their fans' odd behaviour. Then I remember Luton's nickname.

The Hatters.

Tuesday, 26 September 2000

LUTON TOWN 1   SUNDERLAND 2

(Kandol 90)   (Reddy 30, Butler 39)

PLAYED	TRAVELLED	SPENT	POSITION	STATE OF MIND
9	3,733 miles	£494.50	WC 3rd Round	Wet, cold, bored – again

Leicester City (home) – Premier League

Whassupp??! . . . Watchin' the game, singin' a dud

It's Sunday, traditionally the day of rest, of lie-ins, roast beef and washing the car. Now it's just another day for finance, fast food and football. Ah, but there's still the engineering works on the railways. While the former traditions may be consigned to history, Sunday is still the day when the railway companies decide to tear up the tracks. Having limped into Newcastle on the Sunday schedule from London, I discover that the local train to Sunderland has been replaced by a bus service. This takes even longer than the toy train set they normally use. Meanwhile over in Sydney, the public transport system ferried ninety thousand people to the Olympic Games Opening Ceremony with nary a hitch.

Bus travel always seems more personal than the train. You sit physically closer to the person next to you and it's easier to strike up a conversation. Trains, however, encourage and even celebrate mysterious anonymity. You can't really imagine any of those romantic train thrillers happening on a bus: *Murder on the Orient Express*, *The Lady Vanishes* and *Strangers on a Train* would never have worked on the number 78 to Peckham. And yes, I know there was *Speed*, but when was the last time you were on a British bus that went anywhere near fifty?

No, the bus is definitely the mode of travel for the common man. Indeed, 'The Man on the Clapham Omnibus' has defined the English Everyman for over a hundred years. Today I appear to be sitting next to his Millennial descendant: Callow Spotty Youth In Full Techno Mode. He's got the Gameboy, the cellphone and the not-in-the-least-bit-personal stereo.

Ka-ching ka-ching ka-ching – Yo bitch!

Ka-ching ka-ching ka-ching – Mo-ther fu-cker!!

After twenty minutes of 'Bitch Get My Gun', along with assorted cellphone rings and Gameboy pings, I finally snap and really, really lose my temper.

'Er, excuse me, I'm sorry to bother you but would you mind turning down your Walkman just a bit, please.'

I'm confident that I've inputted the information correctly, but the blank response indicates a major malfunction. Perhaps I should have just entered a more basic, single-string command – like 'Turn That Fucking Thing Down!' Fortunately he gets off at the next stop. Maybe it was his RAM or his ROM or his main drive – or complete lack of it. Whatever it was, it was way beyond anything that Dixons could fix.

The Budweiser 'Whassupp?!' craze has hit the terraces and it echoes incessantly around the cavernous North Stand to the point of insanity, each new instigator convinced of his Wildean wit. I think it's a brilliantly simple and clever advertising campaign, but there just comes a point . . . Where once the terraces reverberated to songs of wit, passion and creativity, the decline in singing has now reached its logical conclusion – just a single word.

When Sunderland moved from Roker Park, there were many who claimed its unique atmosphere could never be re-created in an all-seater modern stadium. And while the SOL now does have an intimidating identity of its own, the singing is still sadly lacking. The new stadium took everyone by surprise. Whereas at Roker there had been clear delineations determined by whether you sat or stood and by how much you paid, at the SOL everyone was seated at the same price, so no one knew where they were supposed to go. A die-hard and vociferous Fulwell-ender was as likely to end up sitting next to a stoic Main Stand stalwart, so the old concentrations of those committed to singing were broken up and dissipated. And with most seats reserved by season ticket, you couldn't just move to a better spot.

Gradually, with Bob Murray's declared wish to make the North Stand 'the most intimidating supporters' stand in football', it has become 'the singing end', sort of, but it's still got a long way to go. It's like telling everyone at a party to go berserk when it's only nine o'clock and no one's pissed. It needs time to evolve and find its own identity. And making everyone sit down in a more family-orientated environment has stilted a lot of the old spontaneity. It's like trying to sing on your best behaviour.

Traditionally, there used to be an extensive repertoire of old standards ('We'll Support You Ever More', 'We Shall Not Be Moved', 'You'll Never Walk Alone', 'Molly Malone') mixed in with adaptations of the latest pop songs. But now few know the old numbers and there are no pop songs.

Have you ever heard a crowd singing anything by the Spice Girls, Steps, S Club 7, Boyzone, Madonna, Billie, Britney or Westlife? Their success has been created on image not melodies, and targeted strictly at the under-fifteens, whereas pop songs used to be for anyone who liked a good tune. God, I sound (and feel) ancient. I just miss the singing. Now it's largely just mindless chants (the endlessly tedious 'Red and White Army') or simplistic, one-line, cerebral switch-off numbers ('Super, Super Kev, Super Kevin Phillips').

But all is not lost. The Sunderland fans who travel to away matches seem committed to maintaining a varied songsheet, but interestingly many of the songs are still based on old standards: 'Blue Moon', 'Wild Rover', 'I Can't Help Falling In Love With You', 'When The Saints Go Marching In' ('My garden shed'), 'The Stars and Stripes For Ever' (more commonly known as 'Niall Quinn's Disco Pants') and 'The Red Flag' (well, the Labour Party's given it up so Sunderland might as well have it). Not a lot of Jennifer Lopez in that lot. With time it will hopefully spread back to the SOL, but till then . . . Whassupp??!

One of our centre-backs, Steve Bould, has just announced his retirement at the age of thirty-seven. He joined us a year ago after eleven successful seasons at Arsenal and his first five months before injury saw us rise up the table to second place. His comeback appearance at Man City this season was his last, but fittingly five hundredth, league game in a nineteen-year career. A true pro.

Not all sporting lives last as long or run as smoothly. Leicester have just bid farewell to Stan Collymore, the latest talent to assume the mantle of 'wayward genius'. After turbulent spells with Forest, Liverpool and Villa, Stan signed for Leicester last year and promptly whacked three past us on his debut. Then he let off a hotel fire extinguisher while on a team trip abroad. His history with new clubs of spectacular start followed by spectacular demise has run true to form. Rumours of weight gains, bust-ups and excessive wage demands have seen Leicester's Peter Taylor join a long list of managers to send Stan on his way, unable to marshal one of the few real virtuosi of English football.

Yet while the sport has always struggled with the demons of flawed mavericks, such as Best's booze, Bowles' gambling, Merson's drugs or Gascoigne's whatever, there has at least been an acknowledgement of the problem. When Collymore blamed depression for his turmoil, it was greeted with a universal guffaw. How could anyone be depressed playing professional football and earning twenty grand a week? His Villa manager, John Gregory, was less than sympathetic: 'Depressed is the woman in the twentieth-floor flat with ten kids.' The game seems as unable to cope with the concept of depression as it does with the inevitable truth that there must be gay footballers. Yet as Stan himself protests, 'a footballer can get depression just as the Queen can get cancer'.

But Stan-less and starless, Leicester seem to be thriving. They're sitting second in the table with a defence that would make Scrooge smile. If anything, they are an inspiration to Sunderland and similar teams unable to fork out the equivalent of Brazil's national debt for a player. They play with the kind of hard-graft passion that Reid demands, and while not necessarily a team to fear, have become annoyingly difficult to beat.

Faced with this daunting task, Sunderland have a choice of options. They could modify tactics, team or technique. Or the way they cut the grass. In a cunning ruse to upset the Leicester defence, the Sunderland groundstaff have cut the grass in concentric circles, rather than the usual straight lines. Yep, that should fool 'em.

Leicester's defence have kept eight clean sheets in their last eleven games and it's soon easy to see why. They have two excellent centre-backs in Matt Elliott and Gerry Taggart, while anything in midfield is snapped up by Robbie 'Tan-The-Man' Savage. With a suspiciously blond mane and ludicrously bronzed complexion, he gallops around the pitch like Champion the Wonder Horse. When Leicester get a free kick, he dispenses with the usual hand signals and instead starts pawing the ground.

Rather than batter their way through the middle, Sunderland play it wide down the flanks, but Leicester have put up the shutters everywhere and we can't break into the last third. All that's left is the high-ball to Quinny, but with Elliott and Taggart dominant and their keeper Flowers showing England form, Quinn's getting nowhere. He looks flat, and at times dispirited and uninterested, except when appealing for a foul or engaging in a bit of old-fashioned argy-bargy with Taggart, which results in a booking. Last season he didn't get involved in such fracas, but then he didn't need to. He was unplayable in the air and scoring for fun, but this year he's had as many cards as goals. Now both defenders and refs seem wise to his knack of 'winning' free kicks and, aged thirty-three, one can't help wondering if Niall's sung his swansong as a Premiership striker.

By the end of the first half, both teams have had the odd chance, but despite Leicester's lofty position, it's feeling increasingly like a stalemate mid-table clash.

The second half picks up with a rare Phillips header that goes just wide, but otherwise we're again limited to long-range shots. With Quinn effectively shackled, Phillips is left to wander in midfield, seemingly preferring its wider spaces to the claustrophobia of the penalty area, but that's where we need him. Meanwhile Robbie's rampaging upfield, but fortunately his passes are more equine than efficient.

At last, in the sixty-sixth minute, a chance. A point-blank header from Arca is destined goalwards until Flowers produces a wonder save to deny Sunderland again. Otherwise Elliot and Taggart stifle everything we throw at them and the match ends predictably goalless.

We've no real complaints. Sunderland passed well, but that was all. We're still not good enough and teams now seem wise to us after last season's blazing start, when we were the new boys and taking most of the Premiership by storm. There seem few signs of improvement from last year and our target of qualifying for Europe looks laughable. Meanwhile Leicester have gone top and we're left to ponder what they've got that we haven't.

There are lies, damned lies, and football statistics. On the one hand, we're unbeaten in five games; on the other, we've managed just six points from twenty-one. But the reality is that we're just two points away from the drop zone.

If you find yourself in Newcastle Central Station on a Sunday evening, take a walk over to Platform 3 for the train to London. It's the Platform of Lost Souls. You can't move for couples in farewell embraces after romantic weekends. It's not so much *Brief Encounter* as *Mass Encounter*. And all in Geordie.

'But Jacqué, man, Ah luvs you.'

'Ah knaa, Dennis, and Ah luvs y'too, pet, but it's nae good wi' y'livin' doon London.'

'Then come doon, man.'

'Ah can't, man. Look, the train's here. Ah'll see y'next week . . .'

Cue Rachmaninov Piano Concerto, billowing train smoke and slow tilt up into station roof.

Sunday, 1 October 2000
SUNDERLAND 0   LEICESTER CITY 0

PLAYED	TRAVELLED	SPENT	POSITION	STATE OF MIND
10	4,297 miles	£553.20	14th	Fatalistic – we're a mid-table side

Chelsea (home) – Premier League

Anybody here seen Kevin? K-e-v-i-n . . .

So, bold Sir Kevin has sailed off into the sunset on a tide of media tears. A Nile-full of crocodiles could not have wept less convincingly. There's nothing a hack hates more than someone jumping before they can be pushed. But they could hardly say they hadn't been warned: when it comes to disappearing at short notice, it's a photo between Keegan and Lord Lucan.

For all his *mea culpa* claims of tactical naivety, perhaps the most lamentable excuse of Keegan's reign was his assertion that England were let down by poor passing and a lack of left-sided players. Poor passing? These are the elite of England's professional footballers. Their ability to pass a ball from A to B should be as unconscious as breathing. Passing is what you teach schoolkids. Claiming that international players need to work on their passing is like saying they need to practise tying their laces.

And a lack of left-sided defenders? Just how much does a professional need to be paid in order to learn how to kick with both feet? Obviously upwards of twenty grand a week. If you listen to any of the so-called 'naturally' two-footed players, such as Best, Charlton or Hoddle, they'll talk about the hours spent working on their weaker foot until they could use it without thought. Today such ability seems evidence of alien presence. And as for left-footed full-backs, Keegan could have chosen Michael Gray for Euro 2000; he'd already capped Gray three times but instead elected for right-footed Phil Neville, with predictable results.

The end of Keegan's reign has hopefully at last shed the scales from English eyes, who see huff 'n' puff 'n' courage as substitute for the technique that the French, Spanish, Italians and South Americans regard as non-negotiable. But developing English players with that technical ability and ease on the ball? Well, there's West Ham's Joe Cole and, er . . . come back in twenty years. They aren't even born yet. To groom players like that requires a seismic shift, not just in coaching but in the general English attitude, philosophy and approach to life. At present the Premiership is packed with brave Anglo-Saxon souls who can run and tackle all afternoon, but ask them to hit a first-time, thirty-yard ground pass, quickly and accurately, with either foot? Or sell a feint that would fool a shop dummy? The inbuilt prejudice against Fancy Dan players still reigns supreme in this country. Anyone showing such tendency is not lauded and encouraged, but chastised for being lazy, selfish or arrogant, and usually summarily dumped in a crunching tackle by the kind of journeyman you can see on Hackney marshes any weekend. Just imagine it: Vieira, Kanouté, Di Canio, Zola, Henry, Zidane, all English.

(Climbs down from soapbox, walks off in self-righteous huff.)

The kick-off's been delayed by forty-five minutes. Apparently an engineering contractor has sliced through the main power cable that supplies the stadium. Oops. Being a hi-tech ground, all the turnstiles are electronically controlled, so no one can enter until the fault's repaired. All a bit embarrassing in the week that the SOL came top in a survey of all ninety-two league grounds: 'Sunderland isn't just an away trip, it's an experience not to be missed.' Assuming you can get in, that is.

I use the delay to take a walk around the perimeter to see if I can spot my brick. When the stadium was first built, the Marketing Department came up with the nifty idea of offering supporters their own engraved brick in the stadium walls, thereby literally cementing their support for the club. So, for twenty-five pounds you got twenty letters to express your eternal devotion to Sunderland, although I suppose there was nothing to stop you choosing 'Dave luvs Sharon – true'.

The idea caught on and now some seventeen thousand bricks boast legends of undying loyalty. Most take the form of just a name, and in the midst of this mass fealty there lurks one 'Cwen Least'. Cwen Least? Ever met a 'Cwen Least'? Or even heard of one? Hmm, me neither. It's certainly a name to make you stop and think, though I suppose among seventeen thousand applications it was easy to overlook. Anyway, the quisling now smirks somewhere in the stadium walls, but as anagrams go, it's a bit naff. Was that really the best that the combined intellects of Magdom could achieve? Well, yes, it probably was, but with a bit more thought they could have had Claudette Winsen, Claude Swenstein or the latest arrival on the industrial scene, the German heavy engineering company, Neuwadt Steel Inc. (Marketing Department, you have been warned.)

With the recent North Stand extension, a new section of bricks was made available, offering fame and immortality for half the price of a Newcastle replica shirt. Faced with my own choice of timeless graffiti, I decided upon my name plus some pithy epithet that would encapsulate the grand sweep of my feelings for the club: the pain, the elation, the loyalty – all in twenty letters. 'Rich Hakin – Till Death' seemed a bit morbid, while 'Rich Hakin – For Ever' made me sound like the Bay City Rollers. Or I could have had 'Rich Hakin – Till I Die', both morbid and an apparent declaration never to change my name by deed poll. 'No, I shall never become Brian Sprigsby!'

In the heart of every true fan beats the comforting certainty that they will always have their football club (well, unless it's Accrington Stanley). As the saying goes, 'You can change your job, your wife, your life – but you can't change your football team.' It's an issue of faith. After 1977, I never saw a Sunderland match for twenty years, but they were always my team and always will be. Always faithful – that was it, that's the legend I wanted. But less three letters. Then I remembered the film *Aliens*, where a group of US Marines go into battle yelling 'Semper Fi – Do Or Die!' 'Semper fi' is short for '*semper fidelis*', Latin for 'always faithful'. So I chose 'semper fid' as a closer abbreviation and I had my brick: 'Rich Hakin – Semper Fid'.

Pity I can't find it.

Last season's home game against Chelsea was one of those rare moments of ecstasy that remains welded to the brain. The humiliation of our earlier 4–0 thrashing at Chelsea on the opening day of the season still burned raw. They'd scored four but it could have been eight and I've rarely seen a Sunderland side so comprehensively outclassed. And just to complete the indignity, it was featured on *Match of the Day*. So we wanted revenge. And boy, did we get it. We were 2–0 up after fifteen minutes. We tore Chelsea apart and by half-time it was 4–0. Predictably the second half couldn't maintain the momentum, and the final score of 4–1 spoilt an otherwise perfect match. But that first half – pride restored, the noise and passion 'verging on the sexual', it still has the power to scream the soul.

And today's game erupts at the same heart-bursting clip.

In the opening minutes Arca smashes a shot against the bar, the ball bouncing down agonisingly onto the goal line. Then a Phillips overhead kick is nodded on by Quinn for a certain goal, only for Chelsea keeper De Goey to scramble it away.

For the rest of the first half, Sunderland storm the Chelsea goal, roared on by 'that noise'. I can't believe it's the same lacklustre team that struggled against Leicester. Kilbane is causing nightmares on the right for Chelsea full-back Le Saux, while on the left, little Arca looks the nearest thing I've seen in a red-and-white shirt to a young George Best. In midfield, Rae is running, passing and tackling like a firebrand, but leading them all is Quinn, roaring back to show there's life in the old lion yet. No Chelsea defender can hold him, he's a constant threat on goal and after one bruising challenge with Leboeuf, it is the Chelsea man who has to retire.

Up front for Chelsea, their new signing Hasselbaink is so effectively shackled by Craddock and Thome that he can't manage a single shot, and is taken off at the break. The goalless first half gives lie to Sunderland's dominance, but the shots-on-goal statistic of 8–2 for the home side tells the true story.

Unlike last season, the tempo doesn't drop for the second half, with Kilbane and Arca testing de Goey soon after the re-start. Then Chelsea defender Desailly, struggling again to hold Quinn, fouls him in the box for a penalty, which Phillips calmly blasts home in front of a cacophonous North Stand.

At this point Chelsea, no doubt remembering last year's mauling, become desperate to avoid a repeat. After one clash too many between Le Saux and Kilbane, both are sent off, Le Saux for using his elbow but Kilbane for the more innocuous crime of raising his hands. While no visiting player is ever actually popular, Le Saux seems to receive more than his fair share of vitriol wherever he goes. For all the influence of foreign players in the Premiership, English football still regards any deviation from the working-class norm with great suspicion. Hence Le Saux's penchant for *The Guardian* and a stylish designer lifestyle has condemned him as 'an intellectual'. Or in laddish football culture, 'a bleedin' poof' and thus fair game for unfettered abuse (the existence of a stunningly gorgeous wife and new child seems to be dismissed as an irrelevance). As yet, the first gay professional footballer has still to 'come out' and it's difficult to imagine an environment when that would ever be possible.

Generally Le Saux remains above it all, refusing to play the tabloids' game, but occasionally he can display a petulant chip on the shoulder. While by no means a dirty player, he is seen as 'sneaky', enacting revenge behind the referee's back, as he did with Liverpool's Robbie Fowler last season. This incenses the great football public even further, who prefer villains of the pantomime variety: Nobby Stiles, Norman Hunter, Vinnie Jones and Chelsea's own cheeky chappie 'dodgy geezer', Dennis 'The Menace' Wise.

The double sending-off takes the sting out of the game, but Sunderland continue to dominate to the end. It's been our best display all season and, unlike the opening match against Arsenal, we've come out worthy winners with a victory based not on just guts and running, but skill and imagination. And we're still unbeaten at home. Perhaps there is some hope for the season.

Saturday, 14 October 2000
SUNDERLAND 1   CHELSEA 0

(Phillips 62)

PLAYED	TRAVELLED	SPENT	POSITION	STATE OF MIND
11	4,861 miles	£614.80	10th	Beats me how they did it

Aston Villa (away) – Premier League

Five quid yer Semtex! Semi-automatics in club colours!

I was born with a condition that I like to refer to as 'schizophrenic punctuality'. In my professional life I am never late, but nor am I ever early. I have the nerve-wracking knack of arriving just on time, irrespective of when I leave, how much time I allow, or whatever delays fate, Railtrack or London Transport may devise. A journey that might take the average person thirty minutes, I can do in either fifteen or forty-five, but never thirty. It's like a travel version of Parkinson's Law.

But socially I am, or used to be, a timing disaster. Friends referred to me as 'the late Mr Hakin'. They pleaded, they admonished, they even lied, factoring 'a half-hour for Hakin' into any arrangements in the hope that I might actually arrive on time, but all to naught. With a gift such as mine, the subconscious can always spot these flimsy devices, and I'd arrive doubly late. Then a couple of years ago I discovered the trick of setting my watch five minutes fast. I gleaned it from one of those inevitably American 'Dad's 100 Life Tips' mini-books that only appear around Christmas time as over-priced stocking fillers. I can't really imagine a comparable UK version, as the media image of the typical British dad is of an amiable but genetically gormless creature who stumbles through life in a state of continual bewilderment. (For my own future prospects and sanity, I have to believe this is not so . . . right . . .?)

Anyway, quite how leaving five minutes earlier than I believed it to be cured my condition I'm not sure, but it was so effective that I extended it to ten minutes, which worked even better, and I began to be early! Logic would dictate that should I continue this process then eventually I will cheat time itself and thus become a Time Lord.

I arrive at Birmingham station at noon for a three o'clock kick-off and spend a couple of hours browsing around the city centre (don't bother), before boarding the 2:15 local train to the suburb of Aston. Except at two-thirty we're still stuck at the platform on the last possible train that will get us to the ground in time. Apparently there is a 'technical hitch', which could be anything from a flat wheel to, 'It was the driver's stag night and he's still in Aberdeen looking for his underpants.' All my long-buried punctuality paranoia is coming back, but there's no alternative but to sit here, sweat and silently pray. We finally leave at 2:45 and get to the ground at 3:05. So in one journey I've managed to be both three hours early and five minutes late. So much for your Time Space Continuum, Doctor.

As I rush up to the turnstile, a steward insists on searching me. 'It's not my fault you're late, mate.' At which point I kill him and hurl the body into a passing hot dog van.

There's an extensive list of 'Prohibited Articles' displayed next to the entrance. It starts off relatively sanely, then veers off into the realms of fantasy:

'NO: Cameras
Glass
Bottles
Cans
Knives
Darts
Tools
Gas canisters
Smoke canisters
Fireworks or flares
Golf umbrellas
Flag poles'

So that puts paid to my plans for a televised drunken golfing coup of Villa Park with celebratory flag and firework display. Yet apparently it's OK to take in the odd AK47 and lump of Semtex. It's all a far cry from the '70s, when the only thing you couldn't take into a football ground was a pair of Doc Martens. Now at Sunderland you can't even smoke or swear, although I think you're allowed a certain degree of sarcasm.

The steward discovers an illicit plastic bottle of water and summarily confiscates the cap. Not the bottle, just the cap. Apparently it's to render the bottle harmless as a potential missile, so that all one might achieve in chucking it would be to sprinkle everyone lightly with Buxton Spring. Oh yes, I'm dangerous.

Although I've missed the first five minutes, I was apparently better off stuck on the train. You know it's going to be a dull match because Sky have chosen it for their live coverage. They televised last season's two Sunderland/Villa games, both of which managed to push back the boundaries of boredom. No wonder cable company NTL have withdrawn their £328m bid to screen pay-per-view matches (and they sponsor Villa!). Who'd pay to watch this? Well, apart from saddos like me, of course. For all the heights that football can achieve, it can also be drearily tedious, but therein lies its appeal, because you just never know what's in store. Except today.

To their credit, Sunderland do their best to liven things up by nearly scoring an early own goal, but the match has all the excitement of a bus queue. The personalities on display are of more interest than the game. In goal, Villa have David 'Calamity' James, a tagname borne of displays that swing between brilliance and farce. Or it could refer to his apparent attempts at DIY hair dye, which have left him with a thatch to match his pale green strip. For his full-backs, Villa manager John Gregory obviously decided that you can't go wrong with a pair of matching garden gnomes. At five foot four, with identical builds and bullet heads, Alan Wright and Steve Stone were either separated at birth or came as a boxed set. Then there's midfielder Paul Merson, hugely talented but typically cursed with the accompanying streak of self-destruction. His younger Arsenal days of drinking, gambling and drug abuse thrust him into both fame and the addiction clinic. Now in his thirties, he's an older and wiser family man and playing the best football of his career, perhaps all too aware that he's living on borrowed time. And up front there's Dion Dublin, whose polished shaven head must have rocketed sales of Johnson's Baby Oil. Once brave as a lion, a broken neck last season has understandably dulled his appetite for the physical extremes of the game and his play has suffered accordingly.

Where was I? Oh yes, the match. Well, throughout the entire first half, Villa manage a pathetic solitary shot on target, which is one more than Sunderland. Phillips is playing far too deep to be of any threat while our centre-back, Thome, keeps Dublin well under wraps. The best player on the pitch is Merson, who is dashing around like a teenager, but despite his creative efforts a combination of poor attacking and good defending by both sides keeps the game 0–0 to half-time.

The scoreboard displays a disappointing attendance of twenty-nine thousand, a poor turn-out for a near-forty-thousand-seater stadium. So it's all the more intriguing to see a new stand under construction amid plans to boost the eventual capacity to fifty-one thousand. While Bob Murray's scheme to expand the SOL's capacity to fifty-five thousand is based on the hard evidence of sell-out crowds, Villa Park could well become the Dome of English football. But the man behind the investment decision is no cowering director of the Millennium Experience.

Since taking control of the club in 1968, Villa chairman, Doug Ellis, has steered his own personal course with little time for those who cross or disappoint him. His penchant for sacking managers (or at least persuading them to resign), has earned him the sobriquet 'Deadly Doug' and seen ten managers leave the club under his reign. As rates of attrition go, it's a close call between managing Villa and marriage to Liz Taylor.

The second half starts and Peter Reid is spotted high up in the deserted new stand. With a match this boring he's probably got lost looking for the way out. Yet fortunately the game starts to pick up. Finally Kilbane registers our first shot on target, while Villa wake up and start to play. Quinn stabs a cross just wide then Phillips at last gets in the game with an effort that smacks against the bar.

For the last fifteen minutes it's solid Villa pressure and I resort to the drastic measure of crossing my fingers. Well may you mock, but it works and we hold out for the draw, which as the away side gives us the moral victory. However we've slipped back to thirteenth spot and seem doomed to flounder in mid-table, which is a pity because we could have gone sixth if only we'd won by seven goals.

Back on the train, both sets of supporters console each other on a generally poor match, the first 0–0 draw between the sides at Villa Park for 110 years. And it takes something special to be dull in Birmingham. When a Villa fan expresses interest in a Sunderland lapel badge, the Mackem hands it over in a consoling gesture, acknowledging the devotion of a fellow sufferer.

'Keep it, mate – you've got a lifetime of misery ahead of you.'

Sunday, 22 October 2000
ASTON VILLA 0   SUNDERLAND 0

PLAYED	TRAVELLED	SPENT	POSITION	STATE OF MIND
12	5,102 miles	£660.79	13th	A day at the office

Coventry City (home) – Premier League

Goal? . . . What goal? . . . Anybody see a goal? . . .

It's a week after the Hatfield train crash and the rail system is in chaos. More than two thousand miles of track need fixing, GNER are running a ten per cent service and it's going to take ten years to sort the whole mess out. The only train I can get is the nine-thirty but no one knows when, or if, it's actually going to leave. And the cherry on top of the cake – Sunderland station is still closed for refurbishment, so that even if I make it to Newcastle, I'll have to take the slow bus service to the ground. If I'm lucky I might catch the groundsman locking up.

After Paddington, and John Prescott's 'money no object' pledge, you could have been forgiven for thinking that at last Britain's decrepit rail system was going to be sorted out. Yet twelve months later Railtrack are still three years away from installing the cheaper (and inferior) of two train protection systems, while the 'superior' system, ATP, first recommended in 1988 after the Clapham crash, is now out of date. Its replacement will take ten years to install, by which time it will presumably also be old technology. Now Hatfield has proved the watershed, after years of mealy-mouthed promises to fix the railways while trains kept crashing and people kept dying. Finally the government accept that the pursuit of profit is incompatible with a reasonably priced, reliable and above all safe railway system. Suddenly no expense is spared in checking every inch of line, albeit via the not particularly encouraging method of a man walking very slowly along the track behind what looks like a hi-tech pushchair.

Before Hatfield, the attitude of successive governments and the rail industry to train disasters was alarmingly similar to that of successive governments and the football authorities to stadium deaths pre-Hillsborough: lots of hand-wringing, sympathy and promises but precious little action. Perhaps the rail victims included more of the middle classes, but essentially it was the same callous belief: it's just too expensive to get it right. Ah, but with the four deaths at Hatfield, the magic mark of mortality was finally broached, the level beyond which the authorities seem to decide that perhaps they really can't keep letting people die. From Clapham in 1988, which was about the time the Tories started to run down the railways, to Hatfield last week, ninety-six people died in thirteen crashes. The death toll at Hillsborough was also ninety-six.

With the crossing of the Rubicon comes the finger-pointing and the scapegoating. The Railway Inspectorate blames Railtrack, Railtrack blame their contractors, while the contractors claim Railtrack ignored their repair warnings. The government blames the Tories for privatisation, but have done little to reverse the trend. Then there's the train operating companies, the Strategic Rail Authority, the Health and Safety Executive, the Treasury and Uncle John Prescott and all.

Incredibly, amidst all this crossfire of recrimination, one person seems to have escaped relatively unscathed. Although senior Tories, Bernard Jenkin and Michael Portillo, have admitted to 'some mistakes' during privatisation (hardly a plea for political absolution), the grand architect of the policy to de-invest in the railways as a precursor to selling off British Rail has received barely a mention. When Thatcher announced that 'nothing can stop the great car economy' (except presumably a train passing through red on a level crossing), she started years of neglect, under-investment and a cynical disregard for passenger safety in favour of profits and shareholder dividends.

Now the railways need massive re-investment by private companies who are unable to attract the necessary capital because there's no return involved. Who's going to invest in a guaranteed loss-making venture? The figures just don't add up. It will be left to the government (i.e. the taxpayer) to bail out Railtrack and the train companies, a collection of private monopolies over whom they'll have little regulatory influence. Despite all this, the government wants to plough on with privatising London Underground and air traffic control, where an accident in either sphere would make Paddington look like a parking shunt. Yep, makes sense to me.

I finally make the SOL at ten to three with a couple of fingernails still intact and quickly glance at the programme. I notice that the National Football In The Community Scheme have announced a new partner this week. It's Railtrack. And their slogan? 'Stay safe, play safe'. Now that's what I call timing.

It's a glorious North-eastern autumn day of driving wind and rain, the ideal tonic to lift the spirits after the stresses of the journey. Just to complete the picture, we're playing Coventry, a side that have spent most of their thirty-three years in the top flight flirting with relegation but never quite capitulating. So, top match in store.

However, in an otherwise journeyman side, Coventry boast a couple of jewels in their Moroccan midfielders, Moustapha Hadji and Youssef Chippo, both stars for their country in the 1998 World Cup. And just six minutes into the game, a Chippo cross flies past the entire Sunderland defence to Hadji, who uncharacteristically shoots wide. A few minutes later a Coventry free kick flashes past the post and warning has been duly served.

Sunderland are without winger Kevin Kilbane, serving notice after his little contretemps with Chelsea's Graham Le Saux, a fairly tame confrontation which in football parlance is known for some reason as 'handbags at ten paces'. Without Kilbane we lack any width on the right and look oddly unbalanced, resorting as ever to the long ball to Quinn.

In a reflection of the weather, the game drags on, not helped by referee Wiley's niggling decisions that take no account of the torrential conditions. Every misjudged tackle is penalised and the game becomes a stuttering affair of infringements, frustrating players and spectators alike. At one free kick, Wiley insists on moving the defensive wall back one foot to the supposed exact distance of ten yards. Given the weather, it's like docking fifty pence off Beckham's pay packet.

After half an hour, Coventry's early threats are realised when they score a perfectly good goal with the Sunderland defence nowhere. However that fine, outstanding official Wiley deems the goal offside. It's not often that you see forty-four thousand Mackems looking slightly embarrassed.

In response, Phillips has a solo run which ends in a goalmouth scramble and Arca links well in a move with Quinn and Phillips, but otherwise Sunderland look unimpressive.

The second half threatens to continue in much the same vein, until Thome finally breaks the deadlock with a powerful header. Three minutes later Coventry's Roussel misses an easy chance to equalise and you never know, we might even have a game. Hadji's floating around midfield like a ballroom dancer, while team-mate Bellamy threatens to make amends for his disallowed goal. But the game's still lacking in flow or pattern and Quinn and Phillips are both suffering from a lack of quality crosses.

Coventry press us towards the end but we hold out for a grey win over a grey side on a grey day. But that's now eight games without defeat, we're up to ninth and sometimes you just accept the good luck and a bad win.

After the match we learn that Newcastle have lost to West Ham, so we're now level on points with the Mags. The news sparks an outburst of 'I'm forever blowing bubbles' from the Sunderland fans, complete with attempts at a Cockney accent. And I thought Dick Van Dyke was bad in *Mary Poppins*.

Saturday, 28 October 2000

SUNDERLAND 1   COVENTRY CITY 0

(Thome 51)

PLAYED	TRAVELLED	SPENT	POSITION	STATE OF MIND
13	5,666 miles	£719.39	9th	Damp

Bristol Rovers (away) – Worthington Cup Third Round

Bristol – the land that football forgot
– SUNDERLAND FAN

For all the grandeur of the SOL, there's still a part of me that misses Roker Park. It's where I grew up in football terms and where I first experienced true love's pain and pleasure. It had a passion born of standing terraces, packed crowds, basic facilities and, yes, an undercurrent of violence and danger that the SOL, by the very nature of its comfort, safety and amenities, can never reproduce. Roker was a 'proper' football ground, the like of which no longer exists among the all-seater stadiums of the Premiership. Going to a Second Division ground is a chance to relive those days of standing, stanchions and neck-straining sightlines.

I lived in Bristol for about three years back in the late '70s and have many fond memories, but I never went to see either City or Rovers. I hadn't lost interest in football, it's just that the game has little profile in the city. It's not like London, Manchester, Liverpool or the North-east, where football is omnipresent. In Bristol it's easy to forget that the sport exists at all. Both teams have a history spent largely in the lower divisions and between them can only boast one major trophy, when City won the League back in 1906. It's kind of football's answer to Jurassic Park.

Nevertheless, without clubs like Rovers the game would become a soulless exercise in corporate profit management. They might not win anything for decades and couldn't even be described as a sleeping giant, an epithet that has haunted Sunderland for over forty years. But only eight years ago Sunderland and Rovers were in the same division, so one should be respectful of one's roots. For all that Murdoch and Sky might like to think of football as just Man United, Arsenal and stock options, it ain't. It's about Rovers and Rochdale, Blackpool and Bournemouth. It's pies and programmes, rain and snow, cup runs and glory. It's chest-bursting pride and gut-wrenching sorrow. It's my team, your team and, God, we were crap today. It's more pain and more joy than you could ever imagine. It's facts and figures and did-you-know quizzes. It's taking your kids and passing the torch. It's my club, our club, us. It's tradition, history, identity. That's what football's about.

Although Rovers fans may never see their team win the Premiership or the Cup or be hailed from the heights, they'll still go and yell for the Blues because they love the game, they love their team and the good times will ultimately outweigh the bad. And good on them, for without them the sport would die.

It's an evening kick-off and with no trains that would get us back that night, the London Branch have booked a mini-bus. As we drive through a rainstorm we keep a keen ear to the radio to hear if the match has been called off. The drainage technology of the pitch at the SOL could probably survive Noah's flood, but conventional pitches can only put up with so much. However, when we arrive at the Memorial Ground, the game is still on. Their groundsman is clearly a man with strong religious connections.

When Shakespeare wrote, 'What's in a name?' I don't think he was quite prepared for Bristol Rovers. Formed in 1883, they have over the years acquired what must be the most eclectic collection of monikers of any team in the League. They started off as The Black Arabs (!), a name derived from their black shirts and the neighbouring rugby team, The Arabs. With such an official title you wouldn't have thought they needed a nickname, but The Arabs were also known as The Purdown Poachers. So much for stuffy Victorians. After a year of this silliness, the club officials obviously stopped giggling and changed the name to the more respectable Eastville Rovers, later Bristol Eastville Rovers, to reflect their Eastville location. By 1899 they'd become just plain Bristol Rovers but you can't keep a good name down. Although the new official nickname was The Pirates, the gasometers next to Rovers' Eastville Stadium gave birth to The Gas and their supporters, The Gasheads. Rovers don't play at Eastville any more, so I suppose they're due for yet another bout of lunacy.

The Memorial Stadium is typical of grounds that are the bedrock of English football. Four separate stands of wildly varying design, from the bog-standard corrugated roof and stanchions to something they obviously nicked from Kempton racecourse. The advertising hoardings don't promote major corporations like Sharp, Nike or Carlsberg, but M.J. Wilcox (Electrical Contractors), Cowlin Construction and Bristol Rope & Twine. And we're in the standing section! Brilliant! There's no roof, it's pissing down and we're freezing. I'd forgotten how much I missed it all. In a burst of nostalgia, I cast my vegetarian principles to the darkening skies and wallow in a Bovril.

As kick-off approaches, the sensation of having gone back in time is also enhanced by the music blaring from the PA. It's all from the '60s, so it's The Beatles, The Stones and Jeff Beck's 1967 hit 'Hi Ho Silver Lining'. I couldn't be happier. The last record has clearly been adopted by the home crowd as their own, for as the chorus starts, the whole ground erupts into, 'AND IT'S HI HO BRISTOL ROVERS!' Which is fantastic, but then nothing! The song continues but evidently no one's got around to adapting the rest of the lyrics. For the remainder of the chorus and throughout the next verse, everyone stands around twiddling their thumbs and looking rather embarrassed as they await their next cue. Then they're off again, one rousing burst and then silence. It's a great song, guys, but you need a few more lines.

(To digress for a moment, unsure of whether Mr Beck was still with us or had gone the way of several contemporaries, when I got home I logged on to the web and entered 'Hi Ho Silver Lining'. Happily he's still thriving, but his evergreen classic has now transcended its status as the anthem of choice for late-night revellers and become a standard of the line-dancing circuit . . . the horror, the horror! So forget all that hands-in-the-air stuff, just slip on your Stetson, buff up your boots and it's Pivot 1/2 Turn x2, Jazz Jump Forward & Back With Claps.

'Matron, Mr Beck's asking for more strychnine . . .')

A roar from the crowd signals the entry of the teams, greeted by two lines of very cold and very wet cheerleaders. Some 1,500 Sunderland fans have made the long trip down here for a minor game on a miserable Tuesday night. There's flooding and there's chaos on the railways, but many Premiership teams don't even bring that many to the SOL for a regular Saturday game. Well done, lads.

Rovers may be two divisions below us, but they're at home, with a good crowd and they beat Everton here in the last round. This won't be a pushover, so it's no reserve side for us. Sunderland have put out eight first-team players, including the mighty Stan Varga, making his comeback after *four* operations to repair the injury he incurred at the Man City game.

The match kicks off and within the first ten minutes, young Michael Reddy hits the post for Sunderland and three Rovers players are booked. Fasten your seat belts, we're in for a bumpy night. During an end-to-end first half, Rovers play some good stuff and force Sorenson into several fine saves. Meanwhile Dichio and Reddy threaten for Sunderland and the crowd noise starts to build. Then out of the mayhem, the Bristol crowd start singing 'Goodnight Irene'. Most crowds have a surging battle song to urge on their team, such as 'Glory Glory Tottenham Hotspur' or 'When The Reds Go Marching In', but I've never heard anyone try to lull the opposition to sleep with a ballad. Apparently it's Rovers' traditional theme, hailing from a match against Plymouth Argyle fifty years ago when the song was a contemporary hit and the crowd suddenly burst into 'Goodnight, Argyle, Goodnight'. I guess for a club with their history of nomenclature, they couldn't have just chosen 'The Wild Rover'.

The first half ends with no score and I use the break to have a look at the programme. I must confess to having expected something akin to a Xeroxed effort, but I'm suitably chastened by quite simply the best football programme I've ever seen. Most clubs just put out a bland PR collection of player interviews, 'our visitors today' and advice on how to mortgage your home for next year's season ticket. But this is sixty-four pages of well-written and incisive articles, a staggering twenty-five of them. One particular gem is a question-and-answer session with Rovers player, Ronnie Mauge. Apparently if he hadn't been a footballer he would have become a born-again Christian, which I never realised was an occupational option ('Now, about the pension scheme . . .'). Obviously a sensitive soul, the last book he'd read was *Men are from Mars, Women are from Venus*, but then he describes himself as 'someone not to upset', which presumably wouldn't be the case if he'd followed his alternative career path.

The strains of 'Goodnight Irene' herald the teams back onto the field, although the cheerleaders have some difficulty fitting a raunchy, up-beat routine to a lullaby.

Within minutes, Don Hutchison puts us ahead with a superb low strike from twenty-five yards, his first for the club. That'll be it then, game over. Except no one's told Bristol. With the crowd behind them, they surge back and it's blood-and-thunder football. As Sorenson collects a high cross, he's bundled over by Bristol's Mickey Evans, and drops the ball in front of a grateful Nathan Ellington who slams it home for the equaliser. Hang on, this wasn't supposed to happen. We're the Premiership side here, a bit of respect please. Stuff that. With Rovers in full flow, Reid sends on Phillips for the last five minutes. Twice he breaks clear but is denied by excellent goalkeeping. Two minutes left. A cross into the Bristol goalmouth and Hutchison scrambles it home for a last-gasp winner.

Phew. Well, at least we'll have an easier match in the next round. It's just Man United.

Tuesday, 31 October 2000
BRISTOL ROVERS 1   SUNDERLAND 2

(Ellington 62)   (Hutchison 48, 88)

PLAYED	TRAVELLED	SPENT	POSITION	STATE OF MIND
14	5,896 miles	£743.89	WC 4th Round	Nostalgic

Tottenham Hotspur (away) – Premier League

I come to bury Caesar, not to praise him

It's not been a good week for football managers.

The appointment of Sven-Goran Eriksson as the new England coach has ignited a wave of xenophobic indignation from the Little Englanders. Radio talkbacks are buzzing with protests about this ultimate disgrace to our national pride. Bizarrely the calls seem to come mainly from Chelsea supporters, whose team on occasions have managed to field a side completely devoid of English players.

'Nah, dahn't get me wrong, I ain't racist nor nuffink *but* . . .'

The sweet, sweet victory of '66 has proved just too hard to let go and many cannot accept that in the game we taught to the world, we've gone from masters to pupils. Yet many non-English managers and players have been quite readily accepted into the domestic game, their insight and talents admired and copied. The Arsenal players never bothered stretching down after training until Wenger arrived. The Chelsea players' caff was a haven for fry-ups before the Italian invasion. And then there's that Scottish bloke at United. With the one exception I'll mention, I've never heard supporters of any successful club side object because their manager wasn't born within a free kick of the ground, yet it seems crucial for the national team coach to be a son of the soil.

There were no complaints from the Irish when Jack Charlton gave them their finest hour in the 1990 World Cup. And as a nation we stayed up and yelled the Olympic coxless four to glory, a victory masterminded by their (whisper it) *German* coach. Personally I'd take someone from Planet Zog if they could give us the World Cup, a triumph that would still be achieved by English players. Yet if Eriksson does succeed in winning the trophy that some believe is our birthright, the current dissenters will no doubt be the first to hail his victory. 'I always said he was the Guv'nor. Them Swedes, y'know, they've got it sussed, wot wiv yer Volvos and yer porn and them fit birds from Abba.'

But in a small part of North London, discontent with a manager has arisen not for his distant origins but for their glaring proximity. When George Graham made the one-mile hop from Arsenal to Spurs (albeit via Leeds), you knew it was a good time to get into the knife-sharpening trade. From the moment of his arrival, a section of the Tottenham boys have been waiting for him to fall and been all too willing to help him on his way. In the battle zone of local football, initial allegiance to either camp generally casts one forever *persona non grata* in the eyes of the opposition. Hence Graham, loyal Gunner as both player and manager, was damned and doomed in the eyes of many when he took on the Spurs job in 1998. Even a swift victory in the Worthington Cup in 1999 was not enough to sheathe the daggers.

What the fans don't seem to appreciate is that for the player or manager involved, loyalty to any team has to come second to one's need to make a living. If one lot doesn't want you but their neighbours do, then it's a lot easier to shift camp than to up sticks. For all Graham's fealty to Arsenal, he wouldn't have taken the Spurs job if it pained him that much. The deciding factor was the chance to manage a Premiership side and the no-doubt attractive salary deal.

It's much the same with Sunderland and Newcastle. There's been a long tradition of players and coaches transferring between the two teams, generally towards the end of their careers when they are settled in the area and don't want the hassle of moving. Bobby Saxton used to work across the Tyne. Len Shackleton played for both teams. And for the ultimate example, Sunderland's '73 cup side involved three ex-Mags (two players and the manager).

There are limits. I could never see Shearer or Keegan taking a Sunderland post (or indeed ever being offered one). And when Newcastle midfielder Lee Clark signed for First Division Sunderland in 1997, he ultimately couldn't quell his Magpie loyalties. With Newcastle in the Premiership he was safe, but when Sunderland were promoted two years later, Clark couldn't face playing against his boyhood idols and left under a cloud of recriminations. (Even if he'd wanted to stay, I think his departure may have been inevitable. At the 1999 FA Cup final, Clark was spotted cheering on Newcastle while wearing a T-shirt proclaiming 'Sad Mackem Bastards'!)

So George Graham's not exactly had it easy since his arrival. And his blunt, no-nonsense approach to tactics has jarred with the traditions of stylish play that made Spurs into one of the most attractive, if not successful, clubs of the last few decades. They lie an uninspiring twelfth in the table and have just suffered a humiliating home defeat by Birmingham in the Worthington Cup. The knives are out and glinting, to the extent of today's programme having to issue a warning against anyone planning a protest during the game.

At Seven Sisters tube station, the train disgorges hordes of Sunderland fans who've yet again overcome fuel shortages, a defunct A1 and warnings from GNER not to travel, and made the long journey down. They probably hiked. As we cram onto the upward escalator, a couple of lads decide to bypass the jam and leg it up the alternative but downward-moving staircase. Barry Beergut soon falls back but Jimmy Whippet is gaining ground. Urged on by the rest of us, he bravely battles the opposing physics, eventually emerging triumphant at the top to a huge cheer. And a waiting policeman. In the manner of a long-suffering headmaster, the officer turns the lad around and sends him back down again. As he glides serenely out of view, the last we see of him is arms aloft, bowing to the gallery, bloody but unbowed.

Built in 1899, White Hart Lane is one of England's stately homes of football. By 1909 the capacity was fifty thousand and peaked at a staggering eighty thousand in 1934. It has a grandeur forged from the great Spurs sides of the '50s and '60s, an aura that persists despite Tottenham's fall from grace as one of the country's 'big' clubs. Unlike Arsenal and Liverpool, there are, thankfully, no plans to move elsewhere and the current expansion scheme should see the ground last well into the new century. As you approach, the towering stands dominate and intimidate and you are left under no doubt that you're entering a major football stadium.

Almost without noticing it, Sunderland have put together a half-decent run and we've now gone nine games without defeat. Yes, all right, three of those were Worthingless Cup ties, but we've kept a clean sheet for the last four league games. But today we're battling history and the fates, as we haven't won here in the League since 1978.

Straight from the kick-off, Spurs come blasting out of the blocks and Sorenson makes two phenomenal saves in the first three minutes. We weather the storm for the next ten minutes and gradually get a toehold on the game. Hutchison has a goal disallowed and Quinny goes close, but then Spurs pile back and Tommy makes two more astonishing saves, from a powerful low drive and a long-range screamer that he somehow tips over the bar. I can remember our legendary keeper Monty making some incredible stops, but never with quite the frequency that Sorenson achieves.

After half an hour we start to play, Hutch and Rae passing well in midfield. One move sends the ball into the Spurs penalty area. Their defender, Vega, fumbles and we've suddenly got a penalty for handball. Phillips steps up and while I wouldn't quite put my mortgage on him scoring, I'd certainly consider a hefty deposit – which I then lose when he skies the ball over the bar. It seems to typify his season, close but no cigar. His goal tally of five is not shameful, but it's a world away from last year, when defenders needed counselling after playing him. He looks oddly out of sorts, wandering around midfield when he should be causing mayhem in the box. But that's just my rambling opinion. The guy behind me sums it up far more eloquently: 'The trouble with Phillips is that he doesn't foul enough.'

So, there you go, Kev. You should be giving away more free kicks.

Immediately Spurs storm back and Sorenson pulls off his fifth wonder save, but just before half-time he finally falls to a short-range prod by Sherwood amidst a messy goalmouth scramble. Nevertheless, we start the second half brightly. Rae and Makin go close then Hutch continues his goal spree by heading in to equalise after sixty-four minutes.

Having survived the first-half pummelling, there's now a genuine belief among the three thousand travelling faithful that we can actually pull this one off. With just fifteen minutes left, Craddock heads agonisingly wide for us, a miss that seems to knock the team off their stride. Spurs send on a substitute, Chris Armstrong, an ex-Mag who receives the obligatory bout of booing from the Mackems. He responds immediately by chasing a good through-pass, beats Varga for pace and slots the ball through Tommy's legs for Spurs' second goal. Oh cruel, cruel fate.

There's a brief flurry near the end when Tottenham have Thatcher sent off for fouling Chris Makin, but we know it's not our day.

Perhaps our loss has saved George Graham from a lynching which he doesn't really deserve, but you see that's our trouble – we're just too nice.

Saturday, 4 November 2000

TOTTENHAM HOTSPUR 2   SUNDERLAND 1
(Sherwood 42, Armstrong 78)   (Hutchison 64)

PLAYED	TRAVELLED	SPENT	POSITION	STATE OF MIND
15	5,908 miles	£778.84	12th	We never win here anyway

Southampton (home) – Premier League

Abandon hope all ye who enter here
(Self-service straight ahead)

This is ridiculous. Because of the flooding there are no trains between London and Newcastle. The London Supporters' Branch were planning to hire a coach, but they can't raise the numbers so I've got to make my own way there. I could hire a car, though I don't fancy driving up and down in one day, but the rental charge for two days is prohibitive so I'm left with National Express.

I can't believe the timetables. Apart from the Friday overnight coach, the first Saturday service doesn't arrive until mid-afternoon and the first bus back after the match doesn't leave till midnight. So unless I want two exhausting overnight trips, I'm going to have to go up on Friday and not come back till Sunday. A three-day trip for ninety minutes of football. Against Southampton. I'm reminded of *A Man For All Seasons* and Thomas More's chiding of Richard Rich, when Rich betrayed him to Cromwell in return for an official post in Wales: 'It profits not a man that he sell his soul for the very world – but for Wales?'

If coach travel were as it was in the mid-eighties, I'd be quite looking forward to the journey. The non-stop trip to Newcastle could be done in four-and-a-half hours and featured on-board snacks, videos and ultra-clean toilets, and all for about a quarter of the train fare. The theme was clearly based on the airlines, as the female attendants would wear airline-style uniforms and make similar announcements at the start of each journey, albeit with a healthy dose of Geordie warmth. 'Hello ev'rybody, my name's Sandra and Ah'll be your attendant for wor trip. When we get onto the motorway Ah'll be comin' round with tea, coffee and fresh stotties and then we'll be showin' a video. Wor drivers for today are Bob and Jack. Say hello, Bob.'

'A'reet?'

All-in-all, a real joy.

But now?

Now it can be a seven-hour (or longer) slog with no video, no snacks, no attendant and an obligatory stop at some faceless motorway oasis. You can travel cheaper by train and if there was a pre-journey announcement by the hassled driver, it would likely be no more than, 'Sit doon and shut up.' One hour into my journey, I discover that the on-board toilet lacks soap, towels, water and loo paper. The service used to be called The Rapide. Now it's more The Tediouse.

After nearly five hours on a packed M1 we crawl into a motorway services. I don't know where, I don't care, anything to get out of this damn bus. If there are concerns about deep vein thrombosis in airline passengers, they should look at what long-distance coach travellers have to put up with.

For all the vehement scorn and criticism that's been heaped on motorway service stations, they remain resolutely unmoved. They all boast an identical array of fast food outlets along with, for the 'discerning customer', the self-service restaurant. It's usually given some naff cutesy name like 'The Willows', conjuring up images of home-cooked country fare, but serving up flavours of cardboard and chalk.

As I collect my tray I notice that scattered around the various food counters are pithy quotations from writers and philosophers. I suppose it's some sharp marketing wheeze to take our minds off the food.

'Never go on a trip with anyone you do not love' – Ernest Hemingway. I obviously had some catching up to do with my fellow passengers. 'No amount of travel on the wrong road will bring you to the right destination' – Ben Guage III. Try telling that to our Man City coach driver. When we finally got out of Manchester he somehow lost the M6, then decided that the best route back to London was to head north. 'Grub first, then ethics' – Bertolt Brecht. If he spent any time eating in places like this he'd have the ethics of Hitler.

After eight-and-a-half cramped hours I arrive at a freezing Gallowgate coach station, the new St James' Park looming over me in the darkness. I'm staying with friends and need to catch a local bus, but I'm not sure where to get off. The Geordie driver, ever willing to help a stranger, drops me three stops short of where I need to be.

Next week is the big derby match at Newcastle. Tracey at the London Branch has achieved the impossible and somehow got me a ticket. It arrived completely out of the blue and my reaction when opening the letter on the tube caused several people to move down a few seats.

On the basis of 'know your enemy', I decide to spend Saturday morning taking a look at their new stadium. United are playing away today so the place is deserted. The vast white monolith rises above the surrounding area like the mother ship at the end of *Close Encounters*. As you approach, it resembles a cross between a multi-storey car park and a huge power station, phalanxes of parking bays amid steel and humming generators.

Although the stadium is closed, the club shop is open, famous for selling the fifty-pound replica shirts that cost perhaps four quid to produce. It is a testimony to the blind faith of the Geordie fans that they accepted the scorn of their directors Shepherd and Hall when taunted about their gullibility in parting with so much for so little.

I glance at the opening pages of the official club history, entitled rather strangely, *Newcastle United 1882–92: The First One Hundred Years*. In the early days of designing their strip, they clearly hired only the top couturiers from Paris. Hence, after starting rather conservatively in dark blue, they blossomed, darlings, into chocolate and blue ('Non, really, Monsieur Jackie, it weel look formidable!'), then blue-and-orange stripes ('Trust me, Bobbie, against ze green of ze grass, fantastique!'), before finally, incredibly, red-and-white stripes ('Believe me, it's all ze rage in zese parts!'). At this point I can only assume that the Victorian Geordies finally put their foot down. 'We're fuckin' miners, man. It'll be fuckin' pink next! We just want summat that's not ganna show the clarts – how aboot all black?'

'No, man, we'll luk like a bunch o' refs.'

'Way, stick a bit o' white in – but not much, mind!'

I suddenly realise that I've lost my pen for making notes. There is too much good stuff here to let it pass and a clutch of over-priced Newcastle pens lies temptingly close. My Sunderland principles cringe at the prospect of lining even further the pockets of Snatchit and Grabbit, but here in deepest Gallowgate there aren't too many branches of The Mackem Pen Shop. So I cough up the extortionate price of one pound ninety-five for a simple ballpoint, determined to cast it aside at the end of the day.

Outside the shop I continue walking round the ground. There's a pub only yards away, but I can't believe the name. You'd expect any self-respecting hard Geordie bastard to drink at pubs with names like The King's Head, The Red Lion or The Blacksmith's Arms – but The Strawberry?

We've no Julio Arca today as he's on international duty with Argentina. He's become a crowd favourite and his absence is a real loss. To replace him, Reidy's switched Kilbane to the left and moved Hutchison out to the right.

It should be interesting to see how they cope playing out of position.

If you watch football long enough you occasionally see something quite extraordinary, something you know will only happen once every few seasons. After a bright start by Sunderland, the ball breaks to Southampton's James Beattie. He's forty yards out and no real threat as . . . What!?! From a seemingly harmless position, Beattie has volleyed a dipping, swerving shot that screams over Sorenson and into the net. Bizarrely it is met with almost perfect silence, apart from the faint celebrations from Southampton supporters at the other end. The rest of us are just numb.

Hmm, perhaps strange forces are at work here.

We go back on the attack but are getting nowhere, Southampton containing us with ease. I'm writing notes when I notice the pen. Naah, that's ridiculous.

Another attack breaks down.

It's just a pen – and there are forty-five thousand other Sunderland fans here, God knows what they've got in their pockets.

With Kilbane and Hutchison both largely ineffective on the wings, there is little width or variation to the attack. We're passing well and trying hard, but stalling near goal.

But what if I've brought some accursed Mag hex into the hallowed temple?

The ball comes to Phillips on the edge of the area. Four Southampton defenders close in like traffic wardens on a Porsche. No chance.

I finger the pen. My hands start to exert pressure. It snaps.

Phillips squeezes the ball out to Hutchison, who whips in a low cross. Incredibly, both the Southampton goalie and last defender let it go by and into the path of Quinn, who sidefoots it home. In my joy I stamp the pen to fragments. From snapping it, to the ball crossing the line, was no more than maybe ten seconds. Next time if I've nothing else, I'll write in my own blood.

Free of the curse, we play well for the rest of the half. Phillips goes close, Hutch hits the post from only a yard and the shots-on-goal statistic of 9–1 for Sunderland tells its own story.

In the second half Sunderland inexplicably take their foot off the gas. Phillips misses again from six yards and despite crowd support, the head drops slightly. With last week's penalty miss and his current lack of touch, the seeds of self-doubt must be growing.

Southampton start to come back and go close several times. Our unbeaten home record is under threat. Then, Hutchison makes up for his first-half miss by scoring with ten minutes left. One minute to go and Southampton get a corner. Just clear it, hoof it anywhere, Row Z. The ball comes over and . . . it's in.

Injury time. Tessem breaks clear for Southampton, and now there's only Sorenson, who's out of position, to beat. Oh shit. Tessem shoots . . . wide! I thought only I missed chances like that.

Finally it's over. Our home record is still intact but looking decidedly shaky. If we play like that next week against the Mags we'll get monstered.

Back in Newcastle, I wait for a bus which, when it comes, naturally speeds by. Obviously the same guy as last night. Rather than wait another half-hour for the next chance to be mocked, I start the long walk back, but first fuel myself with some fish and chips. Portions in the North-east are never stingy, and I stagger out of the chip shop with a potato field and a small whale. I trudge up Grainger Street and sit on a bench next to Gray's Monument.

I'm approached within seconds.

There's an unspoken code in the North-east, a bit like that of fireside coffee in the Old West, that you can always cadge a chip off a stranger. It's a charming tradition based on friendship, charity and the threat of getting your head kicked in if you refuse. But it's Saturday night, the lads and lasses are 'oot on the toon' and I seem to be attracting everyone.

Groups of young men go by, dive into my supper and part in good cheer with a wave and a 'Thanks, mate.' I muse that this time next week they'll probably be fighting among themselves to spread my limbs from Carlisle to Calais. Then it's the girls, decked out in *de rigueur* micro-minis and heels higher than United's new stand. 'Ee, can Ah have a chip, pet?'

I love it when Geordie girls call me 'pet', for in that one tiny word lies both the warmth of a cuddle on a freezing Newcastle night and the raunchy come-hither prospect of life-threatening sex. But tonight they're just after my chips. They gather round, twittering like long-legged sparrows at a winter bird table, the combined atmospheres of pungent perfumes dangerously close to critical mass. At one point I must have passed out, for I come to alone, save for the remnants congealing in the flapping paper on my lap.

My simple meal has taken on mystical proportions. Jesus only had five thousand to feed. I'd like to see him face the Toon Army with five chips and a piece of cod. I've fed the whole of Newcastle and there's still plenty left. I chuck the rest and walk away, looking back as a couple of pigeons land on the bin.

Saturday, 11 November 2000

SUNDERLAND 2   SOUTHAMPTON 2

(Quinn 22, Hutchison 80)   (Beattie 12, Richards 89)

PLAYED	TRAVELLED	SPENT	POSITION	STATE OF MIND
16	6,472 miles	£845.68	12th	Sense of Impending Doom II

Newcastle United (away) – Premier League

He that outlives this day and comes safe home
Will stand a tip-toe when this day is nam'd
And rouse him at the name of Sunderland

5.00 a.m.

Urrhh . . .

I thought the whole point of becoming a writer was that you didn't have to get up till noon. The trains are back (sort of) but the London Supporters' Branch has hired a coach, leaving at 6.30 from King's Cross. This not only avoids having to depend on GNER (Going Nowhere English Railways), but allows us to join the convoy of buses that will be leaving the SOL to travel to St James' Park under police escort. The concept was introduced last year to offer the away fans safe passage to the stadium. Fine by me. At last year's derby at Sunderland, about fifty Geordie fans who had eschewed the convoy were surrounded near the stadium by a large and aggressive Sunderland crowd. Any pre-match Broon-fuelled bravado had evaporated and all that remained was a bunch of very scared young men with nowhere to run. The police formed a cordon around them, the scene uncomfortably reminiscent of UN peacekeepers in a Balkan village. Today I don't want it to be me inside that cordon.

King's Cross is not the most salubrious district at the best of times, but at six in the morning it has a ghostly surreal quality. Young men and women seem to materialise out of the walls, wandering around aimlessly. One guy passes me completely bare-chested, oblivious to the biting cold.

Gradually the other twelve Branch members appear, the numbers limited by the few available match tickets. By 6:30 there's still no coach. 6:40: Shit. I've got my ticket, for Christ's sake, I can't miss this game over a stupid transport hitch. 6:45: Come on, come on. Then it arrives – no, that's hopelessly inadequate. It glides like a white ghost out of the morning gloom. It's huge, an 'executive model', with spacious seats, tables with lamps, three televisions and at the back, a kitchen and a bar. It's the kind of coach normally reserved for cup final teams going to Wembley, but certainly not for their supporters. And there are only thirteen of us! It's slightly different from National Express.

For those with no interest in today's game, it's difficult to appreciate just how much is at stake. Describing it as keenly contested is like calling the Cold War a slight misunderstanding. For the Newcastle fans, their team's fall from grace as Premiership contenders in '96 and '97 to relegation prospects in '99 was hard enough, particularly alongside Sunderland's growing success. Then came last year's derby. Amidst monsoon conditions, United manager Ruud Gullit left Shearer on the bench and the Mackems splashed back from 1–0 down to win 2–1.

Now it's payback time and the Newcastle phone-ins, papers and chatrooms have been humming with the desire for revenge. Last year was lucky but now Gullit's gone, Robson's here, Shearer's back and the forecast's fine, and we're going to get the bloody good hiding we deserve. Who the hell do we think we are? We've no quality players, no money and our stadium's crap. There's only one team in the North-east, it's Newcastle United, and the sooner we accept our role as subservient country cousins, the better.

Gosh. They sound quite upset.

We arrive at Sunderland to be met by an army preparing for Agincourt. Banners and colours flutter among the three thousand troops. Roars of hope burst from the throng to stiffen the sinews and summon up the blood. A match ticket changes hands for a hundred pounds. I'm nervous, scared, excited. The convoy waits, ready for the charge: twenty-seven white double-decker buses, fifteen coaches, a phalanx of police cars, vans and outriders. I'm sure I can hear drumming.

The police give the word. The outriders gun their BMWs. The buses rev their engines. A battle cry breaks forth as the first bus moves out. But one of our group is missing.

'Where's Raggy?'

'He's ower the road, gettin' a pie.'

A man has to have his priorities.

'Does he knaa we're gannin?'

'What, with forty buses drivin' past the shop?'

We're just pulling out as Raggy arrives, breathless, pie in hand. The police bikes speed ahead and hold back the traffic. We pass each junction to waves and thumbs-up. Good luck and God speed. We curve out of the town, the long white line snaking its way towards the River Tyne. All we lack are roof-mounted speakers and 'The Ride of the Valkyries'.

On board, several are on cellphones, trying to describe the scene, though one guy is speaking to someone with an optimistic view of the technology. 'He wants us to hold me phone out the window so he can hear what it's like.'

We pass people queuing at ordinary stops. Typical – you wait twenty minutes for a bus then . . .

Along the A1 and past the Angel of the North. When Newcastle reached the cup final three years ago, some enterprising Geordies managed to drape a huge United number nine shirt over the structure, confirming Shearer's status as Geordie deity. Today she's bare and neutral.

The level of anticipation and excitement is palpable and growing. Few made it to last year's game because of the small number of tickets, but with United's new stand the allocation's improved and for many this is their first time on the convoy, unsure of what to expect.

Gateshead and our first sight of the Mag fans. For all their devotion, they are clearly impressed at the sight and unable to repress a smile, albeit accompanied with the obligatory V-signs.

Closer. And then we see it, dominating the distant skyline.

'There it is! Skunk Park!'

The convoy halts at Leazes Moor, some half a mile from the ground. The police spill out of their vans and dispatch one officer to each bus to explain what will happen. It's a huge operation for them today and the logistics are daunting. While most of the fans are grateful for the segregation, there's a significant number from each side who would love the chance of a showdown. An officer climbs on board, his headset and bulletproof vest light years from the traditional bobby.

'Right lads, when you arrive we'll be escorting you off the buses to the turnstiles and once inside, you'll be able to get tea, coffee, alcohol . . .'

'And three points?' a voice interrupts.

The officer smiles. 'Hopefully.' We cheer a fellow Mackem.

I notice movement from the line of buses ahead of us. About a hundred lads, all in replica shirts, have come off the coaches and are now lined up along the edge of the moor, relieving the strain of bursting bladders while delivering a traditional insult. It is surreal, hilarious and perfectly captures the mood of the day.

The convoy moves off towards the ground. More Mags now, more V-signs, a mass of black-and-white venom. We pass a pub, crammed to the rafters with United shirts. We're subjected to a volley of taunts, abuse and threats, yet they can't get at us because the pub door's blocked by a policeman. On horseback. To make eye contact with us, the Geordies have to peer around the horse as it stands oblivious to the madness.

More crowds, more shouts. There's Kate Adie! How heavy is this going to get?

We park the coach and make for the turnstiles. There's a line of riot police just twenty yards away and behind them a sea of black and white hatred. 'You're scum and you know you are! You're scum and you know you are!'

Inside the ground and relative safety. Seven flights up and I emerge into the stadium. Oh. Given its size and the hype surrounding the new development, I'd been expecting more. The scale is vast, yes, the new cantilevered stand the largest in Europe, but the stadium as a whole is dull, dull, dull, a study in grey. Grey terracing, grey seats and a grey roof. A sports psychologist would have a field day with this lot. The SOL is a burst of red and white and the club name, crest and battle cry, 'Ha'way The Lads' have all been incorporated into the banks of seats. Here there's nothing, just 'Newcastle United' on the roof of one stand. And while the new stand is impressive, the other two are much smaller, so the ground has a rather lop-sided appearance. I'm biased, of course, but in the words of former Newcastle Chairman and saviour, Sir John Hall, the whole thing's 'a bit of a carbuncle'.

Three o'clock approaches and the crowd starts to build. The announcement of the Sunderland team is greeted with a cacophony of boos and whistles. Then suddenly the teams march out and the madness peaks, the stadium a cauldron of partisan passion. We do our best to cheer the Lads, but we're three thousand in fifty-two thousand and we're stuck way up at the top of the new stand. I'm glad to see Sunderland have kept their red-and-white shirts, with just a change to white shorts. Call me old-fashioned (and I am), but I hate it when clubs adopt their away strip when the normal strip would suffice. Today of all days is about pride, identity and wearing the red and white.

We've got a full-strength team except for Arca, who's one of the subs. He's still only nineteen and perhaps Reid thinks today's too much for him, although he's captain of the Argentine Under-20 side and they take their footie pretty seriously over there.

From the kick-off Newcastle break forward and within the first minute, Speed is suddenly clear and bearing down on our goal. He's twenty yards out, fifteen. He shoots but scuffs it wide. For the next few minutes they dominate the play with a display of neat, quick passing that has our players running ragged. We manage a solitary attack that Quinn volleys high, but United are instantly back at us. Domi breaks down the right, whips over a cross and there's Speed again, leaping clear of a flat-footed defence. His header thuds against the post and bounces back down into the box. Speed is now sprawled on the ground, three Sunderland players around him. Get rid of it! But Speed sticks out a boot and hooks the ball into the net.

It's strange being in a large crowd celebrating a goal against your team. The shockwave of fifty thousand people yelling 'Yes!' in unison is a physical force you can only appreciate if you're not part of that energy.

For the next ten minutes Newcastle continue to run the game, and nearly score again when Acuna heads just wide, our defence frozen like rabbits in the headlights. The Geordies can smell blood now and crank the noise up another level. They were humiliated last year and now they want revenge. You can taste it, feel it, a tidal wave of chanting rolling down the terraces, a tsunami of 'Toon Army'.

Gradually the storm eases and we start to get in the game. Quinn goes close with a clever chip from outside the box that keeper Given just tips over. Our defence settles down and significantly Shearer's not getting a sniff of anything, thanks to Thome and Craddock. Then after half an hour Craddock bursts into the Newcastle box to meet a Gray free kick. He reaches the ball just yards out and is about to shoot when Shearer hauls him back at the vital second. It's a clear penalty but Shearer's conned the ref with the old pro's trick of holding out his arms in innocence the split-second after doing the deed, making it look like he never touched Jody.

For the remainder of the first half it's pretty even. United keep threatening with long passes that split our defence, but we keep scrambling the ball away. At the other end Quinn's winning his battles, but his knock-downs aren't being picked up by anyone.

Whatever adjectives Reidy's used in the dressing-room seem to have an effect, as we start the second half looking more effective and better organised. Quinn is still our main target and from a Kilbane free kick, he powers down a header that has goal written all over it, until Given scoops it away from the foot of the post. This is more like it. Come on, lads, come on! We're yelling our hearts out, singing every song, every chant in the book, although it's unlikely we can be heard this high up.

Reid sends on Arca. He shuffles on, looking like he's wearing his kid sister's socks, yet the moment he gets the ball, he seems to mesmerise three defenders just a yard away. His ability to work in close to players is extraordinary, always confident that he can whip the ball away from any lunging tackle.

With Arca playing, the balance suddenly shifts. He hustles Solano into an error and the ball breaks to Quinn just inside the box. He lays it off to Phillips who dummies a defender and whips over a curling cross. The ball beats Quinn and two United players before reaching Hutchison at the far post. It's travelling high and fast, difficult to control, but Hutch just lashes it into the net.

The release of tension around me rips the air like a thundercrack. We're on our feet and screaming, bugger the rules about having to sit down. Now we've got a match.

After a period of shocked silence, the home fans roar out their indignation as United go back on the attack. Within a minute of our goal they get a free kick, thirty yards out. Solano bends it round the wall and it smacks against the post as fifty-two thousand hearts miss a beat.

With a quarter of an hour left, Mickey Gray's got the ball in defence. If we can hang on for a draw we'll have won the day. Gray slips the ball to Alex Rae. Any away draw's good, but here it's like a win. Gray takes off like a train down the wing. What's he doing, stay back for Christ's sake! But Gray's running flat out as Rae feeds him an immaculate thirty-yard pass through three black and whites. Go on, Mickey! There's a defender coming in, but without breaking stride Gray belts a cross into the centre. Big Niall's waiting, flanked by two defenders. He leaps, meets the cross perfectly and lobs a header into the top corner.

My eyeballs are trying to explode.

GEEETTTT!!

And my chest cavity's just erupted.

IIIINNNNNNN!

I'm thirty feet up in the air.

YOOOOUUUUU!

And my hair's all fallen out.

BASTAAAARRDD!!

I am surrounded by, and part of, complete and utter mayhem. If the world were about to end in five seconds, it would be calmer than this. The goal is one of sublime perfection. A perfect pass, followed by a perfect cross, finished by a perfect header. It simply could not have been done better if we'd had Pele making the pass, Bestie down the wing and King Kong in the middle.

Ten minutes left. Come on, lads, we can do it, we can do it.

Eight minutes left. United stalwart Lee breaks into our box, but Quinn's forcing him wide. Then out of nowhere Quinn launches a crude tackle and Lee crashes to the ground. Penalty. The Geordies are ecstatic while we're just numb, but there's not a word against Niall.

Up steps Shearer.

I've never seen him miss a penalty. Or rather I've never seen a keeper save one. Or even get near one. They're always hit high and left but at blinding speed, so it must be maddening for the goalie because you know exactly where it's going, but there's bugger all you can do about it. Oh well, a draw's OK, I guess. Sorenson waits, long arms dangling, tensing for the leap. Shearer places the ball on the spot like a sniper loading a bullet. I remark aloud to no one in particular: 'He always blasts them high and left.'

He sidefoots it low and right. And Tommy dives low. To his left. And knocks it away.

Well fancy that, I never knew I could spontaneously combust.

It's even better than the goals. It's Monty's save in '73. Shearer, hands to head in horror. He's blown it and he knows it. Around him, hearts sink and heads drop. They won't beat us now. The last few minutes pass in a blur and when the whistle blows, we are delirious beyond measure. Handshakes and hugs, yells of delight and more than a few tears. Oh joyous, rapturous victory. We few, we happy few. And gentlemen in Sunderland shall think themselves accurs'd they were not here – but they couldn't get a ticket.

The police hold us back until the Mags have dispersed, but we're happy to stay. It's a moment to savour like a rare vintage. The stadium is empty now but we linger, singing our anthems to the echoing stands. Then finally down the stairs and out of the ground. There are some United fans waiting, but with the massive police presence there's little they can do but stare. They haven't even the heart to hurl abuse, but their faces – I've never seen such hatred. We taunt them in the cruellest way possible. 'Shearer! Shearer!'

On the bus everyone's grinning like idiots or yelling down cellphones. I call Anna at home to let her know I'm OK. I'd said I wouldn't tell her the result so she could watch it on *Match of the Day*, but the background din and my breaking voice give the game away. 'We won! Two–one! I love you!'

Back into Sunderland. The Colliery Tavern is next to the stadium and everyone's come out to welcome us home. Drinks in hand, they cheer and wave, feting each coach as conquering heroes. God, this is good. It makes up for all the bad times, all the heartache, of which no doubt there'll be more to come, but it's exactly those moments that make this one so precious.

Finally we're on the motorway for the long drive back. We've at last calmed down, the wild euphoria now a gentle glow. The radio's on and Reidy's being interviewed about the penalty incident: 'I saw Quinny go in for the tackle, but he's never been able to tackle and I thought "Oh flip . . ."'

Yeah, right.

The coach is warm and comfortable. There's a card game going on and someone's just cleared a big pot of fifty pence. Raggy sits back, tired but happy, basking in the memories of an incredible day. 'If I've won the lottery tonight, that would be quite nice – but it wouldn't be as good as this.'

Which I think sums it up rather well.

Saturday, 18 November 2000

NEWCASTLE UNITED 1   SUNDERLAND 2

(Speed 4)   (Hutchison 68, Quinn 76 – and Sorenson 82!)

PLAYED	TRAVELLED	SPENT	POSITION	STATE OF MIND
17	7,042 miles	£923.47	9th	Ecstasy beyond imagination

Charlton Athletic (away) – Premier League

Meanwhile, at the other end . . .

The reverberations of last week's victory have thudded through the North-east like a sonic boom. The hysteria of the win and the bitterness of the loss have continued unabated, and will remain so for the next five months until the return match at the SOL in April. In the interim, workplace banter will be both agony and ecstasy and I just wish I knew a Mag I could annoy. So with one down, let's move on to the next debt that needs to be repaid.

The 1998 First Division play-off final between Charlton and Sunderland has been acknowledged as one of the best ever Wembley finals. The events of the day forged a bond between both sets of supporters, each recognising that they had witnessed something special. All very noble and praiseworthy of course, but I think those applauding such sportsmanship couldn't have been watching the match from my perspective – in the middle of twenty-thousand Charlton fans.

I hadn't been back in the country long and had only seen a few games at the SOL, so in the Mackems' scramble to get tickets, I was a complete non-starter. The only alternative was to go through a London ticket agency, who traded under the unusual name of Rip-Off Scumbag Bastards Ltd.

'Twenty-pound ticket, sir? No problem. That'll be fifty pounds, please.'

'Fifty quid? For a twenty-pound ticket? What's the extra thirty for?'

'Service fee, commission, administration charge and delivery, sir.'

'Who's delivering it – the Queen?'

But there was a bonus. I was going to be slap-bang in the middle of the Charlton fans, all psyched up for one of the most important games in their club's history with a ten-million-pound place in the Premiership at stake. Oh joy. But hang on, this was the '90s, aeons away from the fear-filled '70s when going to an away game was akin to a tour of 'Nam. The morons had been weeded out and the game had gone all middle-class and families with stewards, police and CCTV. And at Wembley cup finals everyone's always on their best behaviour.

I decided against wearing my replica shirt.

Walking down Wembley Way I chided myself and wished I'd worn something red and white after all. The sun was shining, with everyone in fine humour, and the banter between the fans was good-natured. Some lifelong supporter I was.

Inside the ground my seat was high up in the stand, only accessible after a long climb up an enclosed concrete stairwell. But at least I wasn't entirely alone; about a dozen other Sunderland fans were scattered around me. The agency must have made a nice little earner. Gradually we started to relax, confidence growing in our unity. Jackets came off to reveal a scarf, badge or replica shirt. A few throat-clearing chants to stake our allegiance. A few heads turned, but it was OK.

The game began, Sunderland nervous and scrappy, unable to string two passes together while Charlton were playing with fluent ease and after twenty minutes, they scored. Taunts that 'we weren't singing anymore'. We'd have had to be Pavarotti to be heard among that lot. Unfortunately one of our number, high on beer while low on brow and brain cells, reacted to the time-served teasing with a volley of violent abuse. This did not go down well. I reminded him of our situation, twelve of us and twenty thousand of them. They had better odds at Rorke's Drift.

Second half. A quick equaliser. Our celebrations were greeted with total silence and accusing stares. Five minutes later we were ahead and our Neanderthal Fan began taunting the Charlton faithful with a flurry of insults. Good move. His opposite numbers rose off their knuckles and made towards us, challenges spitting through twisted faces. 'Come on then! Come *on* then!' Stewards rushed to stem the surge and we ended up inside a police cordon as large-scale chanting burst out of genuine anger: 'Get 'em aht, get 'em aht, get 'em *aht*!' From that moment on it was clear that any hope of a good-natured victory had gone. There was too much tension, too much to lose. The game became a heart-pumping rollercoaster of emotion. They equalised 2–2. We went ahead 3–2. With five minutes left they equalised again. In extra time our fourth goal was swiftly matched with yet another equaliser. By the time we got to penalties there were sick faces everywhere. No one wanted this. Ten spot kicks, all converted. After nine months, forty-six games, three play-off matches, extra time and eighteen goals, it came down to sudden death. With no quick exit, our police cordon gone and all the stewards now pitchside, I realised I faced a personal choice of some difficulty. Either we lost or I risked a serious kicking from vented bitterness. Hamlet never knew when he was well off.

Two more penalties. Both successful.

They scored again, seven in a row, which must be some kind of record. Then up stepped Michael Gray. And I was safe.

On reflection it was probably the best result for both clubs. Charlton won a brief taste of the Premiership which allowed them to regroup and prepare a more viable challenge, while we had an extra season in the First Division to consolidate and strengthen, ensuring our eventual return to the top flight was on a firm footing.

But I still wish we'd won.

My personal trauma aside, I'm actually a big admirer of Charlton. Like us they've fought their way up from Division One without money or stars and play a similar blend of fast-running, hard-tackling football. And they have a wonderfully ridiculous nickname: The Addicks. Allegedly this 'Sarf Lunnun' moniker derives from an early tradition of both teams sharing a post-match supper of haddock and chips. Their fishmonger would attend games with a haddock nailed to a stick. Classy.

Above all, Charlton are a club of their community. When The Addicks were forced to leave their beloved Valley Parade ground in 1985, their supporters mounted a seven-year rescue campaign that involved raising one million pounds, putting up candidates for local elections and clearing the debris from the decaying stadium. Now they're back with a new set of stands and plans for expansion, an inspiring example of the bond between team and town.

As we wait for kick-off, the PA asks the home crowd to applaud the Sunderland fans in recognition of our sporting behaviour at the play-off final. Dammit, will you stop being so *nice*, I'm starting to like you guys.

Until yesterday, today's game was actually in doubt. A survey during the week discovered that roof supports in one of the stands had just been welded rather than bolted. They'd been like that since 1994. Gulp. The emergency repair work was completed in time but the previous scenario doesn't bear too much thinking about. For six years, six thousand people have been sitting under a roof that has, in effect, been glued on.

For all of last week's glories, I'm expecting us to struggle today. Charlton are unbeaten at home and I suspect our players are still on Cloud Nine. As usual I'm proved wrong when we go straight into attack and a Hutchison drive skims just past the post. However, the rain and a soggy pitch make play difficult. The opening football is slippy and scrappy, and it's almost twenty minutes before the first shot on target, when a Quinn effort is cleared off the line.

Events pick up just before half-time when Phillips is foiled by a superb last-ditch tackle. Then Kilbane hits the bar and Phillips snaps on the rebound, but his tight-angle shot flashes across the front of goal.

As has become the pattern, Sunderland lift their game in the second half. The passing starts to click and a spectacular Rae bicycle kick makes clear our intent to win this. Ten minutes later and Rae seals his man-of-the-match award with what is popularly known as 'a screamer'. Collecting the ball inside the Charlton half, he heads for goal then lets rip with a thundering effort from twenty-five yards that fairly flies into the top corner.

For the rest of the game we stay in control, with Craddock in particular superb in defence. It's seventy-four minutes before Charlton manage their first shot on goal and though they press towards the end, we hold firm for the three points. Amidst all the euphoria of last week, no one seemed to notice that it was also our first away win of the season and now we have two. Whoa, heady stuff.

Saturday, 25 November 2000
CHARLTON ATHLETIC 0   SUNDERLAND 1

(Rae 57)

PLAYED	TRAVELLED	SPENT	POSITION	STATE OF MIND
18	7,054 miles	£955.07	9th	On a roll

Manchester United (home) – Worthington Cup Fourth Round

And Buddha's alive and well and working for Sony

It's been a few years since Sunderland beat Man United outside of a regular league match.

Bill and Monica, Charles and Camilla – and Diana. GM, New Labour and United's Treble.

Sunderland 1 Manchester United 2.

Maggie out, Mandela out. The storms, the Crash and the fall of the Wall. Hillsborough, Tyson and the Hand of God. OJ, BSE, HIV.

Manchester United 3 Sunderland 0.

Torvill and Dean, Charles and Di, Reagan and Gorbachev. Thatcher and the Falklands, Lennon and The Pistols.

Manchester United 1 Sunderland 0.

Watergate, *Jaws* and the Sea of Tranquillity. Dirty Harry, Basil Fawlty and Bleedin' Harold. Vietnam, Prague and Paris. John and Paul, Eric 'n' Ernie, Mick and Keef. Bond and Bestie, Moore and Mohammed.

Manchester United 5 Sunderland 1.

JFK and Supermac. Martin Luther and The King. Marilyn, Frank and Ella. *Psycho*, Suez, Korea. Churchill's Curtain and Hitler's holocaust. A *Farewell to Arms* and farewell to Edward. Noel and Gertie, Fred and Ginger, dancing cheek to cheek.

Votes for women but not for Chatterley. Penicillin and talking pictures. The Jarrow March and the General Strike.

Manchester United 2 Sunderland 1.

Chaplin, the Charleston, the BBC. Ypres, the Somme, Mons. *Titanic*, Marconi and Henry's Tin Lizzie. Monet, Cézanne, Matisse. Kitty Hawk and Marie Curie. Chekhov, Shaw and the death of Wilde. Queen Victoria. The Boer War.

Monday, 26 April 1897. Sunderland 2 Newton Heath 0. (Newton Heath became Manchester United in 1902.)

While all the others were cup ties, this was a test match, the last in a series of games to determine relegation and promotion between the First and Second Divisions, sort of Victorian play-offs. The bottom two in the First (Sunderland and Burnley) played the top two in the Second (Notts County and Newton Heath). Sunderland had to win this final encounter to avoid relegation, but their very presence in the test matches was mystifying. They were the 'team of all talents', ironically the Man United of their day. The previous five seasons they had finished first, first, second, first and fifth. They'd even won 'The Championship of the World' in 1895 when, as English title-holders, they beat Scottish Champions, Hearts. The season after this relegation struggle, they were second again. Following Sunderland has never been for the faint-hearted. Or the impatient. But after 103 years, it has to be our turn tonight . . . doesn't it?

I can't get a train so I'm back on National Express. I'm sitting next to a slight, neatly dressed man in his early thirties, whose business suit and haircut are both classic British middle-management, beyond Marks and Sparks but not yet Savile Row. If the trains were running, he'd be relaxing in First Class with *The Times* and a decent cup of coffee, but today he's having to slum it with the plebs.

In that curiously British way, we manage to spend the first five hours of the journey without exchanging a word while merely inches apart. Somewhere around Middlesbrough, he notices my screenwriting magazine.

'Are you a writer?' It's a slightly strangled, caught-in-the-back-of-the-throat voice of the sort much used by Monty Python when depicting accountants.

'Well, a sort of struggling unknown one,' I reply.

'It's just that our church group is putting on a play . . .'

Uh-oh. I know I'm being ungracious, but I don't want to spend the remaining two hours talking about letting Jesus into my heart and I quickly change the subject. It transpires that he's just returned to England after some years abroad, but is considering leaving again.

'Where would you like to live?' I ask.

'Probably Japan, because they are the most civilised nation on earth.'

Any alarm bells that had been tinkling faintly start to clang loudly. I take him to task about Japan's treatment of prisoners of war in World War II. He spouts out stuff about the Japanese belief in country being everything and their despising of anyone who wouldn't die for their nation. 'However, I do accept that they have a rather racist and xenophobic outlook.'

So, racist and xenophobic then, but in a civilised sort of way. I push on. 'But why do they regard themselves as superior to everyone else?'

'Because there is a direct father-son blood link going back four thousand years between the present Emperor of Japan and the Son of God.'

There's a sudden movement around us as the other passengers start hurling themselves towards the emergency exits. I'd join them, but I'm trapped in the window seat doing a fair impression of Munch's *The Scream*. *Help, help, for pity's sake someone help me. I'm stuck in a bus next to Loopy Larry.*

I'm literally shocked into silence. When someone believes something that extreme, you know it's pointless trying to convince them otherwise.

Bloody Man U supporters.

There are certain footballing legends whose exploits far outlive their careers, becoming part of the game's mythology that is handed down with appropriate embellishments. One such character is Len Shackleton and there is genuine shock when it's announced that he's died just hours before tonight's match. Mention Shack's name to anyone and it invariably brings a knowing smile, even among those too young to have seen him play. A talented maverick of the '50s, he inevitably clashed with the authorities at a time when players were regarded as little more than journeymen. With the maximum wage in force, Shack lacked the economic clout of a current star, and hence the power to call a manager's bluff in any stand-off.

He spent nine years with Sunderland, making millions laugh with his on-field antics and his off-field wit. Almost as an aside, he also scored enough league goals to remain the club's post-war record-holder. When I ask those who really did see him play, they just smile wistfully and say, 'He was better than Best.'

Before kick-off there's a one-minute silence that farcically has to be re-staged for the sake of Sky. That must have given Shack a good chuckle.

Since their losing appearance in the League Cup final of 1994 and the subsequent demands of the Champions League, Manchester United have placed little importance on tonight's domestic irritation. While they've never actually fielded their Under-12 Girls XI, their teams have invariably had an anonymous quality to them. We should be flattered that tonight's Reds include three first-team regulars: Phil Neville, Dwight Yorke and Ole Gunnar Solskjaer.

But whoever we're playing, it's still Man United and it's still a big occasion, so having both Quinn and Kilbane injured is a major setback. From the kick-off our missing target man and lack of width are painfully evident, as all our attacks funnel through the middle and are easily stifled by United's defence. Conversely, their attacks snap like a sprung trap. Reserves they may be, but the visiting players still ping the passes and run the spaces like their senior colleagues.

Inevitably United score first when Yorke breaks free and heads goalward. A brilliant tackle by Craddock forces the ball away to the touchline, but the Sunderland defence freeze as Jonathan Greening picks up the loose ball and feeds it to Yorke who prods it home.

In the next ten minutes, Greening fires just wide, Sorenson denies him with a brave dive and Yorke misses an easy chance to put them two up. United are cutting through our defence at will and history looks like maintaining its depressing tradition.

Finally, just before half-time, Phillips collects the ball on the edge of their box. He dummies a United defender then whips in a swerving shot that smacks against the post. Apart from the penalty against Chelsea, he hasn't scored since his wonder goal ten games back at Liverpool, yet his margin of failure has often been mere centimetres.

For the second half, Sunderland come out buzzing and within the first five minutes, Phillips has two good efforts foiled again, but you can't help thinking that last year he would have buried them both.

Fifteen minutes left. Phillips collects the ball wide on the right and curls in a cross. You'd normally expect Quinny there, but tonight it's little Julio Arca who nicks a header into the bottom corner. To hell with history, we can win this.

A minute later Greening dances through our defence again with just Tommy to beat. He pushes the ball past Sorenson who brings him down with a flailing dive. It's a clear penalty but, incredibly, is not given. The United players are incensed at being denied their birthright of favourable decisions, and within minutes Dwight Yorke launches an X-certificate tackle into Emerson Thome. Yorke is sent off, while Thome hobbles off and the incident cranks up the passion for the remaining ten minutes.

In injury time, Phillips nearly sneaks a winner with a free kick that zings past the post and we're into extra time. Even with just ten men, United keep threatening, but when Phillips is brought down in the box, he finally delivers with a calmly taken penalty to give us the lead.

Then it's the last five minutes, and the crowd's baying for a win as United storm for an equaliser. They hit the bar, they hit the post, but ultimately it's our night. It's a victory that's been a long time coming and hopefully we've made Shack smile.

Tuesday, 28 November 2000

SUNDERLAND 2   MANCHESTER UNITED 1 (Extra time)
(Arca 74, Phillips 100)   (Yorke 30)

PLAYED	TRAVELLED	SPENT	POSITION	STATE OF MIND
19	7,570 miles	£1,010.96	WC 5th Round	Knackered but happy

Everton (home) – Premier League

What do 'F' and 'A' stand for in the table?
Is that the proportion of football to art?

Into the life of most male football supporters there comes a moment of destiny, a fateful arrival at the crossroads of fealty to stand before the archway of allegiance. Beyond this portal lies the land of loyalty where only the devoted may tread. But behold the dreaded gatekeeper, a hooded figure of terrifying aspect. For he alone can grant salvation for the pure or damnation for the cursed. He alone can bestow happiness or misery. He alone can answer the question: 'Is my girlfriend unlucky for my football team?' (There are those for whom this query holds little fear. A Newcastle supporter, recently married, made clear his priorities to his new bride: 'I've supported The Toon for thirty year. We've been married for six month. Get the picture?')

When I first met Anna she'd never seen a football match – of any description. Never been to a game, never seen one on the telly, never even watched kids playing in the park. Her slate of soccer knowledge was as clean and pristine as a fresh fall of snow. Apparently on our second date I spent two hours talking about the '73 Cup final, but I think she's exaggerating. The match only lasted ninety minutes. The fact that she agreed to see me – or even talk to me – again was a clear indication that this was the girl for me.

Inevitably the time came to invite her up to the SOL. Past attempts to introduce girlfriends to my team had not gone down well. The proposal to travel six hundred miles to watch the Lads had been greeted with a degree of enthusiasm normally reserved for dental treatment. But Anna was willing to venture into the frozen north, so I got two tickets for a home game against Liverpool. Bias aside, I genuinely believe that if you've never been to a football match, there is no better introduction than a day at the SOL. It's a magnificent arena that still gleams like new, there's not a bad seat in the ground and it's reasonably priced. It's safe, good-humoured (except on derby days) and at its best has an atmosphere to exhilarate the soul.

On the day, the sun shone and the stadium sparkled. With a full house against a big team, the place was buzzing. Ten minutes into the game, I had to know.

'So, what do you think?'

She turned to me, her face bright with excitement.

'I can't believe they don't rehearse it!'

Which is one way of looking at training. And it did conjure up a delicious image of Kevin Phillips and Peter Reid 'in rehearsal'.

'I'm sorry, Boss, but I just don't feel that my character would head the ball at this point. During the second act perhaps, but not here.'

'Kev, just put the fookin' ball in the fookin' net.'

Three more matches and Anna was hooked, with all the zeal of a new convert and all the innocence of the new born. 'Am I shouting too loud?' 'I wouldn't want to be the goalkeeper – you don't get to run around with everyone else.'

Her final acceptance into the tribe came during the fourth game. She was sitting next to an old guy who'd probably enjoyed the heydays of both Shackleton and the shipyards. When Phillips wasted an easy chance, he turned to her in a spirit of kinship, 'How did he miss that?'

But there was a problem. We'd lost the Liverpool game 0–2. The next three matches Anna saw went 2–2, 1–2 and 2–2. Not only had we never won when she was there, but the opposition always scored twice. Four times in a row was more than coincidence. Could I really stay with a girl who hexed my team just because I loved her?

Next match, Everton at home last season. Twelve games without a win, we were free-falling down the table. Desperate times call for desperate measures. If we didn't win this and Everton scored twice, I'd be looking at a very tough decision. As we entered the ground, Anna handed me a folded piece of paper. 'I dreamt about the game last night. Put it in your wallet.'

We scored early on but then Everton equalised just before half-time. And Anna was smiling! 'It's OK . . .' she began, then stopped herself.

Second half, and Phillips scored an absolute peach from outside the box in the seventy-seventh minute to finally give us a victory of 2–1. After the game, Anna reminded me about the note, which read as follows: 'Sunderland 2 Everton 1. Everton equalise just before half-time. Second Sunderland goal is a penalty by Phillips in the seventy-eighth minute.'

Which just goes to show that girls know nothing about football.

This is extraordinary. In the space of just a few weeks, we've gone from mid-table muddlers to a top six spot if we win tonight. And Europe! Eighteen months ago we were in Division One playing Grimsby. This time next year it could be Barcelona in the Nou Camp. Waaaahhhhhh!! After an inauspicious start, we're now looking solid with just one defeat in the last fourteen games. The squad is strong, particularly in defence with Thome, Varga, Gray, Makin and especially Jody Craddock, who has improved beyond all recognition. Phillips might not be scoring for fun as he was last season, but the goals are still coming from others in the team, which stuffs all the experts who said we'd struggle if Kev lost his form.

My memories of former Sunderland teams showing any league prowess are that they'd bottle it at the merest hint of a good run. They might stretch to three games without defeat, but give them a home game against a poor side and they crumble magnificently under the weight of dormant hope and expectation. But not tonight. Tonight we take off like an express train.

Quinn goes close, then Arca, then Quinn again when he takes a high ball on the chest and turns and volleys against the bar. It rebounds awkwardly to Phillips, just yards out from goal, but he snatches at it and it bounces clear.

Everton are also lively on the break and seem able to thread passes through our back four with ease. Their main striker, Kevin Campbell, is a constant threat and nearly scores with a clever lob. One minute later and there are three unmarked Everton attackers falling over themselves in front of our goal, but incredibly they all miss and the ball slips away.

But it's Sunderland who dominate the first half, with Quinn in superb form. His every touch is quality and after half an hour his magnificent header forces a brilliant save from Everton keeper Gerrard.

Finally a breakthrough. Quinn flicks another high ball to midfielder Gavin McCann who lines a shot up for Alex Rae on the edge of the box and . . . bang! Rae rifles in another bullet to match last week's goal against Charlton. In injury time, Phillips brings another good save from Gerrard and although Kev might not be scoring, he's looking sharper than he's been all season.

In the second half Sunderland play as if they're Man United at home. Apart from one long-range effort which Sorenson tips over, it's all red and white and it's all about Phillips. He stumbles over a skewed shot from Quinn as it whizzes through his legs when he's just a yard out. Then he rounds the keeper but hits the side netting. Finally, after sixty-five minutes, an Arca shot is deflected into Phillips' path. He's got so much space he must be offside and so much time he could sign the ball, but he's onside and on target as he slots it coolly past Gerrard. It's his first league goal from open play for ten games and the noise that greets it is as much in relief as celebration.

For the rest of the game, Everton are never in it and for Sunderland it's just a question of how many. Arca's tormenting their midfield, Rae is having his best match ever and Quinny's unbeatable in the air. At the back, our defence is a rock with Sorenson supreme. Ten minutes left and Phillips nearly grabs a third, but a sublime save by Gerrard forces his shot against the bar. Everton hold out to finish just two goals down, but it's our most convincing win of the season.

Strikers blow hot and cold and Phillips could be criticised for missing several easy chances, but at least he's in the thick of the play. I'd be more concerned if he wasn't getting any chances at all. He's just half a yard off the pace and his shots are mere inches wide. One day soon he's going to click back to form and somebody's going to suffer badly – and I think it might just be Middlesbrough.

Monday, 4 December 2000
SUNDERLAND 2   EVERTON 0
(Rae 44, Phillips 65)

PLAYED	TRAVELLED	SPENT	POSITION	STATE OF MIND
20	8,134 miles	£1,079.67	6th	In Reid We Trust

Middlesbrough (home) – Premier League

I'll have a double Y chromosome, pet

For all of football's recent revolution, one tradition remains as the bedrock of going to the game: the pre-match pint or ten. On match days, any hostelry near the SOL will be packed to its red-and-white rafters with a heady mixture of bodies, sweat, testosterone and above all, noise, a cacophony of yelled conversations, thumping music and Sky TV, with everything louder than everything else. It's probably not too dissimilar to inviting Motorhead and their mates into your local sauna and saying, 'OK, guys, exactly how loud can you play?'

The one trait common to all the pubs is the level of swearing. As you walk through the door, you're suddenly engulfed in a wave of expletives.

'Haddaway three pints y'wanker.'

'Y'knaa that gobshite fuckin' tosspot?'

'Fuckin' two pies bollocks, man.'

'Crappin' useless granny shagger.'

'Bloody salt'n'tossin' vinegar, y'bastard.'

As every conversation sounds like this, it's impossible to determine whether they're ordering a pint, deriding Newcastle or discussing the US presidency. But it's all done without a hint of offence. Swearing is so casual and universal as to be a token of affection. One young lad spotting a mate across the road will yell at full volume, 'How, y'fat get!' Two middle-aged men will greet each other with effusive smiles and 'Y'sexy bastard!'

While the atmosphere in those pubs might initially intimidate, it is suffused with friendliness, good humour and unfailing politeness. Those squeezing their way through the crush will invariably evoke a chorus of 'Sorry, matey', 'Thanks' and 'Mind yersel', pet.' Try the same in a London pub and all you'll hear is 'Farkin' shift' and 'Wos your game?' In the capital, any semblance of public good manners has long disappeared, but it's a trait that's common throughout the North-east. In shops and take-away bars, hard-bitten Mackems and Geordies of all ages consistently display the signs of parental lectures. They wait their turn, are unerringly polite and always say 'please' and 'thank you', because they know that if they don't they'll get a smack from their mam.

Having conducted my own brief survey of the town's watering holes, I became aware of one particular pub that was spoken of only in hushed tones. At the very mention of its name, grown men went quiet and stared down into their pints. Not even the Sunderland fans went there. It was a pub so rough that it attracted the local bus drivers.

It wasn't difficult to find; the van-full of police outside was as good as a neon sign. Given its reputation, I was thinking of sending Anna in first but she disappeared off for some fish and chips. It was now or never. I walked in, expecting the piano to stop playing and all eyes to turn in my direction. Instead I encountered a guy coming out with his ten-year old son. 'Try not to sway too much, son, or he'll think you're pissed.'

What? This is The Really Scary Pub?

Inside, while I wouldn't advise wearing a Newcastle shirt, it had the same boisterous bonhomie that pervaded everywhere else and I couldn't understand all the fuss. Back outside, I quizzed the police in the van.

'Oh, aye, it used to be a bit rough, like, but it changed hands about a year ago. It's OK now.'

'So why are you parked here?'

He indicated an approaching fellow officer, a bundle of paper in his arms.

'It's next to the chip shop.'

Today's match is Sunderland's two thousandth home league game. The first was against Burnley on 13 September 1890, and while we haven't exactly set the football world alight of late, we are still the last team to win the championship wearing stripes (i.e. a 'proper' football strip). It's just a pity it was in 1936.

Our anniversary is in danger of being upstaged by the debut of Middlesbrough's new coach, Terry Venables. With Boro anchored near the bottom of the table and just one point from their last twenty-four, they desperately need a saviour. Enter El Tel, complete with his media commitments, short-term contract and a not inconsiderable portion of humble pie for incumbent manager, Bryan Robson. I wouldn't envy Bob Murray asking Peter Reid to step aside for another coach if there was a corner flag anywhere handy.

For all Boro's plight and poor form, one shouldn't underestimate the spark that can be ignited by a new manager. It might splutter and die after briefly flaring, but we could get our fingers burnt today. I think it's going to be difficult and from the kick-off Boro do not disappoint. Their plan is clearly to disrupt the flow of the game and, to their credit, they are dreadful. I don't know exactly what Terry said to his players beforehand, but it was apparently something along the lines of, 'Right lads, remember, if it moves, kick it and if it doesn't, oh what the hell, kick it anyway.'

The game commences as a stuttering series of free kicks and when play does get going, the ball spends more time flying around than the Red Arrows. However Boro's tactics backfire when defender Ugo Ehiogu kicks one of his own team-mates in the head. The fact that the unfortunate victim was called Stamp is probably mere coincidence. Thereafter Boro calm down slightly – they stop decking their own players – but the game retains a certain agricultural quality.

Up front, Boro have Hamilton Ricard, a muscular player who is proving a handful for Craddock and Thome. He blasts over the bar early on and after twenty minutes blows an excellent chance by choosing to shoot (and miss) with two unmarked team-mates waiting in the six-yard box.

Sunderland are scrappy and not coping well with Boro's 'direct' approach. Then, after thirty-six minutes, Ricard heads in from a packed goalmouth. This does not look good. Hang on, yes it does, it's been disallowed, apparently for shoving. It could be for bad breath, I don't care, it's a huge let-off.

Just before the interval, Ricard forces a brilliant low save by Sorenson, who tips the ball just round the post. But overall the first half's not been pretty and a mere five shots by both teams tells its own sorry tale.

In the second half Boro actually manage to lower their standard of play. The tackles are still flying and referee Poll is losing his grip of the match. But at last Sunderland start to assert themselves and a McCann drive is tipped over the bar by keeper Schwarzer. Then Arca and Gray combine in a good move down the left. It appears to break down inside the Boro penalty area, but Mickey keeps going, beats the defenders to the ball and hits a low hard shot through Schwarzer's legs into the net. Oh the ignominy, oh the relief.

Deprived of their spoiling tactic, Boro are now forced to start playing, allowing Sunderland to do likewise. Five minutes later, a superb passing move gives Phillips a chance, but his shot is deflected just past the post. This is more like it and with ten minutes left, Phillips goes close again. Boro make a spirited push to the end and may have had a penalty had Ricard not exaggerated his fall with a dive worthy of an Olympic springboard final. But thankfully it ends without Boro equalising and a match I'd been dreading all week is over.

The Boro fans are rightly silent and sick, with a paltry one point from nine games. For us, it's now five wins on the trot and to get a result when you don't play well is a sign of a good team. We look strong and cannot be intimidated by anyone. Sorenson is a giant in goal, the defence looks good and Phillips keeps threatening to give someone a damn good thrashing. (Yes, I know I keep saying that, but one day it will happen, honest!)

Saturday, 9 December 2000
SUNDERLAND 1   MIDDLESBROUGH 0
(Gray 53)

PLAYED	TRAVELLED	SPENT	POSITION	STATE OF MIND
21	8,680 miles	£1,141.72	5th	Another one bites the dust

Leeds United (away) – Premier League

Or we could call it 'Lovely Lovely Leeds' . . . no?

It's another coach trip with the London Branch, as there's a problem with the train to Leeds. Apparently the guy with the red flag has sprained his ankle. Actually it's a blessing in disguise, as the prospect of walking the mile from the station to the ground holds no appeal. There's little love lost between Leeds and Sunderland fans, but then there's little love lost between Leeds and just about everyone. Our particular animosity has been forged over decades of bad-tempered cup-ties, battles for promotion and, of course, the '73 final. Along the way, two Sunderland players, Willie McPheat and Bobby Kerr, suffered broken legs, although Kerr was to exact the ultimate revenge as our cup-winning captain.

As for the rest of the country, their own vendettas probably arose through similar conflicts. The Leeds team of the '60s and '70s were renowned for their cynical professionalism (or as Norman Hunter recently described it, 'bending the rules a little bit'). They were respected, feared and loathed by everyone outside Yorkshire, yet dismissed their unpopularity with arrogant disdain. Team and supporters bonded alike, and their fans earned a reputation for trouble and violence. Today, for all David O'Leary's crafting of a skilled side, old enmities die hard, while in players such as Bowyer, Batty and Smith, there's more than a hint of the old 'Nobody Loves Us And We Don't Care'. A number of their fans seem equally resistant to change, the playground bullies who never grew up, with a racist minority destructive as ever. In the 'nature or nurture' debate, Leeds radiate the former, their 'Yorkshire grit' impervious to fate, fashion or personnel. Quite how Rio Ferdinand, a product of West Ham's more cultured approach, will adapt to the Leeds way is anyone's guess. At present, he looks like a concert pianist in a heavy metal band.

We arrive a couple of hours before kick-off, so I take a walk round the stadium. Elland Road is one of those grounds that suffers from Forth Road

Bridge Syndrome. Each stand is developed in turn, so by the time the last is improved, the first looks dated and disjointed. Hence the vast and impressive East Stand of 1994 looms over its opposite number, built in 1957. The exterior walls range from ultra-modern to grey concrete and traditional red brick. If you can imagine a large firm of architects having an internal tiff that ends with each partner storming off to design their own section, you'd come up with Elland Road.

The club shop stocks the usual cornucopia of clothing and paraphernalia, without which it is apparently now impossible to support one's team. In the videos section, there are umpteen copies of Leeds' 1972 FA Cup win over Arsenal, but oddly not a single tape of their appearance the following year. Obviously a big seller. For magazines, you can choose between two staggeringly original titles: *Super Leeds* and *Leeds Leeds Leeds* (presumably the first two launches didn't quite take off: 'No really, CK, I'm sure if we add one more "Leeds" it'll do the trick!'). Perhaps I should just have called this book *Sunderland Are Fab*.

On leaving the shop, I notice a commotion by the club car park. The Leeds team coach has arrived, which seems a bit odd considering they're playing at home. Apparently all the players drive to the ground early, leave their cars and then go off by coach to the training ground for a final session and pre-match discussion. The coach drives into a cordoned-off area to be greeted by a waiting crowd of home fans. Their cheers as each player descends from the bus are met with sulky indifference. Young Rio almost smiles for a moment, then suddenly remembers who he's playing for now.

About thirty yards away is the players' car park. It's some way removed from Arthur Daley. Two Leeds stewards hover nervously, but otherwise I'm free to wander among a million quid's worth of motors. Just for the record, there's one Roller, two Jags, three Porsches, four BMWs, five Mercs and a long black Corvette (Harry Kewell's). Obviously a Leeds wage packet doesn't stretch to a Ferrari (downright scandalous, I call it). Stanley Matthews used to take the bus.

Given past encounters, there seems little point in us even turning up today. Leeds have won the last nine games against us (both home and away), while we haven't won a league match at Elland Road in the top division since 1934. For all of O'Leary's blarney about his team being 'just kids', Leeds have become a tough, skilful and professional outfit who've established themselves as a top Premiership side with a place in the Champions League. Our only hope might be to catch them while they are suffering from a touch of the 'Chelseas': dazzling in Europe (a win at Lazio), disappointing in England (a loss at Leicester).

When the Leeds team is announced, I realise it's going to take more than a bout of jet lag to stop them. Not only is Ferdinand making his home debut, but David Batty's back from injury, as is Wizard o' the Wing, Harry Kewell, thus affording O'Leary a first opportunity to play his Holy Trinity of Kewell, Smith and Viduka.

From the off, Leeds are zinging passes around the park and O'Leary's Dream Machine are purring like their expensive autos. In the opening ten minutes they threaten with efforts from Viduka and a long solo run by Dacourt. We're struggling to keep up and an early tackle by Thome earns him a yellow card, putting him on the back foot for the rest of the game.

The first goal arrives after twenty-two minutes with a depressing inevitability. Leeds surge down the right, then Smith and Viduka break into our penalty area with a couple of ping-pong passes. Craddock hesitates to clear and Bowyer pounces to blast clinically past Sorenson.

Five minutes later Smith goes close and we've barely had a nod at goal. Then Gray and Arca perform another of their double acts down the left. Gray blasts in an excellent cross (will somebody tell me why he isn't playing for England?) and little Phillips beats two Leeds defenders to knock the ball down to Quinn. Niall's just ten yards out and unmarked. The ball's falling kindly for him. This is it, our chance to get back – and he skies it high and wild. Ah, big fella, we love ya, begorrah, but you should have stuck that away.

But it's a start and we begin to compete on more even terms. Rae and McCann have a couple of pops from distance, while Leeds continue to exceed the speed limit. They are faster than us and better at the physical stuff, which is no mean feat against a Peter Reid side. At full-back, Darren Williams is struggling as a replacement for Makin and every Leeds attack threatens a heart attack. Another surge, Smith's coming through and Thome blocks him off with an illegal challenge. The ref reaches for his pocket and brings out the second yellow card – which he shows to Craddock! Ssshh, nobody say anything! Incredibly the Leeds players let it go, either through ignorance or some hitherto well-hidden code of honour, but Thome's escaped and we're still a full team.

The match screeches to a halt at the break without a further score, although just before the break Kilbane completes his disappointing first half by failing to equalise from close range.

I'd love to know what they put in the Lads' half-time cuppa, as yet again we storm out with all guns blazing. After ten minutes, Quinn appears to equalise but is ruled offside. The double rush of adrenaline and despair hurts more than not getting the goal. The pace of the game steadies, probably under doctor's orders, and Leeds show their class with Dacourt dominating midfield. Sorenson makes a brilliant save in a goalmouth scramble and we narrowly escape again when Bakke backheels a pass against the post.

A minute later and Quinn has another great chance to equalise. A pass from Arca finds him just five yards out, but perhaps mindful of his earlier miss, he takes a touch to control the ball. In that vital half-second, Ferdinand appears like a rocket to block the shot.

With Phillips kept quiet by the Leeds defence and Quinn wearing the wrong boots, it's down to our defence to keep us in the game. We're living on borrowed time. Ten minutes from the end, Kewell skips down the right, chips over a cross and the incoming Viduka heads home Leeds' second. Thank you and goodnight.

To their credit, Sunderland fight on to the end. Danny Dichio, on for Quinny, nearly grabs one back when he heads against the bar, but Kilbane's wild volley off the rebound rather sums up our afternoon: lots of passion, lots of energy, nothing to show.

Outside the ground it's starting to get dark. I pass a group of lads, wearing no colours, but their accents are clearly Mackem. They draw the eye, their loitering a contrast to the passing crowds eager to get away. Then another joins them, clearly the leader. 'They're just where he said they would be. Is everybody ready then?'

As one, they zip up jackets and pull up hoods, anonymous yet distinctive, ready for the rumble. They move off, and for a second I'm tempted to follow, the professional voyeur. But this isn't me. I head off back to the coach.

Saturday, 16 December 2000
LEEDS UNITED 2   SUNDERLAND 0
(Bowyer 22, Viduka 76)

PLAYED	TRAVELLED	SPENT	POSITION	STATE OF MIND
22	9,082 miles	£1,199.07	6th	Battered and bruised

Crystal Palace (away) – Worthington Cup Fifth Round

This golden goal – do you want it 24-carat or just gold-plated?

Ask any Sunderland fan to nominate their least favourite ground and up there along with Oxford United's Manor Park and, of course, St James' will be Selhurst Park, joint home of Crystal Palace and Wimbledon.

It's not that it's particularly grotty, although it's no picture book. It's a fairly average First Division ground with a mixture of old and new stands. Nor is it necessarily the distance. Sure, it's a trek to the capital and then even further into the hinterland of south-east London, but for supporters who've spent years schlepping down to Bristol and Plymouth, a mere 600 miles is a trip to the shops. It's not even that Selhurst Park is a graveyard for Sunderland. Yep, it's where we were relegated in 1997 and knocked out of last year's Worthington Cup, but it's not like Leeds or Spurs where you have to go back decades to find a win. It's the fact that it's all of the above: a dull ground, a long hike and a good bet for a loss. That's why it's a top three contender.

So when Wimbledon were relegated last year to join their co-tenants in Division One, there was a general sigh of relief that no more would we have to visit their hated stadium. Until now, that is, with a visit to play Palace in the fifth round of the Worthington Cup. Still, just about worth it for a place in the semis and a sniff at a trophy and Europe.

But now standing in the teeming rain outside the ground, with the game cancelled a mere ninety minutes before kick-off, the old resentment returns and there is no contest for that number one spot. Not so bad for me as I live in London, but for the two thousand Mackems who've taken the afternoon off and braved the weather and the trains, it's an appalling insult. It's been raining solidly for three days, but there was no mention either this morning, or at lunchtime or this afternoon of even the possibility of a pitch inspection. Yet suddenly, just before kick-off, the groundstaff realise they have a problem. Palace manager, Alan Smith, blames Sky for insisting that the pitch inspection be delayed until the last possible moment. Whatever the reason, it's a wasted six-hundred-mile journey that will have to be repeated next week.

The next day, Sunderland announce that they'll be giving free third round FA Cup tickets (ironically against Palace) to all those who made the trip. Note that it's Sunderland making the gesture, not Palace. That's what's called looking after your supporters.

There's a fondly held belief among football fans that their beloved club can rise above any financial slings and arrows of outrageous misfortune. You can't kill off a team because ultimately it is an ephemeral being. It's not the players, or the manager or the directors, all of whom come and go. Nor is it the ground, as Sunderland have proved with their move to the SOL. A football team is merely the physical expression of the faith, love and devotion of their fans, indestructible abstracts that can never be touched by the sordid aspects of money and commerce.

If only.

In June 1998, businessman Mark Goldberg bought a financially troubled Crystal Palace for about twenty-three million pounds. It was, to be generous, an investment decision of some optimism. Nine months later the club was in administration, with debts of twenty-two million and losing five hundred thousand pounds a month. Nine months after that, Goldberg was declared bankrupt.

By March 2000, Palace had been in administration for a year. Despite much talk of rescue packages, the reality was that unless a wealthy saviour could be found within three months, they would not be allowed to compete in the new season. The Football League is rather fussy about professional clubs actually being able to pay their players.

The Palace fans formed a Supporters' Trust. Within a month they had raised an incredible one million pounds toward buying shares in the club, so that its future would, to a degree, be in their hands. But the dosh required was way beyond a mere million and the Trust still needed their angel investor. Once the Administrator pulled the plug, Crystal Palace would cease to exist. A new team called Crystal Palace might rise again, but they'd be a semi-professional outfit slumming it outside the League. Palace would have died.

Then in June 2000, behold, there came from the East a wise man. Well actually it was Croydon, which is more south-east, and there are some who would question the wisdom of his decision, but mobile phone entrepreneur and Palace fan, Simon Jordan, bought the club for £10.6m. Cue Hallelujah chorus. And he shall reign for ever and ever.

Which is where the story should have ended, with happy supporters rejoicing tearfully in the streets and holding up infants to be kissed by their benefactor. Not quite. The Supporters' Trust didn't get their seat on the board, manager Steve Coppell was sacked for the third time and by October a bad run of results saw Palace fans *spitting* on new boss Alan Smith, while Smith described his players as 'lazy whingers'. But you get that in the best of families.

What the Palace saga hammered home was that ultimately a professional football club is not just the body corporeal of its fans' hopes and dreams, but a very expensive ticking bomb that can explode with relatively little warning. In 1998 Palace were still a Premiership side, yet within two years came within a whisker of going under. They were lucky – this time. Others have not been so fortunate: Accrington Stanley (1963), Newport County (1989), Aldershot and Maidstone (1992) all lost their League status due to money problems. Bournemouth, Luton and Portsmouth have all had recent visits from the Receiver or Administrator.

The repercussions of a financial crisis can last for years. During the 1950s, Sunderland became known as 'The Bank of England Club' for their extravagant spending in the transfer market. They'd reached two FA Cup semi-finals, finished fourth in the League, had massive support and boasted a team of internationals. This was a big club.

Then in 1957 the Football League received a letter from an unknown 'Mr Smith' alleging illegal payments by Sunderland to its players. The resulting investigation expelled four of the club's wealthy directors, forced the manager into retirement and suspended several of the team. The following year, Sunderland were relegated for the first time ever and entered a forty-year wilderness of minimal success (one trophy), falling crowds, struggling finances and seven relegations, including one spell in the old Division Three. Only in the last four years has the club shown signs of revival with the new stadium, a healthy bank balance and consolidation in the Premiership. The identity of Mr Smith is still a mystery.

It's now a week later and the red and white army are back, but they're not happy – again. As they swarm around the Palace programme sellers, indignant cries of protest burst forth. 'Three quid? Yer bloody kiddin' tho' but?' Surprisingly, the pages are not embossed with gold leaf. If Palace keep selling programmes at this price, their financial worries are over.

We're starting without five regular players tonight (Quinn, Hutch, Makin, McCann and Craddock), which is going to make a hard task even harder. Palace may be First Division, but they're having a good run in the League and have already knocked out Leicester in the Cup. With just two games to the final, they are looking for a storybook ending to their near-death experience.

The game begins at full pelt but soon speeds up. An early Palace break leaves leading striker Clinton Morrison with just Sorenson to beat. His shot is partially deflected by Tommy but is rolling towards the net. Suddenly there's a blinding flash and Darren Williams, faster than a speeding bullet, hooks the ball away just in time. Give that man a pair of bright red underpants.

Sunderland have a couple of half chances, but it's Palace who seem to want this more. Their forwards are fast and dangerous and our attempts to play the offside trap result in Tommy making several last-ditch saves. It's thirty minutes before we get our first real chance: a defensive slip leaves Arca unmarked just ten yards out, but his attempted lob goes tamely over the bar.

Palace continue to threaten but at half-time it's still 0–0. While Sunderland have the better technical skill, Palace have energy, commitment and will to win, and that's often all you need in a cup-tie.

Three minutes after the re-start and a dodo lands on the pitch. Not quite, but an even rarer event occurs: Sorenson makes a mistake. His weak goalkick barely clears the box and goes straight to Morrison, who quickly crosses for Forsell to tap in the first goal. The Palace fans erupt in a blast of belief that this really is going to be their year. The noise is still reverberating when Darren Williams crosses, Dichio heads down and Alex Rae scores from close in. We've equalised in under a minute, the Palace roar stops and ours takes over.

Ten minutes later we nearly snatch the lead when Dichio and Phillips collide going for the same ball. Palace respond by hitting the bar twice in a minute and this cup-tie is going down to the wire. Phillips finally gets into the game with a saved low drive from twenty yards, then minutes later he's clean through, chasing a pass into the area. The goalkeeper makes a clumsy challenge, but rather than allowing himself to be fouled for the penalty, Phillips hurdles the keeper and in doing so, loses control of the ball. It's a commendable piece of sportsmanship but there's many a striker who would have gone down.

Eight minutes left and Morrison again bursts into our penalty area. He twists away from Thome, then flashes a low shot into the net. If they were fired up before, they're like a furnace now and despite a late rally, we fail to equalise. Palace take the tie and now face Liverpool in the semi-final. Just for their sheer refusal to die, both on and off the pitch, I hope they make it all the way – and that we've seen the last of Selhurst Park.

Tuesday, 19 December 2000

CRYSTAL PALACE 2   SUNDERLAND 1
(Forsell 48, Morrison 82)   (Rae 49)

PLAYED	TRAVELLED	SPENT	POSITION	STATE OF MIND
23	9,094 miles	£1,228.27	Out!	Not again!

Manchester City (home) – Premier League

And here's to you, Mrs Thatcher . . .

I've just finished Colin Shindler's book, *Manchester United Ruined My Life*, which describes growing up within Manchester's Jewish community while discovering the joys of following Manchester City. It's an enjoyable read, but I've got a bit fed up with City fans being awarded Most Favoured Martyr status by the nation. Suffering? Ha! Luxury, more like. Let's look at the facts. Shindler saw his first match in 1955 and I'm writing this in December 2000. In the interim, City have been relegated four times and had twenty managers, but won the Championship, the FA Cup, the European Cup-Winners Cup, the League Cup (twice) and the Charity Shield (twice). By comparison, Sunderland have been relegated seven times, gone through twenty-three managers and won sweet FA (just the once). When it comes to wandering in the wilderness, at least Shindler's tribe have seen the Promised Land. The Makemites just have an old postcard.

During the lean years, support for Sunderland certainly dipped (if you were one of the 8,192 souls who saw us beat Portsmouth at home in 1974, I think there's a reunion next Wednesday). There's always been a symbiotic relationship between team and town, inexorably linked but occasionally drifting apart. As long as the town had the shipyards, the mine and Vaux Breweries, the community had an identity outside of the football club. Then came Thatcher, with a slash-and-burn policy for the North-east that would have done credit to Hitler's Blitzkrieg. The Sunderland shipyards went from producing the world's highest tonnage during the '50s and '60s to oblivion in the '80s. The Wearmouth Colliery, the last surviving pit in County Durham, closed in 1994. Vaux served their final pint in 1999. The only large-scale replacement for these core industries has been the Nissan factory near Washington. But it is the basket with all the eggs, and foreign car companies are not renowned for hanging in there when times get tough just for the sake of the local workforce.

Ironically, as the town's economy struggled, its profile prospered. The local college became a university in 1992 and the town a city the following year. Yet all that this new city can now depend upon is its football team and it has embraced them as a drowning man grabs a lifebelt. Since moving from Roker Park in 1997, the average attendance has gone from twenty thousand to forty-six thousand. The Premiership has brought money into Sunderland and the team's appeal is now worldwide. Yet unlike the Board of Manchester United, Bob Murray recognises that club and community need each other if both are to survive and prosper. It's not like Newcastle, a large confident city that could carry on without United. If Sunderland AFC died, so would the area.

To this end, the club has developed the largest community programme in British football and employs nearly fifty people in projects that embrace education, health, coaching and crime prevention. Too often, such schemes either receive scant lip service or become blatant PR exercises, but the sheer scale and detail of Sunderland's venture would impress even the most cynical (so if the following all sounds rather worthy, that's because, well, it is – very worthy).

Within the stadium are two purpose-built classrooms for visiting children on school trips, while a fleet of vehicles take the education and coaching programmes to seventy-five schools a week, covering an area from Edinburgh to Yorkshire. The programmes include the first anti-drugs initiative in football and the first CD-ROM produced by a football club to aid numeracy and literacy, using the game as a learning tool ('If it takes Kevin Phillips thirty-eight games to score thirty goals . . .'). A reward scheme tackles truancy by offering free match tickets and stadium tours for schools with good attendance records (Newcastle are the only Local Education Authority in the North-east not to have adopted this scheme, as they were concerned that it would *increase* truancy). When I was growing up, girls didn't play football. It was a boys' game. Girls didn't play because . . . well, they just didn't. But the times they are a-changing. Now Sunderland's coaching schemes include girls-only sessions, with a feeder system leading to Sunderland AFC Women, who now play in their equivalent of the Premiership. A major complaint about Premiership football is the cost of tickets and season ticket 'lock outs' which prevent fans from attending games on a match-by-match basis. At every Sunderland game there are twenty thousand concessionary seats and about six thousand tickets available for match day sales.

And if that lot weren't impressive enough, the club even have the nets for the SOL and all their training pitches made by inmates at Durham Jail, as part of a successful rehabilitation scheme.

Murray's 'family' policy of making football safe, pleasant, affordable and accessible to the whole community has produced capacity crowds with the youngest average age in the Premiership and the highest proportion of female season ticket holders. None of this would have been possible without the SOL, yet ironically, for all Thatcher's destruction and her rejection of 'society', she is indirectly responsible for the club remaining a part of the town.

Originally, the new stadium was going to be located next to the Nissan plant. It would no doubt have had many excellent features, bar one – the heartbeat of being inside the city walls. With the closure of Wearmouth Colliery, suddenly a location arose within the town, making the SOL one of the very few new stadiums in the country to remain in its community. It overlooks the River Wear and embraces the mining heritage that gave the town its prosperity and the team its support. A large replica Davy Lamp stands outside the stadium, while the NUM Lodge banner hangs inside the main entrance.

But the strongest link is the one which cannot be seen, the spirit of over 200 miners who died under the very ground on which the SOL now stands.

Manchester City is one of those clubs with whom Sunderland share an unusually high number of coincidences. The two managers, Reid and Joe Royle, are fellow Scousers, and have both played for, and subsequently managed, City. When Sunderland were relegated in 1991, the final match was against Peter Reid's City side which contained a certain Niall Quinn, whose two goals that day sealed our fate. The Lads' fifth-round FA cup-tie against the Blues in 1973 was voted The Greatest Ever Game at Roker, and when Sunderland opened the SOL, their first opponents were . . .

Traditionally, games played close to Christmas were always in danger of being called off due to snow or frozen grounds, but with the advent of under-soil heating, the show now always goes on. However, there is a nod towards the season with a good sprinkling of Santa caps among the crowd and one group of lads in full Saint Nick regalia, albeit with Blues Brother sunglasses. (I think they may be the same lot who attire themselves variously as Arab sheikhs, Elvis and the Teletubbies.)

Following the hiding we got at Maine Road, I'm grateful to see that City's hitman that evening, Paulo Wanchope, isn't playing today. To counter that, we're without Kevin Phillips, suspended for one game. It's the first match he's missed all season, so it should be interesting to see our tactics without him.

We start well when Gavin McCann has a chance, but get caught ball-watching as Shaun 'The Goat' Goater almost gives City the lead after ten minutes. The first break comes when Don Hutchison is fouled just outside the City penalty area. He gets up and stands waiting to take the free kick as Weaver in goal organises his wall – and it's in! With an almost magical sleight of hand, Hutch has taken the kick with City still sorting themselves out, and the ball has screamed into the top corner past a bemused Weaver. The City players protest, but referee David Elleray waves them away in his best housemasterly fashion. 'Stop whining, boy. And take fifty lines: "I must pay attention at free kicks".'

Two minutes later, McCann zings a great ball out of defence to Arca, who finds Gray, who then hits a low hard cross into the goalmouth, straight into the path of the advancing McCann. He's just yards out, this is going to be one of the goals of the season . . . and he skews it wide!

Although Quinn is without his buddy Phillips, he is still a threat. On the half-hour, he takes a ball high on his chest some thirty yards out with his back to goal. In one sublime move, he turns and volleys a screamer towards the City net for a certain goal, yet at the last instant Weaver arches back and tips it over for an incredible save.

For the remainder of the first half, Sunderland are in complete control. City are totally reactive, as if their whole game plan had centred on how to stop Phillips, and now he's not here they are completely stumped.

The second half couldn't be more different. From the whistle, City are sharp and aggressive, forcing Sunderland to up their own game, and the first fifteen minutes ding-dongs merrily on high. Hutch has a great chance for his second goal with only Weaver to beat, but chooses a weak pass instead of shooting. The next minute there's a scramble in the Sunderland goalmouth, leading to a City corner from which Sean Wright-Phillips is mere inches wide. Inspired, the Blues press on, twice bringing good saves from Sorenson and nearly forcing Thome into an own goal, when his defensive header just scrapes over the bar. From cruising it in the first half, we're now on the back foot and the home crowd are getting tense and nervous, which they express in the time-honoured tradition. 'Get stuck into them, man!'

Quinn misses a couple of chances to increase the agony and for the last twenty minutes it's nail-wracking, nerve-biting stuff. Alfie Haaland scuffs a shot for City in front of goal then, with just ten minutes left, Wright-Phillips flashes a header goalwards with Sorenson nowhere. That's it, it's in – till the ball thumps against the post and away.

More City attacks, more near misses and finally, thankfully, it's over. The shots-on-goal tally of nine apiece shows how close it was, but we've dug out a win and settled the account from the Maine Road match. We're now just three points off second place. It's a very merry Christmas.

Saturday, 23 December 2000
SUNDERLAND 1   MANCHESTER CITY 0
(Hutchison 18)

PLAYED	TRAVELLED	SPENT	POSITION	STATE OF MIND
24	9,667 miles	£1,278.22	6th	There is a Santa Claus

Bradford City (away) – Premier League

'Is that a streaker?'
'What, in this weather?'
'No, hang on – it's Elvis.'

So, we're off to watch the Lads play Bradford at Valley Parade. Sorry, the Bradford & Bingley Stadium. Which used to be called The Pulse. Now there's a name to strike fear into the hearts of the opposition.

'Who we playing next week, Boss?'

'It's a tough one, lads – we're going to The Pulse.'

'Is that some specific kind of pulse, Boss, such as lentils or haricots, or are we talking in the generic sense of the edible seeds of any pod-bearing plant? Boss?'

In the wake of the Taylor Report, the need for clubs to attract major sponsorship became paramount in order to finance the stringent new safety requirements. Naturally the deals involved a prominent display of the sponsor's name within the stadium. Thankfully the SOL has limited this to just the stands (Carling, Metro), but several clubs have gone the whole hog and handed over their identity (and arguably their dignity) to the highest bidder. So there are the Reebok, McAlpine and JJB stadiums, but I think The Pulse takes The Biscuit (apparently a deal with a local radio station). And it didn't stop there. When The Queen visited Bradford City in 1997 to open their new stand, she was faced with the fraught-ridden task of announcing, '. . . so it gives me great pleasure to declare this Allied Colloids Stand open'. She probably spent the entire speech thinking. 'It's Colloids not haemorrhoids, Colloids not haemorrhoids'.

Being Boxing Day, there's a good spirit among the crowd, further enhanced by various Santas and pantomime dames. There's a good relationship between the two clubs, kindred spirits who epitomise the hardworking ethos of traditional English football. And we both play in stripes. Some of the Bradford fans get a bit sniffy about their team's perpetual portrayal as brave, gritty battlers of little sophistication, but among the Sunderland fans there is genuine respect and a desire to see them stay in the Premiership. Hell, we almost (but not quite) didn't mind when they beat us last year as part of their last-ditch survival campaign.

Such touching sentiment, however, obviously does not extend to all clubs. Just outside the stadium is the burnt-out shell of a car, which is attracting some attention.

'Weren't that from t'Leeds game?'

'Dunno – but it's a Nissan Twin-Cam 16-valve. Our Brian were after one o' them.'

'Well tell him you've found a do-up.'

Unfortunately, this year has again found Bradford struggling at the foot of the table. They've just appointed their third manager in six months and it looks like they'll need another miracle. But lacking in ambition they're certainly not, with a new shop that is heralded as the largest club store in the world. Now, granted, I never pursued my accountancy career, but if you've been struggling to get crowds of eighteen thousand, what's the point of having a larger store than Man United who regularly get sixty-seven thousand? The plans for their stadium seem equally optimistic. A vast new stand is under construction among plans to boost the eventual capacity to thirty thousand, yet they're hardly turning people away at the moment. Meanwhile their fans complain of tickets that are among the most expensive in the Premiership and prices that have doubled in two years. Perhaps it's an act of faith akin to 'if you build it, they will come'.

The store itself is a veritable emporium, with an inventory that extends way beyond the normal football paraphernalia. Golf clubs, luggage and even Bradford City's own-label wine. Mmm, Yorkshire Chardonnay, now there's tempting. Among the footie stuff is the *City Gent* fanzine. Started in 1984, it's the oldest fans' publication in the country and, I'm afraid, looks it. An old-style typeface, black-and-white photos and solid, unremitting blocks of text don't exactly leap out and grab you, but perhaps the design is a deliberate attempt to remain unique among the raft of subsequent flashy imitators.

With kick-off approaching, Anna and I head for the turnstiles. The stewards outside are doing rather casual body searches that seem more for show than effect. Anna, as ever, is waved straight through. Good job I gave her the Uzis. One extended family are going through the ritual, when the steward gets to the grandfather. The official begins patting him down, extending his arms round the old man's back, and receives in response a big hug.

With the stadium in the midst of its expansion plans, it's very much like sitting in the middle of a building site. And at twenty-seven pounds for an uncovered seat in the full blast of an icy wind, it is definitely a memorable experience. Still, there's a nice view of the valley beyond the stadium, some cheerleaders are freezing on the pitch and we're being entertained by Lenny The City Gent, Bradford's 'adult' mascot. A rotund figure in full Bradford City strip complete with umbrella, briefcase and bowler hat, Lenny was inspired by the club's early cartoon mascot. He's certainly a refreshing change from the usual rather naff animal characters, most of whom seem to end up either confusing or scaring the smaller kids. With Lenny you get a show, which consists of him revealing his considerable midriff and consuming a large pie that he keeps in his briefcase. And they say that music hall is dead.

For the first time all season, Bradford have a full house, thanks largely to the travelling contingent who are divided between the Symphony Stand End and the 'Norman Corner Corner', named after a former Bradford player. With impressive bouts of stereo chanting, we cheer the Lads onto the pitch for a match that could spiral us to even dizzier heights. We've no injuries for the first time all season, we've won here on our last five trips and everyone's fired up for a good game.

Within the first five minutes, Phillips is just beaten by the keeper to a through pass and Hutchison makes a solo run into the penalty area, only for his shot to be deflected away. Hutch's play over the last few games has improved dramatically and, equally important, he has proved himself committed to The Cause. His goal against Newcastle and his exuberant celebrations for Quinn's winner made clear his allegiance and quelled any prejudice about his Geordie antecedents. He's now showing why Reid bought him and is another endorsement for the manager's canny ability to pick quality players.

The game continues briskly with Sunderland passing well and generally showing their superior pedigree. After seventeen minutes, Alex Rae rockets a low cross into the goalmouth where Phillips is standing just a yard out – yet he manages to scoop it over the bar. It's an extraordinary miss, the latest in a saga of chances over the last few games that should have been buried.

Bradford are struggling to keep up, but at least they aren't resorting to Boro's tactics the previous week of 'if at first you don't upend, kick again'. For the next twenty minutes, Sunderland dominate and restrict Bradford to just one shot on goal.

With half-time approaching, Gavin McCann has two good attempts, but it's looking like 0–0 for the break. Then a long cross by Mickey Gray lobs over Walsh in the Bradford goal to find Quinn at the far post, where he stabs in from close range to give us the lead.

If we dominated the first half, the second is a procession. Within minutes, McCann sends Phillips scampering clear and he pokes a shot past Walsh. Two–nil. Five minutes later and it's Hutch who delivers a brilliant forty-yard pass for Phillips again. Three–nil.

Now we really start to turn on the style. In midfield, Hutch and McCann are controlling the play, Rae's providing the steel and Arca's doing the fancy stuff. But with quarter of an hour to go, it's Bradford who pull one back after a goalmouth scramble. Their crowd have seen enough comebacks in recent games to believe that they might just do it again. The noise picks up, the Bantams press forward and go much too close for comfort. If they snatch another one, we could be facing a very embarrassing draw.

But with five minutes to go, Phillips nails the win with an excellent run and shot from outside the area. With only one goal in the last nine games, a hat trick looked about as likely as a sighting of Elvis. Oh, and there is Elvis, as a white-suited clone runs onto the pitch and pays homage to the King. Though someone's on the pitch who thinks it's all over, there's a final sting when Rae is brought down for a penalty. Phillips prepares for his 101st goal in 139 matches – and misses. Ah well, we'll settle for just the four.

I have to pinch myself. After a poor start, we've hauled ourselves up to third place with six wins out of the last seven. Ironically we're in the same position as last Christmas when we suddenly nose-dived into a twelve-game run without a win. But these are rare and heady moments to be enjoyed to the full. We play Arsenal next in a top-of-the-table clash, and it feels good to be in the limelight.

Tuesday, 26 December 2000

BRADFORD CITY 1   SUNDERLAND 4

(Blake 75)   (Quinn 45, Phillips 48, 55, 86)

PLAYED	TRAVELLED	SPENT	POSITION	STATE OF MIND
25	9,747 miles	£1,333.22	3rd	Jingle bloody bells!

Arsenal (away) – Premier League

OK, so Arsenal are going to Wembley, Wimbledon are moving to Highbury which means that England will be playing at . . . Plough Lane?

'Tickets for the match, who wants a ticket?'

'How much, mate?'

'Hundred sovs, guv.'

Well, well, it seems we've arrived in the big time.

Highbury on a match day feels like the real McCoy of those street festivals that the tabloids keep forcing on us for occasions such as a Royal wedding, beating the Germans or anything to do with the Queen Mum (Gawd-bless-her-she-dahn't-look-a-day-over-ninety-she-stayed-wiv-us-durin'-the-Blitz-ave-a-banana). In several front gardens, stalls have been set up and are doing a brisk trade in burgers, hot dogs and footie merchandise. One stall manages to combine the lot with a sign proclaiming: 'Sleep Football, Drink Football, Eat Burgers'. There's a guy offering bags of peanuts for fifty pence, reminiscent of the man who used to sell them for a tanner from the edge of the pitch at Roker Park, money and peanuts being thrown expertly over the heads of the crowd. The fanzine sellers are out in force with a selection of Arsenal publications: I generally don't bother buying a fanzine unless the title is particularly arresting – and they probably don't come much more arresting than *Up The Arse*.

And for the travelling Sunderland fans, there is even a rival garden shed, the headquarters of Arsenal Supporters Club, which sits crammed into the garden of a red-and-white terraced house. (Incidentally, the 'garden shed' song now has accompanying gestures, seemingly inspired by the title sequence from *Playschool*. You have to see it being performed by several hefty Mackems to fully appreciate its lyrical glory.)

It's all very lively, loud and colourful, but at the same time quite in-your-face and intimidating. We are the Arsenal, this is our patch and outsiders aren't welcome. While Spurs do a nice line in Jewish irony (Ginola on a Star of David badge) and Sunderland engage in self-mockery (T-shirts proclaiming 'I was here when we were shite'), with the Arsenal it's arrogance and who-you-lookin'-at? There aren't many Sunderland shirts visible and given the importance of today's game and what happened when the teams met at the SOL, there's revenge in the air.

But going to Highbury is one of the highlights of the season, like Anfield or Old Trafford. However well or badly Arsenal may be performing, you're always aware of their past glories that have established them as a perennial 'big' club. They began life in Plumstead in 1886 as 'Dial Square'. What, just that? Given the Victorians' propensity for assigning silly names to a new football team, I would have expected Dial Square Dribblers, Dry Cleaners or Deep Sea Divers. By 1913 they were Woolwich Arsenal and in trouble. Newly relegated and facing bankruptcy, this south-east London club were only saved by the intervention of a wealthy football-mad entrepreneur . . . hang on, I've just done all this in the Palace chapter. They moved to North London, had a tube station named after them and, well, you know the rest.

Now they're moving again, their success and popularity having long outgrown Highbury's modest capacity of just over thirty-eight thousand. Initial plans in 1997 for expanding the stadium could only offer an increase to fifty thousand plus the prospect of a long drawn-out battle with local residents. Over the next two years, fifteen alternative sites were considered, including King's Cross and Wembley, with plans at one point for Wimbledon to move into Highbury (a bit strange perhaps, but not nearly as wacky as the proposal in 1997 that the Dons move to Dublin). Finally Arsenal have settled on building a new sixty-thousand-seater stadium on an industrial site a mere five hundred yards from Highbury (and Wimbledon might be going to Milton Keynes – now there's a marriage made in Hell).

The move is planned for 2004, but thankfully Highbury will to a large extent remain. The facade of the East Stand, built in 1936, is one of the architectural glories of the game and is rightly protected as a listed building. Although both the Clock End and the once-mighty North Bank will go, the East and West Stands will be converted into luxury flats overlooking the famous turf which will become a communal garden. It all sounds very stylish and upmarket, likely to involve names such as Highbury Mews or Highbury Court, rather than Midfield Drive and Promotion Close. I'm sure Nick Hornby will be one of the first tenants as the next step in his apparent desire to become organically bonded with the Highbury pitch.

Walking round the stadium, I skip the cloned club shop in favour of the

Arsenal museum, which claims to be the largest of its kind in the country. Yet today, of all days, it's closed. The North-east is shamefully lacking in any collection of football antiquities, oddly so given the area's passionate heritage. But we might be a bit pushed for a notable silverware collection. We'd probably end up with cases displaying 'Bag of peanuts, Roker Park, circa 1913' or 'Pie crust, St James' Park, 1955. Kindly donated by Jackie Milburn'.

Inside the stadium, it's clear to see why Highbury was once lauded as the best in the country. The four large separate stands are classics of their kind, but now look dated compared to the new breed of all-enclosed stadiums. Like the Anfield Kop, the North Bank has been subdued by seating, moved upmarket and bought a nice little cottage in the country with a retriever, a cardie and a pair of slippers. But it still has the best pitch, an immaculate verdant swathe that makes your average bowling green look like the Somme. For the last three years it's been voted top turf in the Premiership, a lawn to die for. And therein lies the secret of its success. Every close season, the top four inches are removed and the assembled ashes of gone Gooners are liberally sprinkled before a new turf is laid down. The pitch is now consecrated ground and will become a memorial garden for the new flats. I like that.

But to business. The opening day's fixture ended in acrimony with Vieira being banned for three matches. Even the seemingly mild-mannered Arsene Wenger received an incredible twelve-game ban from the touchline following an alleged dispute with the fourth official. What on earth do you have to say to get that kind of ban? Reidy's comments after the game made it clear that there's little lost love between the two camps and if that weren't enough, we're set up today as third versus second. It's a real test of our calibre and of any pretensions we may have to being a top six side.

Arsenal start off at a pace. Vieira's controlling midfield and Henry's making life hell for Makin, his first dancing run down the left wing forcing an early corner. The ball comes over, Vieira leaps and it's in, simple as that. We had two guys on Vieira, but they might as well have been playing chess.

The next minute and Stan Varga heads back into the path of Pires, who is only stopped by a quick-thinking Sorenson. For the next quarter of an hour it's Arsenal, Arsenal, Arsenal. Pires blasts the side netting, and Sorenson tips over a Kanu header and then stops Henry when he's clean through. I have to keep checking the scoreboard to remind myself it's just 1–0. Arsenal have won their last two home games 5–0 and 6–1 and this has all the hallmarks of a similar thrashing.

Sunderland seem completely overawed in such heady company. The only players making any impact are Varga and Sorenson – Varga for his mistakes and Sorenson for his miracles. Poor Stan seems destined to have both his best and worst games all season against the same side.

Arsenal attack twice more with Kanu and Ljungberg, but both shoot wide. It's over twenty minutes before we even get a sniff at goal when Quinn hustles their keeper into an error, but he quickly recovers. Phillips hits a curler over the bar from long-range, but immediately Arsenal cut through us again. Ljungberg beats Varga with a shimmy that sends Stan off to the corner flag, then blasts over the bar from just ten yards.

Then finally we have a real chance. Our Swedish midfielder, Stefan Schwarz, making his first start all season, nutmegs Tony Adams with a clever pass to set Phillips free on goal. Kev bangs it in first time, cleanly and on target. Manninger in goal gets his body in the way but can't hold the shot. The ball bounces back to Phillips at speed but he's unable to control it. The guy next to me seems to draw inordinate strength from this one chance, insisting 'We'll win 2–1.' At which point Varga makes another mistake and Arsenal miss again.

With five minutes to half-time, it looks like we might just hang on to 1–0, when Henry skips past Makin for the umpteenth time and sends over a long cross. It beats everyone in the box but falls nicely for the incoming Dixon, who guides it through the crowded penalty area for their long overdue second goal.

I never thought I'd be relieved to be just two down after forty-five minutes. It should be about five. We've been completely outplayed, just as on the first day, but this time it doesn't look like we're going to get away with it.

Sunderland launch into the second half with their customary renewed vigour, which seems to catch Arsenal by surprise. The Gunners have obviously decided the game is over and they're going to cruise the second half, maybe tuck away another two just for show. But Rae and McCann start to exert some influence for us in midfield and we're actually starting to attack. Arsenal fail to clear a long throw-in into their box and Vieira and Quinn both go for the falling ball. Quinn tries to control it but only succeeds in knocking the ball against Vieira's hand. And we have a penalty. It's a tough call, one you certainly wouldn't get at Old Trafford, but nevertheless very, very welcome. Phillips steps up and with no sign of nerves from his Bradford miss, tucks it cleanly away. Incredibly, we're back in the match.

A minute later, Phillips is clear and shoots. Manninger parries but can't hold it and the ball is still loose in the area. Arsenal defender Stepanovs hoofs it away towards Row Z, only for the ball to ricochet off the incoming Quinn and on to the post!

It's a different game. We fight for and win every ball, Arsenal now in shock – we were supposed to be dead and buried, not running the show like this. Vieira, sublime and unflappable in the first half, is now getting caught in possession with Rae snapping at his ankles.

Eight minutes left. Rae robs Vieira again, the ball breaks loose and from twenty-five yards McCann scoops a long curling shot towards goal. It goes on and on, time seemingly on hold, before finally sneaking into the top corner. It's an unbelievable goal. The players all pile on top of McCann, we all pile on top of each other, in an explosion of joy.

Arsenal pound forward, clearly furious with us and themselves. The nerve of these guys! In the last minute, Hutch feeds a superb long pass to Phillips on the right wing. He skips over the flailing Stepanovs and shoots as Adams slides in with a last-ditch tackle. The ball beats Manninger but just shaves the far post. For a second I'm convinced that my heart has actually stopped.

The match ends 2–2. We're not the best team in the Premiership, or the most gifted, but with the exception of Man United we've become the most difficult to beat, eleven stubborn Peter Reids who never, ever give up, and I've rarely been more proud. Today might not have hit the emotional high of the Newcastle game, but it's our best result all season and now we fear no one. Ha'way the Lads!!

Saturday, 30 December 2000

ARSENAL 2 SUNDERLAND 2

(Vieira 5, Dixon 39) (Phillips 53, McCann 82)

PLAYED	TRAVELLED	SPENT	POSITION	STATE OF MIND
26	9,759 miles	£1,403.42	4th	Proud, defiant, unbeatable

Ipswich Town (home) – Premier League

The Antarctic has the reputation of being the coldest place on earth. Even without the wind chill factor, temperatures can drop below –100 Fahrenheit. Throw in winds that can reach two hundred miles per hour, and it can get a little nippy. Sudden blizzards create whiteout conditions that distort all perspective, leaving any hapless victim to stumble around blindly, gradually succumbing to frostbite, hypothermia and eventual death.

Or you could spend New Year's Eve on Newcastle quayside.

I have vague memories of North-east winters from twenty-odd years ago, but it's only since returning that I've been able to fully appreciate their deep-frozen qualities. And there's no denying it, I've got soft living down south, even more so since being in New Zealand, where the Auckland winters plummet to a horrifying 45 Fahrenheit. Whenever I go up to Sunderland between October and March, I wear more layers than Ranulph Fiennes. Meanwhile, the local lads are wandering around in short-sleeved replica shirts eating ice creams. You can tell when it's really cold, because that's when they go topless.

With no public transport for the home game on New Year's Day (or none that I'd trust), Anna and I elect to hire-drive up the day before and join in the local celebrations. A large area around Newcastle quayside has been cordoned off for a big New Year's Eve party, with two stages, street bands and the inevitable fireworks.

It's a tad chilly. Several similar events around the country have been cancelled due to high winds, but it takes more than a seventy-mile-per-hour winter gale to stop the Geordies having a party. After seven layers I have to stop simply because I've run out of clothes, but it's still bitingly cold. Yet as we mill among the revellers, it seems we're the only ones feeling the freeze. The girls are wearing the usual backless, strapless, minimal threads, but also, more noticeably, open sandals as they wade through three inches of snow and slush. Antarctic explorers have lost toes in warmer conditions. So if you reckon the lads are hard, don't even think about messing with the lasses. Perhaps the alcohol works as anti-freeze and the tan as a form of insulation.

Compared to my youth, Newcastle quayside is now the height of trendy sophistication. Thirty years ago it was an area to be avoided, and only the hardest of hard-drinking Geordies would dare venture into the waterside pubs. But now it's an elegant promenade for idle gambolling on a Sunday morning or wild nights in the pubs and bars. There is also a range of smart offices, one of which immediately grabs my eye, a law firm called Hadaway. Hadaway? In the North-east that name is usually found in the less delicate popular phrase, 'Hadaway and shite, man,' which translates roughly as 'Honestly, Simon, you do sometimes talk the most utter poppycock.' However, a legal firm called Hadaway & Shite does have a certain ring to it. (Mere jovial conjecture, of course, and in no way a reflection of the fine services – and so reasonably priced – provided by said company.) Anyway, we continue on past Gannonman Chartered Accountants and the Yebuggermar Insurance Company.

Further down the Tyne is the new pedestrian bridge, a Millennium project of gleaming white and stunning design. Destined to be known as the 'blinking eye bridge' (as opposed to the Dome's bleedin' eyesore), its two long curved sections resemble the outline of an eyelid. Both are connected by a series of steel cables, so that the bridge also compares to a giant avant-garde harp. The really clever bit, the 'blinking' aspect, occurs when a ship needs to pass underneath: the 'eyelid' then tilts up around its two axis points on either bank, raising the pedestrian walkway in a gigantic wink. As far as I'm aware it doesn't wobble like its Thames counterpart, but you can't have everything.

As midnight approaches we head back to the Tyne Bridge for the celebrations. People are dancing along the quayside, probably as much to keep warm as to enjoy the music. The police profile is high, but they seem to be enjoying themselves. The only dodgy moment is when one guy, in an optimistic view of the evening's bonhomie, breaks into a Sunderland song. No sooner has he got the first line out than his two more sober mates clamp their hands over his mouth, with stage whispers of 'What the fuck d'ye think yer deein', man?' In Newcastle it may be the season of goodwill to all men, but not to all Mackems.

Midnight arrives with an explosion of fireworks from the Tyne Bridge in an attempt to re-create those of Sydney Harbour's Olympic farewell. There's a popular belief that the Tyne Bridge, built in 1928, was the inspiration for the Sydney Harbour Bridge, completed four years later. However, the Australian design was actually submitted in March 1924, nine months before that for the Newcastle bridge, which might win you the odd pub bet.

For all our brilliant performances over the Christmas period, today looks like being a tough one. Ipswich are one of the surprises of the season, having scraped into the Premiership via the play-off final, but now sitting above us in third. They've got the second-best away record in the League (after you-know-who) and recently had a couple of great wins at Liverpool and Leeds. Meanwhile, we're without Niall Quinn, who has finally given in to a persistent back injury that has seen him substituted with alarming regularity. In his place we've got Dichio, tall, brave and powerful, but lacking Quinn's finesse and touch. Or, as one Sunderland fan put it during the game against Coventry, 'Bloody Dichio lumbers around the pitch like a friggin' hippo.'

So today is not a day to be starting with an apparent hangover from the night before. From the off, our midfield is not connecting, the defence has gaping holes and Ipswich's clever play is causing us problems. After just five minutes, a neat through pass catches Jody Craddock out of position, and Ipswich forward Marcus Stewart lobs over the advancing Sorenson to score.

For the next twenty minutes, while Phillips shows a couple of promising bursts, it's largely Ipswich who run the show, their clever, confident passing controlling midfield and posing a constant threat to our defence. Then we get a free kick on the edge of the Ipswich penalty area. An impressive seven-man wall blocks the path to goal, but Julio Arca sends a gem of a free kick around the wall and into the top corner. Mr Beckham could not have done better. The goal gives Sunderland a much-needed boost, but Ipswich are no mugs, and the play is pretty even to half-time.

For the second half, Sunderland pull their usual stunt of sending on eleven hyped-up doppelgangers and Ipswich don't know what's hit them. The star of the show is Phillips. His movement, control and passing are immaculate and it's easily his best display of the season. He's sharp around the box, but also dropping back to midfield and directing the play with a confidence that borders on arrogance, teasing defenders into fruitless tackles then whizzing off to create havoc in the penalty area. Unfortunately Dichio cannot match him and squanders a superb chance from just ten yards out, after Phillips had done all the work. But Dichio soon makes amends in flicking a pass to Phillips, who loses his marker in a flash and nonchalantly sidefoots the ball past the keeper as if passing it into the net. That's now his seventh goal in eight games and his 102nd for Sunderland, making him their joint post-war top scorer. I told you he'd come good.

Within minutes Phillips is off again. He muscles away from his marker and pulls the ball back for an unmarked Dichio to score. After that, it's like watching Man United. The crowd is up as Sunderland drive relentlessly forward. Players are moving off the ball and creating spaces as Ipswich are left chasing shadows. With twenty minutes left Reid makes an audacious three substitutions, a brash sign of confidence that nearly backfires when Ipswich twice go close in two minutes. But then Stefan Schwarz volleys in our fourth from the edge of the area with three minutes left and now it really is all over.

No one's taken Ipswich apart like this all season. It's confirmation that there's more to Sunderland's game than just hard running and tackling, and that on our day we can play excellent football against a top side. Reid has proved himself an astute tactician, a superb motivator and a shrewd trader in the transfer market. Our third-place position feels more legitimate than this time last year. Then we were the novelty newcomers who were ultimately found out. This year it's a better squad and, apart from the early Man City anomaly, no one's hammered goals past us to the same extent. It's looking good.

The bookies have stopped taking bets on Man United for the Premiership, as they are eleven points clear of both Arsenal and Sunderland. It seems rather rash, given the events of recent years. In 1998 United were similarly eleven points ahead of Arsenal, yet still lost out. And United themselves won the Championship in 1996, having been twelve points behind Newcastle in January. But then, have you ever met a poor bookie?

Monday, 1 January 2001

SUNDERLAND 4	IPSWICH TOWN 1
(Arca 25, Phillips 56,	(Stewart 5)
Dichio 63, Schwarz 87)	

PLAYED	TRAVELLED	SPENT	POSITION	STATE OF MIND
27	10,332 miles	£1,477.62	3rd	And a very happy New Year

Crystal Palace (home) – FA Cup Third Round

It's the AXA-sponsored magic of the
AXA-sponsored FA Cup, sponsored by AXA

What on earth have they done with the FA Cup?

When I left England in the '80s, The Football Association Challenge Cup was the oldest and most revered football competition in the world. It epitomised glory, romance and the utterly English concept of plucky underdogs overcoming impossible odds. It was unique in its global appeal. I always used to go all patriotic just as the final was about to kick off, when the commentator would announce, 'And this final is being watched in 952 countries around the world.' It was the best and it was ours, the undisputed birthright of every English football fan.

I came back to find the film star doing daytime soap. A competition smothered by sponsorship, with many of its traditional elements repackaged into a brighter-than-white new box that shook with an ominously hollow rattle. The marathon replays that became national sagas now reduced to one replay and penalties. Holding the third round in *December*. The final itself, once the season's finale that brought down the curtain, now squeezed into a schedule of Premiership matches and play-off preliminaries.

The draw for every round used to be broadcast on the radio, on the Monday lunchtime after the Saturday cup-ties. If your team had won, you had the whole weekend to endure and enjoy the agonies of anticipation as to which team you might get next. The draw itself was a piece of radio theatre: the wood-panelled chamber deep in the heart of FA Headquarters; the collection of distinguished and long-serving ancients of the FA Challenge Cup Committee. And, most evocative of all, the rattling, clicking sound of the ivory balls as the velvet bag was shaken to signal the start of the draw. Then it would begin, a voice of appropriate gravity announcing the procedure.

'I shall now ask Mr G.A. Pembleton to make the draw and Mr C.P. Harrison to announce the teams.'

Rustle, rustle, click, click.

'Number fourteen.'

'Bolton Wanderers.'

Rustle, rustle, click, click.

'Shall play number thirty-six.'

'Sheffield Wednesday.'

And so it would progress, excruciating in its drawn-out detail, every announcement preceded by racing pulse and crossed fingers. Is this us? At home? 'Crewe Alexandra.' Be a drag to have to go there. 'Will play Lincoln City.' Phew. 'Manchester United.' Here we go, a glamour tie. But do we want them this early, and away? 'Will play Tottenham Hotspur.' And even in the august setting, there would be a little ripple of reaction at the prospect of such a cracking match.

Now what do we have? A Sunday afternoon 'TV event' with sporting celebs from rowing, boxing and cricket doing the honours, and a corralled studio audience of minor football folk who have to suffer the indignity of being asked inane questions immediately following the draw. 'So, away to Stockport, how do you feel?'

Occasionally some of the previous round's matches haven't even been played before the draw for the next round is made. Add in the odd stalemate from the Saturday (or Sunday) games and you can end up with meaningless fixtures such as, 'Leicester City or Chelmsford will play the winners of Kettering or Chelsea versus Rotherham or Newcastle'. There's no mystique, no suspense, and the whole event has the dignity of the Saturday night Lottery Draw.

You can't even call it 'The Cup' anymore. Now it's got to be 'the AXA-sponsored FA Cup' or 'the FA Cup, sponsored by AXA'. I can accept that it needs a sponsor, like every other competition, but while it seems perfectly adequate to refer to the Carling Premiership, the Worthington Cup or the Nationwide League, AXA insist upon this linguistic pedantry. Whenever I see that Nice Mr Lineker or that Lovely Mr Lynam struggling with the 'AXA-sponsored' phrase, I sense a couple of AXA Thought Police standing just off camera in black leather trenchcoats.

They can't even leave the trophy itself alone. Traditionally, the cup had just a couple of ribbons in the winning colours, and obviously no sponsor's logo. Now it's festooned with so many strands of satin that it looks like something Mr Mainwaring would hand out for the

Walmington-on-Sea Morris Dancing Tournament. Sponsored, of course, by AXA.

And what do you get for winning it? Entry into the UEFA Cup. You'd be better off coming third in the Premiership and making the Champions League. The cup itself can be booked for promotional appearances. There was a time when only those who sweated and fought and won the old Tin Pot were allowed to touch it. Even the losing finalists never got a sniff. Now it's a corporate marketing device that can be hired out for lunch.

And the FA and AXA wonder where the magic's gone. For all their mantra-like pronouncements of 'The magic of the Cup is back! The magic of the Cup is back!', it quite patently isn't. The falling attendances and second-string Premiership teams of the early rounds show how devalued it's become, the third-place prize behind the Premiership and Europe. It's now being hyped in an effort to revive that magic, but for over a hundred years, you never had to 'sell' the Cup. In that very tradition lies the answer to restoring the status of the competition. Put It Back The Way It Was! Bring back unlimited replays. Not everyone's involved in the UEFA Cup or the Champions League, and if a replay clashes with Europe, then tough, work round it – that should be the price for entering the competition. Restore the draw to a Monday. Stick it back on the radio and give it some gravitas. Make the final the last match of the season and the showpiece it deserves to be.

Give us back our Cup and you'll get back your magic.

Well, seeing as we're here, we might as well try and win it. And first up, our old buddies, Crystal Palace. Time to teach this lot a lesson.

Sunderland certainly start with that intent, with swift neat passing that has Palace defenders scrabbling all over the park. This is clearly going to be an easy run-out and suitable revenge for our Worthington Cup defeat. I reckon we'll get about four.

After just twelve minutes the first goal almost arrives when Dichio, in for the still-injured Quinn, misses the Miss of Misses. Six yards out, unmarked, a ground pass straight to his feet. He swings at the ball and . . . well, you can guess the rest.

Several other chances fall to Phillips and McCann, but still we don't get off the mark. Palace's tactics are clear: defend to the last man. It's twenty minutes before they get a shot on goal. With Sunderland lacking both Arca and Kilbane, we have no width to our play. Everything's going down the middle but running into the Palace gates. After half an hour we've lost our confidence and our shape, and the match has descended into a full-on cup-tie of little finesse. Palace keep hoofing the ball upfield for their young nippy forwards to chase and we resort to little better, the high ball to Dichio.

With half-time approaching, Palace twice nearly snatch a goal and Sunderland go off to the rare sound of boos from the home crowd.

At the re-start, Sunderland get back to some neat passing and put the Palace goal under siege. But keeper Alex Kolinko has decided he's going to be Superman. In the first ten minutes he makes incredible saves from Phillips, Rae, Hutchison and McCann. Then Varga hits the post. This is not what was supposed to happen.

With the increasing tempo, there's a scuffle between McCann and Mullins and the Palace man is sent off. OK, that's it, they've only got ten men now, so just pass it around until the gap appears. Except nobody's told Palace. They fight even harder. Waves of Sunderland attacks are booted away. We bring Kilbane on as an extra attacker and take Williams out of defence, leaving just three at the back. Still Kolinko stands firm.

Seven minutes left. Palace forward Mikael Forssell breaks through our meagre defence and has only Sorenson to beat. Tommy brings him down but, incredibly, incurs no penalty. Five minutes later, Palace are clear again. Freedman's heading for goal when Varga brings him down with a 'professional' foul, for which Stan is sent off.

The tie ends scoreless but has cost us dearly. We've got a key defender banned for at least one match, while Hutchison has picked up his fourth yellow card, so is close to suspension. The replay's an extra game we don't need right now and, best of all, we've got another trip to Selhurst Park. Ah, the magic of the Cup.

Saturday, 6 January 2001
SUNDERLAND 0   CRYSTAL PALACE 0

PLAYED	TRAVELLED	SPENT	POSITION	STATE OF MIND
28	10,878 miles	£1,525.27	FAC 3rd Rd	Somebody shoot this team

West Ham United (away) – Premier League

You're just a small town in Scotland
— TAUNT BY WEST HAM FANS

I've never to been to West Ham before, not just the ground, but that part of London. My sum knowledge is Alf Garnet, Moore, Hurst and Peters and Sunderland's worst-ever defeat in October 1968. It was 4–0 at half-time, so obviously you doubled the score for full-time and ended up with 8–0. My father, who ostensibly supported Newcastle, but only as a flag of convenience to wind me up, asked me the result, but I refused to tell him. So he sat on me until I confessed. I'm still in therapy.

I've arrived early at Upton Park tube, so decided to take a look around the area. Next to the station is Queen's Market, a vast collection of stalls that buzzes with noise and smells. It's largely fruit and veg, but in the middle is an imposing display of fashion watches from the likes of Giorgio, Pico and LA Beverly Hills (no, I've never heard of them either). Every item drips with gold and jewels. There's a pair of matching his 'n' hers solid-gold watches encrusted with diamonds for just thirty-five pounds. Amazing – one for thirty-five pounds, sure, but two . . .

Back outside I mingle with the crowd heading for the match. There's a noticeable lack of Sunderland shirts and I could be in a foreign land.

'So 'e clocks me Chevy in the bazaar and 'e wants 'is sausage. I said, "Fark orf, Tel, I just done a Leo in me sherbert, do us a cheesey. I'll 'ave an Arthur then you'll get yer Bugs." Well 'e goes radio bleedin' rental, 'e was well Alan Border.'

Another local warns the young lad next to him, 'It's a rough area, son.' Christ, if the natives say it's bad, it must be serious. The number one haircut is the number one choice and I'm off to watch a team sponsored by Doc Martens. Welcome to Geezerland. After passing a laundry with the sign, 'Don't Kill Your Wife. Let Us Do It', I arrive to find the ground is next to the Co-op Funeral Parlour. But I'm sure everyone's smashin' and sends their muvvers flahrs 'n' fings.

Every team needs a local rival. It strengthens a club's identity and gives them a derby game, and in its own perverse way, being loathed is a sign of respect. London clubs are spoilt for choice: while Spurs and Arsenal are clear-cut foes, everyone else seems to have a transferable vote when it comes to nominating their nemesis. Geographically West Ham's derby should be against either Millwall or Charlton, but as both have been out of the top flight for years, The Hammers have had to create a new opponent: the enemy of my enemy is also my enemy. So Chelsea have been the stand-in antagonists, but in today's programme West Ham's young midfielder, Michael Carrick, thinks that it's Spurs. Of course, being a Geordie, he'd know all about that. So who do I find is most vilified in the merchandise stalls around the ground? Man United. Stands to reason, dunnit.

It's a good job I've arrived early, because getting into the away fans' section of the ground is like trying to crash Madonna's wedding. After passing through the first set of security guards, I walk down an access-way lined with ten-foot-high steel walls and barbed wire. My ticket is checked again. I walk another twenty yards. A third check. But then it's probably not this lax when they play Millwall.

Finally, I'm allowed to enter Upton Park. Or is it the Boleyn Ground? No one seems quite sure. The programme boasts a special insert: 'Inside! Extra eight-page Chairman's statement!' as if it were a Pamela Anderson centrefold ('Phwoar! Look at those retail figures!'). Yet while the Chairman consistently refers to the Boleyn Ground, the rest of the programme calls it Upton Park. A steward informs me that the stadium is officially called the Boleyn Ground, but the area is Upton Park. So everyone calls the stadium Upton Park . . .

On the pitch, the cheerleaders are providing a distraction from the January cold. Generally English cheerleaders have all the zip and pizzazz of contestants in *The Generation Game*, but this lot are clearly a cut above the norm and a match for their American counterparts. For these are 'The Hammerettes!', a professional dance team who also perform for Warrington and Saracens rugby clubs and London Leopards basketball team. But today they're at Upton Park and wearing a version of the West Ham kit I've never seen before. Those shorts are nearly as brief as Di Canio's. And apparently they aren't cheerleaders but 'sports dancers', although I suspect the guys in the crowd know little of the difference and care even less. The group even run their own community programme, which apparently involves a bit more than just taking leotards to the underprivileged. But at least the troupe maintains some of the traditions of all-girl dance groups, with names such as Dannie, Donna, Dee and Dawn. Wot, no Debbi?

As the girls finish performing to 'Dancing Queen', the PA announces the arrival of another Swedish success, new England manager, Sven-Goran Eriksson. The standing ovation is both warm and genuine, and an uplifting swipe at the xenophobes who objected to his appointment. With West Ham having won the '66 World Cup (according to Alf Garnett), Eriksson's obviously made a canny nod to tradition in coming here for his first Premiership game, but hopefully he'll also cast an eye over Phillips, Gray, Craddock and McCann.

The teams come out to a rather funky version of 'I'm Forever Blowing Bubbles', the heavy bass beat several Coladas away from Chas 'n' Dave. West Ham are something of a conundrum: on paper they have the perfect blend for a successful side. They've got Cole and Lampard for youth and skill, Pearce and Winterburn for steel and experience, and Kanouté and Di Canio for match-winning brilliance, yet still they're muddling around in mid-table. Quinn's returned for Sunderland, but it's debatable how long his back will hold out against professional defenders who know of his Achilles heel.

West Ham presumably win the toss as they elect to change ends, an unusual sight nowadays when teams seem happy to start off in the halves in which they warmed up. The reason soon becomes clear when they win an early corner. The low winter sun is shining directly into Sorenson's eyes and he only makes the subsequent save with difficulty.

The opening phase is fast and furious, with one West Ham player booked and Winterburn clearing a Hutchison header off the line. West Ham make most of the play, with Cole and Di Canio running the midfield and creating chances for the ever-dangerous Kanouté. Then, after twenty-two minutes, McCann swings in a free kick and Varga's six-foot-five frame rises above the rest to hammer in a header. Time to dust off the impossibly optimistic songs.

'Now you're gonna believe us
We're gonna win the league!'

But it's still a long way from over. Joe Cole is all trickery and brilliance, zipping and skipping away from tight corners and tackles to set up chances for his team-mates. Fortunately for us, West Ham's finishing is terrible and may explain their under-performance.

In the second half, Quinn nearly snatches a goal when he controls a Phillips cross and volleys straight into the face of the keeper. As the game progresses, Hutchison and co. grab the midfield and West Ham's frustration erupts with some stupid fouls and off-the-ball incidents that see three more players booked.

Cole isn't buzzing quite as much as in the first half, but he's still a threat. He gets the ball on the edge of our penalty area, feints left, but then dummies the whole stadium with a reverse pass to Di Canio on the right. The Italian's in the box, unmarked and advancing on Sorenson. He shoots past Tommy, but the ball hits the post and ricochets behind Sorenson across goal. It strikes Darren Williams and zings back towards the net, before Thome finally hoofs it clear. Aarrggh!!

The near-miss lifts the Hammers briefly, but it's still Sunderland in charge. On one attack, Quinn is fouled about thirty yards out. As West Ham organise their wall, the Sunderland players mooch around the free kick as if on a fag break. A sudden movement, and Hutchison curls the ball around the defenders and into the net, a replica of his goal against Manchester City. Hutch's transition from early-season villain to present-day hero is complete, and for the first time the Sunderland fans grant him the honour of his own laudatory song.

Five minutes later, Pearce thunders a free kick that Sorenson can only save one-handed, but to be honest, West Ham haven't really looked like a team who believed they could score. We finish easy winners and are now second, two points ahead of Arsenal. Of course, not everyone sees it that way. As we shuffle towards the exit, one obviously long-suffering Sunderland fan sums up his view of our win. 'That's it, forty-two points – we're safe!'

We are now eleven points behind Man United, who visit the SOL in ten days' time. Before then, we have an easy three-pointer against Bradford, so we might even sneak up a little more. If we can beat United, the gap will be just eight points with fourteen matches left. We maintain our good run, they slip up a couple of times and . . . Understand what I'm saying here. It's not impossible that we could, that we might . . . no, no, whisper it, whisper it, he who dares . . .

Saturday, 13 January 2001
WEST HAM UNITED 0   SUNDERLAND 2

(Varga 22, Hutchison 68)

PLAYED	TRAVELLED	SPENT	POSITION	STATE OF MIND
29	10,890 miles	£1,563.77	2nd!!	The Impossible Dream

Crystal Palace (away) – FA Cup Third Round Replay

Men who know the score, score with
the great smell of Palace

Now I'm not going to get caught out again. Before leaving home, I phone Crystal Palace to check that the game is actually going ahead.

'Oh yes, no problems,' replies a cheery voice.

Hmm, just a bit too confident there.

'So it's not being postponed because it's too wet?'

'No.'

'Or too cold?'

'No.'

'Or too dark or too late?'

'No, no, kick off 7.45.'

And, like a fool, I believe them.

This is the third time in five weeks I've made the trip to this God-forsaken outpost and I still manage to get the wrong train. It's obviously my subconscious screaming, 'No, no, please, not again!' The intricacies of the South London rail network have remained something of a mystery. It's so mind-bogglingly complex, it should have its own Open University course (M.Phil. Connex Trains And Depressive Behavioural Psychosis). Several stations apparently exist in triplicate (Streatham, Streatham Hill, Streatham Common, Beckenham Junction, Beckenham Hill, New Beckenham), but the Crown of Confusion lies with Clapham (Clapham South, Clapham Common, Clapham North, Clapham High Street and Clapham Junction). There are probably hordes of missing tourists just riding round South London trying to find Clapham West.

Naturally, the train out of Victoria station is late. After years of poor performance, Connex South Central have just lost their operating franchise, although that hardly seems fair. A public flogging on the station concourse of all their senior management, now that would be fair. But then I'm just an old wishy-washy liberal.

At every ground, I always try and get to the club shop. Apart from a match programme, I've never actually bought anything, but I'm on a quest to find the Holy Grail of Naffness, the tackiest bit of football merchandise anywhere in the country. And I have to admit, a life-size cardboard cut-out of Neil 'Razor' Ruddock, Palace's tough-guy defender, is a tempting contender. But then I spot it, a sure-fire finalist for the Top Ten of Tat: Crystal Palace Shower Gel – 'With the Official Fragrance of Crystal Palace Football Club'. The mind boggles. Sweaty jockstraps? Hot dogs with onions? The whiff of bankruptcy?

'Mmm, Mike, new aftershave?'

'It's Palace.'

'Pallis? I like it. Say, I might be free for that drink after all.'

But here's the clincher: not only does it smell of . . . something, but it's also 'Cruelty Free'. After suffering three relegations in five years and the near extinction of their club, I think the Palace fans have a bang-to-rights claim under the Trade Descriptions Act.

I get to my seat at 7.30 p.m. because I don't want to miss the absolutely-sure-to-go-ahead-on-time kick-off. On the pitch, several of the groundstaff appear to be struggling with one of Peter Stringfellow's hairdryers. Three guys are hauling a huge silver-tubed hot-air blower over the grass, while trying not to dry-roast themselves in the process. According to a steward, the pitch has 'areas of surface water' and the referee has yet to deem it safe for play. With fifteen minutes to go. Oh, and my view of one goal is completely blocked by a huge stanchion. Please, somebody, just kill me now and let it be over.

At five to eight, the Blaster Boys finally leave the pitch and a rather limp firework display indicates that the match is actually going ahead. The teams emerge for the third and positively last time this season, with a result guaranteed by the guillotine of penalties. Sunderland don't have a great record in penalty shoot-outs with South London clubs.

Palace are on a high after their recent win over Liverpool in the first semi-final of the Worthington Cup. Sunderland are taking no chances and are fielding a full-strength side. The match erupts into FA Cup thunder, with Sorenson whacking his buddy Varga while punching away a Palace attack. As in the previous games, we start impressively, passing the ball about cleanly and crisply, while Palace simply hoof and hope. We look as if we can open them up easily, and after ten minutes Quinn volleys just wide, then

Rae misses a long-range lob with the keeper stranded. If it were anyone but Palace, I'd be confident of an easy win, but twice burned . . .

Sure enough, after surviving the early onslaught, Palace force their way back into the match, with the pacey Clinton Morrison again causing problems for our defence. After twenty minutes, he beats the offside trap to force a brilliant low save from Sorenson. Warning duly posted. Five minutes later, Rae sends a stray header back over his own defence, Morrison is onto it in a flash and he thunders home a shot from twenty yards.

Here we go again. Between you and me, if we're going to get knocked out, it might as well be in the early stage of the competition. Sunderland's recent record in the FA Cup is pretty much all or nothing. Since losing the final in 1992, we've never got beyond the fourth round, so if we have to go, then let's go now. We're poised at a crucial stage in the Premiership and the last thing we need is extra cup matches, in which key players can get suspended or injured. Five minutes later, Phillips turns quickly with nobody near him and falls instantly to the ground, clutching his knee in apparent agony. See what I mean? Probably twisted knee ligaments, so that's him out for the season and we've no effective cover.

OK, so I'm a pessimist, but look who I support. After treatment, Phillips gingerly gets to his feet. Within minutes, he takes a pass from Quinn and blasts a shot that Kolinko in goal does well to parry. But for the rest of the half it is mainly Palace who run the play and we do well to hold out without further loss until half-time.

While it would be going a bit far to say that the Sunderland fans are revolting, the troops are definitely becoming uneasy.

'Ha'way Reidy, wake these bastards up.'

'Ha'way Sunderland – Newcastle's gettin' beat.'

'Ha'way Sunderland, a bit o' pride.'

This encouragement, along with Mr Reid's Bottom-Kicking Seminar, sees Sunderland start the second half with an excellent four-man move that ends in Phillips shooting just wide. Then it's like the SOL all over again. Sunderland hammer the Palace goal, but Kolinko produces a string of saves from McCann, Williams and especially Hutchison, whose screaming volley the keeper tips just round the post.

Another attack and Quinn takes a high ball on his chest with his back to goal. In one move, he turns and volleys a brilliant shot into the corner. Yes! The goal signals the usual bout of stranger-hugging and . . . Quinn has scored! Amid the celebrations, Phillips has scampered away and scored another in just fifty seconds.

A minute to go. Now that we're ahead, I obviously want us to win, my basic instincts overriding any former calm analysis. Next round is a home tie against Ipswich, whom we've just hammered, and then it's the fifth round, just three games from the final and . . . Palace have just equalised. Bastards. Extra time, penalties – I love Selhurst Park.

Into extra-time and it's full-on FA Cup fervour. They miss a chance, we miss two, Darren Williams nearly scores an own goal – what more do you want? In the second period, Ruddock misjudges a long Sorenson clearance and Phillips nips in to score his 104th goal to become Sunderland's post-war top scorer. Meanwhile Dichio comes on, gets booked twice and goes off, all in just fourteen minutes. You take my point about us needing some cover for Phillips?

With five minutes left, substitute Kevin Kilbane runs through a tired Palace defence and coolly beats Kolinko with a low drive to settle the match. That's it, we've finally beaten this team and this place. Let's get outa here.

Wednesday, 17 January 2001

CRYSTAL PALACE 2   SUNDERLAND 4

(Morrison 24, Thomson 89)   (Quinn 71, Phillips 72, 102, Kilbane 114)

PLAYED	TRAVELLED	SPENT	POSITION	STATE OF MIND
30	10,902 miles	£1,592.17	FAC 4th Rd	At last!

Bradford City (home) – Premier League

You'll not write many chapters on that match
– TRAVEL TRACEY

Alongside the growing influence of money in the game, there developed a paranoia among clubs over any voice of dissent, lest it damage expensive reputations, particularly where a club was listed on the stock exchange. This desire to control all information, good or bad, resulted in the lack of any means for the ordinary fan to express their opinion. Local media toed the party line, while official match programmes often became just bland collections of press releases and asinine player interviews.

'New signing Dave Talent is really happy to be playing for Northford: "They're a great set of lads and we all get on really well. The supporters are fantastic and it's a brilliant stadium. I'm hoping to score lots of goals and help the lads get into Europe." Rovers boss, Ron Hardman, said "He's a great lad who gets on really well with the lads. I'm hoping he'll score lots of goals and help us get into Europe."'

Out of this was born the fanzines, independent supporters' publications which could not only voice uncensored opinion, but also discuss rumours and raise issues that would otherwise be kept firmly under wraps by the club's Press Office. From Bradford's *City Gent* in 1984 have sprung hundreds of siblings and, with the Internet, the fanzine websites, although the published versions are the real McCoy. By definition, the fanzine is an anarchic beast, a spirit often reflected in the title. In the Premiership there's *Gary Mabbutt's Knee* (Coventry), *One Flew Over Seaman's Head* (Spurs), *Goodbye Horse* (Charlton) and, of course, *Up The Arse*. Similar gems lurk in the lower divisions: *Colin's Cheeky Bits* (Blackburn), *Bob Lord's Sausage* (Burnley) and *Tora, Tora, Tora* (Chesterfield). Up in Scotland, the city of Dundee is blessed with both *Can I Bring My Dog?* (Dundee United) and the wonderful *It's Half Past Four And We're 2–0 Down* (Dundee). I don't know what these guys are on, but I'd love to try some.

Sunderland is equally well served. The large supporter base has seen the rise and occasional fall of five fanzines. Sadly, *It's The Hope I Can't Stand* is no more, but we currently have *The Wearside Roar*, *A Love Supreme* and the oh-so-true *Sex & Chocolate Aren't As Good As Football*. *A Love Supreme* is arguably the best supporters' magazine in the country, having won 'Fanzine of the Year' six times since its birth in 1989. Its success gave rise to *Sex & Chocolate* in 1998 and both have grown from modestly produced booklets to full-colour editions that locally outsell *Loaded* magazine. I'm not sure how they stand up against chocolate sales, but commercially, sex is clearly not as good as football.

Both publications give voice to supporters' opinions, whether positive or negative, while also being an excellent source of rumours, hidden truths and scurrilous gossip. The opening editorials are generally reasoned and considered, the authors clearly devoted to the cause, yet not blind to the club's failings. And as you move through the pages, there are similarly rational pieces on transfers, racism, match tickets and the growing influence of Sky. Then you notice the more offbeat stuff: 'You The Jury: The People versus Darren Williams', a close-up of Don Hutchison's rain-soaked buttocks and 'Hairstyle Options For Stan Varga', until finally you arrive at the Letters Page. Virtually all correspondence seems to fall into one of four categories: 'Reid is crap', 'Reid is brilliant', 'Newcastle are crap' and 'I love Kevin Phillips'. Each letter begins with a personal history of allegiance that vies to outdo the rest:

'I've been watching the Lads now for thirty years and I can remember . . .'

'I was a season ticket holder three years before the club was formed . . .'

'I live in Peru and I haven't missed a match since before I was born . . .'

'I finance away trips by selling my own body parts . . .'

As with all good letters pages, correspondents engage in fierce debate, with exchanges zinging back and forth in a flurry of low-flying insults.

'And if you think Peter Reid is crap then you're clearly just a plastic Mackem, you tosser. Yours respectfully . . .'

Which will produce a response of:

'I cancelled my own funeral to watch the Reserves play at Huddersfield, so I'm no plastic Mackem, you wanker. I remain, sir, your obedient servant . . .'

An exception to this mayhem was a meticulously researched letter that analysed the forty-year correlation between the respective fortunes of Sunderland AFC and the Labour Party. So we're probably safe from relegation till about 2005.

Each matchday the fanzine sellers are out in force, although I think the editors might have a quiet word with some of their female sales staff. A degree of confusion is likely to arise from teenage girls standing on street corners shouting, '*Sex And Chocolate*, one pound eighty.'

'Er, how much for just the chocolate, pet?'

Paradoxically, Sunderland's current success is making life difficult for the fanzines, as there is little ground for complaint if you're lying second in the Premiership and unbeaten at home. And this afternoon promises to be something of a formality against a Bradford side still bottom and still reeling from our recent victory. A good win today will set us up nicely for the big one against Man United next week.

Everything starts well, as Sunderland dominate the opening play and promise a similar result to Boxing Day. But the chances aren't coming and it's actually Bradford who force a couple of saves from Sorenson in the opening twenty minutes. Then Hutchison crosses for Quinn who is unmarked six yards out, so here's the first. But he heads wide. Then Bradford's keeper Walsh makes a close-range save from Alex Rae. Hmm, not good.

The first half is a generally dour struggle with Bradford a completely different proposition from the team we hammered 4–1. They've shelved the flamboyant talents of Collymore, Petrescu and Carbone in favour of a dose of Yorkshire grit and it's paying off. A very determined wall keeps blocking our attacks, and with Sunderland playing their dangerous offside game, we nearly get caught with a couple of Bradford breakaways. Phillips is buzzing around nicely, but it's all in midfield where he can only create rather than destroy and the break arrives with a disappointing 0–0 scoreline.

There's a bit of light relief at half-time with the free kick competition. Two opposing fans try to score into an open net from initially twenty yards, then thirty, forty and so on. It's a bit naff, but it's better than facing the crush in the bars or the toilets. Bradford's fan is, of course, the City Gent while Sunderland are represented by Gary 'Sunderland AFC' Lamb, whose recent deed poll change of name has granted him a brief burst of fame. I just pity him if he's ever stopped by any Geordie police who ask to see his licence. In keeping with the first half, both competitors are challenged in the skill department, neither able to hit the net from forty yards. It doesn't bode well for a skill-packed second half.

Two minutes in and Quinn has another chance that he heads straight into the goalkeeper's arms. Five minutes later and one more Walsh save denies a Quinn header, which the big guy would normally have buried. Then, suddenly, Bradford beat our offside trap as they've been threatening to do all afternoon. A cross leaves Sorenson stranded and lands at the feet of striker Dean Windass. He's five yards out, unmarked and Sorenson's nowhere. Shit, he can't miss. But he does. When it was easier to score than not, he elects the harder option and blasts into the side netting. A few minutes later Tommy has to produce a superb save to deny another Bradford chance. Come on, guys, get a grip or we could actually lose this.

We keep hammering away and have the odd chance, the odd goalmouth scramble, but we're getting nowhere fast. With Arca away on international duty and Kilbane on the bench, Reid's playing Hutchison and Stefan Schwarz out wide when both prefer to be in central midfield. So there's little width to our play and we keep running into a ten-man defence that is quite happy to hoof the ball away whenever we attack.

With fifteen minutes left, Dichio comes on for Quinn, falls over, handles the ball, but does little else. Kilbane also appears and nearly scores when his first attempt is deflected just wide of the post. But it's not our day and the match ends scoreless. Maybe the Lads were too confident, or perhaps their minds were on Manchester. Or possibly it's just that Bradford played well. They've become something of a bogey team at the SOL, the last club to win here, and they have not conceded a goal as visitors for three years.

Luckily Arsenal drew, so we're still second. But we're now thirteen points behind Man United and our brief, mad dream of catching them is over. There's only one faint glimmer of hope: United still have to play Bradford at Old Trafford.

Sunday, 21 January 2001
SUNDERLAND 0   BRADFORD CITY 0

PLAYED	TRAVELLED	SPENT	POSITION	STATE OF MIND
31	11,448 miles	£1,653.97	2nd	Blown it

Ipswich Town (home) – FA Cup Fourth Round

And we could use his Second Symphony for Darts Night

'You're going to a strip club?'

Anna's never been one for the subtle approach.

'It's not a strip club,' I reply, 'it's an adult-themed sports bar.'

'What's the difference?'

Damn.

'It's a modern pub environment catering for a pre-match, adult male clientele with a range of entertainment, such as . . .' I read the ad from the back of a fanzine. 'Such as football fun and bargain beer.'

'And "Topless Totty"? I've seen the ad.'

'Oh.'

'You don't think you'll look rather sad,' she continues, 'standing around with a bunch of guys watching girls take their clothes off. At your age.'

Ouch.

'Ah, but that's where you're wrong, my little angel of the North. As a sociological study, I'll be watching the men watching the girls taking their clothes off.'

She looks unconvinced. I'm not surprised. I struggle on.

'It's for the book.'

She looks even less convinced. 'Don't forget your raincoat.'

While the traditional pub still reigns supreme as the supporters' drinking den of choice, its role has been supplemented by sports bars, large open-style bars where the emphasis is on cheap beer, music, drinking games and big-screen sport. The target audience is generally the sports-mad male, eighteen to thirty-five, and as many of his mates as can be crammed in. With the advent of all-seater stadiums, the sports bar is probably the nearest in spirit to the old-style football terrace, with its physical proximity, camaraderie and overwhelming maleness.

Negotiating my way past the door security ('Sorry mate, no raincoats'), I squeeze to the bar and order a half of testosterone and lime. Nah, what the heck, make it a pint. While virtually all the clientele conform to the marketing profile, the bar staff are exclusively young women, whose close-fitting attire of tops and shorts seems likely to seriously threaten their circulatory systems. Against one wall is a small raised stage, perhaps only ten feet in diameter. I think the bar must originally have been a fire station, as they seem to have kept part of the old pole. Nice to see a touch of heritage. On stage the MC/DJ is holding court, revving up the crowd with a selection of jokes that range from the unprintably filthy to the charmingly silly ('Two blokes were nicked for stealing car batteries and fireworks. One was charged and the other was let off'). The crudeness of the gags eventually becomes funny through sheer saturation, and I find myself transforming into Sid The Sexist of *Viz* fame.

The lads who have glued themselves to the front of the stage in anticipation of the main event are hauled up to take part in a 'yard of ale' competition. I have vague student memories of witnessing such trials, and success seemed to involve combining techniques of twirling the yard glass with opening one's gullet and literally pouring the beer down the throat. Unfortunately none of today's contestants possess either the knack or the epiglottal control, as each attempt ends in dismal failure and a sodden shirt. Which is probably preferable to the likely consequences of downing three-and-a-half pints of fizzy lager.

Next up is 'Punch The Maggie's Lights Out'. This involves a four-foot-high cartoon cut-out of a stereotypical Newcastle fan, all cropped hair, beer gut and tattoos. In place of the eyes are two small red light bulbs rigged to pressure sensors, which switch the lamps off when struck with sufficient force. While the preamble is overladen with macho tones, the pay-off is disarmingly tame and rather quaint. I imagine the challenge to be some trial of strength or aggression, but contestants are required to extinguish the rage in their rival's gaze with nothing more threatening than three bean bags. I haven't seen those since junior school.

Of course, all this is only a warm-up for the star turns. This must be the only bar where the girls take the stage to the strains of Prokofiev's 'Dance of the Knights'. But if it's good enough for Kevin Phillips, it's good enough for 'the lovely Tanya', who engages in a routine with the pole that probably contravenes most Fire Station Regulations. Around me, guys are respecting the obligatory spilling-of-the-pint-down-the-front that is all part of the ritual. I spot the occasional bored girlfriend viewing the proceedings with a mixture of disdain and 'mine are better than hers' jealousy.

With kick-off approaching, there is a mass exodus for the stadium, the departing atmosphere heady with beer and machismo. I doubt whether Prokofiev foresaw his music as a backdrop to football and sex, but I bet his spirit's rather chuffed.

Traditionally, Sunderland just getting past the third round would be enough to light the blue touchpaper and spark talk of '73 and another tilt at the Cup. The ticket queues would form overnight and cup fever would grip the town, feeding off its own momentum. An attendance today of a miserly 36,005 for a fourth-round tie against a top Premiership side says more about the status of the competition than any 'magic of the Cup' hype. Sunderland drew bigger crowds in their First Division days against Grimsby, Crewe, Port Vale and Swindon, with ticket prices that exceeded today's ten-pound bargain. The FA have similarly announced cheaper tickets for the final and a greater allocation for the two teams. The Cup final used to be the FA's licence to print money, with both clubs grateful for however many tickets the ruling body deigned to distribute. But then in those days, there was never any fear that the game's greatest showpiece might not actually sell out.

In recognition of his team's performances in December, Peter Reid has been awarded Manager of the Month. While always an honour to receive, the award appears to be cursed, with subsequent poor results haunting past recipients. Of more pressing concern is the situation regarding Niall Quinn. His back is now so bad that he is unable to last a full ninety minutes, nor play more than one game a week. Meanwhile our only cover is Danny Dichio, in whom Reid seems to place inordinate faith, but who has yet to convince the Sunderland crowd of his Premiership credentials. One easy goal against Ipswich does not a striker make.

In contrast, Ipswich themselves have Marcus Stewart, attempting today to equal a club record by scoring in eight consecutive matches. And after fifteen minutes he nearly succeeds when his low drive is tipped just round the post by an alert Sorenson. Otherwise the first twenty minutes is a dour midfield conflict, with only Titus Bramble for Ipswich catching the eye, his darting runs from the back threatening as in previous encounters.

As Varga breaks down another Ipswich sortie, he sends a signature long pass out to Hutchison on the right. With deceptively lazy control, Hutch kills the pass first time then swings over a looping cross into the Ipswich penalty area. Normally he'd be looking for Quinny, but today it's Dichio who dives full length to head the ball low into the net for an excellent goal.

Two minutes later and Dichio nearly snatches a second when he nips in behind Bramble and slips a shot just wide of the post. Where the hell has this guy been all season? The remaining twenty minutes see only a chance apiece as the first half plays out in a struggle to control midfield.

With Phillips substituted for the second half, the burden is now solely on Dichio. After ten minutes, Hutchison lobs another clever ball over the Ipswich defence and Dichio is off, chasing it with new-found speed. It's a fifty–fifty challenge with the keeper, but Danny never flinches. As the two collide, the big striker just gets a toe to the ball and pokes it goalward. It rolls on, it's going in, then at the last second it hits the post and Bramble nips in to clear.

The near miss lifts the game as Sunderland take charge. Ten minutes later Dichio shoots just wide again for what could have been his fourth goal. While he's no Ronaldo, the Sunderland crowd love a trier and for the first time all season get behind him as the noise starts to build. For the last twenty minutes, Ipswich push for an equaliser and nearly grab one when a stray pass by Alex Rae leads to a goalmouth scramble. But otherwise they never really look like scoring and we hold out to the end for the single-goal win.

While it wasn't a great match, there were some good individual performances. Craddock and Varga excelled in defence, while in midfield Hutchison and McCann were stylish and composed. But the day can only belong to Dan The Man, who has put us through to the fifth round for the first time since 1992.

Saturday, 27 January 2001

SUNDERLAND 1   IPSWICH TOWN 0

(Dichio 22)

PLAYED	TRAVELLED	SPENT	POSITION	STATE OF MIND
32	12,012 miles	£1,714.44	FAC 5th Rd	It'll do

Manchester United (home) – Premier League

I'm sorry, Officer, I have no idea how she got there

Following Arsenal's win last night, we've slipped back to third, but can regain second place if we beat Man United this evening. Our recent run of success seems to have invoked the wrath of both the southern-based media and the football establishment in general, who all seem incapable of giving credit where it's due. After we beat West Ham to go second, all Lineker and co. could talk about was Joe Cole. That Sunderland have had the temerity to gatecrash the constitutional hierarchy of Arsenal, Chelsea, Leeds and Liverpool has seen us dismissed as a bunch of kick-and-rush hicks, the bastard progeny of Wimbledon FC. The only possible explanation for our rising to second is not any merit on our part, but the 'low' standard of the usual suspects. The fact that Leeds and Arsenal are going well in the Champions League, and Liverpool similarly in the UEFA Cup, is conveniently overlooked. No, we just have to accept that we are merely, in the words of David Mellor, 'a meat and potatoes side'. Which presumably puts his Chelsea, six places below us, somewhere around the level of Spotted Dick.

Tonight we're obviously going to have to rely upon more than our limited talents of hard running and tough tackling, tactics that have proved so successful for Man City, Bradford and Coventry . . . Tonight will require alternative sources of inspiration. Superstition is rife in football, both on and off the pitch. Players' match-day rituals include Andy Cole being last out of the tunnel, Paul Ince coming out bare-chested and George Best sleeping with a blonde (just in case of another comeback). Old Trafford is supposed to have immaculate feng shui, being bang in the middle of an old Druid ley line.

I'm equally susceptible to irrational belief. Fortunately Anna proved herself (eventually) not to be the cause of the opposition always scoring twice, but there are many other quirks to which I desperately cling. The easy ones are items of clothing. I don't have a lucky hat, but Anna does, a woollen Sunderland beanie that I insist she dons whatever the weather. Several Mackem T-shirts, choice on the day to be determined by nothing more than whim. This allows their powers of good fortune to be retained, as obviously if we lose, it's because I chose the wrong shirt. The inevitable lucky underpants and the replica shirt that is never washed until we lose (this doesn't apply to the underpants). The right foodstuffs are vital. Every home game requires a visit to Roker Fish And Chips of Roker Avenue, but not more than ninety minutes before the match. And it's no coincidence that Sunderland's superb run over Christmas coincided with my taking a few chocolate coins to each match, which I refrained from consuming until the final whistle. The London Branch have a similar routine with prawn cocktail crisps, eaten only at the start of the second half (Roy Keane please take note).

There was a time when it seemed that Anna's mother, another recent convert, was the crucial factor, as every game she attended produced a great result. Matters came to a head when I failed to get her a ticket for the Arsenal game, but fortunately the Lads still managed their superb draw despite my failure to smuggle said mater into Highbury.

'Excuse me, sir, could I have a look in your bag.'

Night matches are always a bit special, the darkness and the cold seeming to intensify every sensation. The air is crisper, smells are sharper, sounds louder and sights keener. It is at night that the Stadium of Light lives up to the hype, with four of the world's most powerful searchlights tracing the sky with the strength of a billion candles (reputedly sufficient to read a newspaper six miles away). In the streets around the stadium, long lines of the faithful trudge towards the ground, drawn inexorably to the bright oval in a scene of almost primal symbolism. Inside, the pitch seems to glow, as if the groundsman got his fertiliser from Sellafield, while the floodlights enhance the mood of theatre, the brightly lit stage awaiting the players.

Although any chance of us catching United has gone, a win tonight is still vital to maintain our position ahead of the chasing pack and keep alive the chance of Europe. Plus, of course, everyone wants to beat Man U. Sky are broadcasting the match worldwide and Sir Alex has paid us the compliment of fielding his strongest team. Curtain up.

Instantly United attack with Giggs flashing down the left, but his cross is cleared by Craddock. Sunderland respond when Phillips nips in behind young Wes Brown in the United defence to volley over the bar. For the next fifteen minutes it is thrust and counter-thrust, the speed and fervour living up to expectation, while the sell-out crowd cranks up the volume.

The first incident comes out of nothing, when United's eccentric French keeper Barthez receives a harmless throw-in down by the corner. Rather than taking the ball back into his box, he casually clears upfield and trots back towards goal. The ball loops down to Alex Rae who volleys it straight back, with Barthez still out of position. It falls harmlessly wide, but Barthez is clearly shocked to discover a fellow spirit on the pitch.

Five minutes later Barthez comes out to pick a Michael Gray cross from the heads of Quinn and Jaap Stam. He catches it cleanly, but then drops the ball in front of Quinn with the empty net beckoning. As Quinn goes to score, Stam hauls him back, yet referee Graham Poll blows not for a penalty, but for a foul on Barthez. Obviously United have brought some of that feng shui with them.

For the first half-hour Sunderland have the upper hand and it looks as if we might actually pull this one off. The defence is solid, the midfield strong and up front Quinn and Phillips are a constant threat. Then the inevitable: Quinn's back gives way and he has to go off. In that instant you can feel the crowd sink. For all of Phillips' superior goal tally, it is ultimately Quinn upon whom Sunderland depend the most, and without him we tend to struggle against anyone, let alone the best side in Europe.

United too sense the moment and seize hold of the game. Keane and Scholes take over midfield and the pendulum starts to swing. In the last ten minutes of the first half, United press forward and Sheringham nearly scores with an audacious back-heel at the end of a classic six-man move. But we hold out to half-time, honours even, each with four shots on goal. It's been fast, furious and skilful and the game is all set up for a great second half.

In United's first attack, Sheringham flicks a pass to Cole who blatantly controls it with his hand, but referee Poll, only fifteen yards away, sees nothing. The ball breaks to Keane who nods it forward again. Craddock makes to belt it clear, but his wild slash misses completely and the ball goes through to Cole. As Sorenson advances, Cole chips over him into the net. All this within the first forty-five seconds.

In the mayhem of protest following the goal, Sunderland skipper Gray runs forty yards to argue with Poll about the handball and is immediately sent off. Meanwhile, somewhere in the crowd, one particular spectator is getting particularly angry.

Part of Bob Murray's campaign to make Sunderland a family-friendly club is a much-vaunted social behaviour policy. Its zero-tolerance approach to anti-social behaviour forbids swearing, smoking, standing, excessive drinking, offensive chanting or indeed anything that may be deemed 'anti-social'. To back this up, a large team of stewards patrol the seats and have, on occasion, been criticised for being a shade over-zealous in enforcing the policy.

So, imagine you're a steward at pitchside and you notice a large man leave his seat. He walks down the steps, then climbs over the fence onto the perimeter track (in itself an offence normally invoking the death penalty and the withdrawal of one's season ticket). The guy is gesticulating wildly and heading onto the pitch with the apparent intention of decking the referee. Do you:

a) Look the other way and warn the five-year-old kid that if she rustles that sweet paper one more time . . .

b) Look the other way and tell the guy in the wheelchair to oil that annoying squeak; or . . .

c) Look the other way and haul off the nearest silver-haired granny for questioning in relation to the disappearance of Lord Lucan?

Hmm, not easy, is it? Well, actually it's a trick question because all of the above are correct. You not only don't bother to stop the guy going on the pitch, you don't chase after him either. You leave it to one of the players to hustle him off and into your incapable hands.

The controversy of the goal, the sending off and the pitch incursion have thrown Sunderland into disarray and United storm forward, with Sheringham heading just over the bar. Gradually Sunderland pull themselves together and a Hutchison free kick skims just past the post. The next minute, Beckham threads a forty-yard pass through our defence to an unmarked Keane. Sorenson charges out, forcing Keane to shoot just wide into the side netting. This match needs more excitement.

Two minutes later, Giggs sends a high cross into the Sunderland area. Cole loses out in a challenge with Sorenson but it seems fairly innocuous. Suddenly Rae and Cole are exchanging pleasantries and engaging in a bizarre bout of head-pushing, foreheads locked like fighting bison. There is no actual butting or punches thrown, so it's perhaps a yellow card each. Instead Mr Poll sends them both off and inflames the crowd even further.

And now we have nine. With so few players the game has taken on a surreal quality, with spaces everywhere but Sunderland lacking the numbers to find a way through United's defence. We keep fighting and suddenly Kilbane is in the box. He rounds Barthez and shoots, but somehow the Frenchman forces the ball away for a corner.

What do we need now, with the game so finely balanced? Ah yes, a female streaker. From the same part of the ground as before. After the first guy, you would expect the stewards in that area to be so fired up that they'd make Islamic Jihad look like the Wombles. But no. She clambers over the fence, wanders onto the pitch and walks towards the Sunderland players. Meanwhile the stewards look on. First she goes up to Chris Makin and then to Stan Varga, who tries to move away without actually breaking into a run. Still no move from the guys in yellow. Bored at not having persuaded any of the Lads to marry her, our visitor wanders into the centre circle and starts waving at the United fans. She's been on the pitch for a full minute when finally, a lone steward walks on with a coat and takes her off.

With this latest farce, the game could have ended as a competition, but Sunderland keep pressing, a goal down and a man down against the best in the business. In the dying minutes Hutch flicks a header into the path of Phillips. He's clear and in the box with the kind of chance he thrives on. He makes to shoot, but at the last second Wes Brown dives in and forces the shot wide.

Sunderland now fling everyone forward, Sorenson pushing up like a sweeper. Hutchison is bundled over in the penalty area but Poll gives nothing. A Varga free kick is only parried by Barthez and the ball bounces around the box as if in a pinball machine, before Keane belts it clear. A final header by Phillips goes over the bar – and that's it.

As a piece of entertainment, the match has delivered in spades, but if you've booked to see Shakespeare, you don't expect music hall. United are about a thousand points clear and might as well collect the trophy now. Sunderland battled well in the face of a ref making Harry Potter judgements, but ultimately United are an extraordinary side. You have to beat them on so many levels: skill, determination, luck, karma, intimidated referees and just sheer bloody fate. But our day will come.

Wednesday, 31 January 2001

SUNDERLAND 0   MANCHESTER UNITED 1
                    (Cole 46)

PLAYED	TRAVELLED	SPENT	POSITION	STATE OF MIND
33	12,567 miles	£1,789.83	3rd	We Wuz Robbed

Derby County (away) – Premier League

And another fiver on Peter Reid for Prime Minister

I was out of the country during Matthew Bannister's culling of Radio One's DJs, so I never knew what became of any of the Smashey and Nicey brigade. Until now.

'And good morning everyone and welcome to this Midland Mainline service from St Pancras to the fabulous city of Derby. My name's Trevor and I'll be your Customer Service Manager, along with the lovely Lizzie, who'll be serving you with tea, coffee and light refreshments. But mind your ankles on that trolley, folks! Just as well she isn't driving the train! But seriously, it's a brilliant day here in London and with the time approaching 10:03 we'll be leaving in a couple of minutes, so just sit back, relax and let the train take the strain. Coming up, we've got new stops at Luton, Bedford, Wellingborough and Kettering, so lots to look forward to over the next couple of hours. Enjoy your journey and thanks for choosing the best main line to the midlands, Midland Mainline.'

Although officially a city, Derby bustles like a cosy county town, confident that it neither wants nor needs the attractions of a big metropolis. The older red-brick Victorian buildings display the solid assurance of carved names across their fascias, so certain were their owners of their permanence in the world. The Midlands Railway Institute still stands proudly outside Derby Station, despite its current role as a wine bar and gym – sorry – health and fitness centre. The town's pedestrianised centre retains a post-Christmas holiday feel, with a kids' fairground, busy shoppers, and the inevitable busker trying to sound like an off-key Stereophonics, and succeeding. Small narrow streets boast stores that proclaim and maintain the area's heritage, such as Ye Olde Video Shoppe, while the spirits of several older buildings are still in good spirits as trendy pubs and bars. And there are churches everywhere. What is it in Derby's past that requires so much blessing and forgiveness (apart from letting Cloughie go to end up with Forest)?

Generally it's overwhelmingly *nice*. You can't move for Laura Ashley and bespoke sweet shops. The centre is dominated by the old Guildhall building and the restored Market Hall, a huge cavernous Victorian trade hall with magnificent wrought-iron beams in burgundy and cream. Here you can relive the essence of Derby's commercial past with Keith's Kave, the Feng Shui Shop and La Terrazza Espresso. The Guildhall Theatre has played host to Shakespeare and tours by the National Theatre, but occasionally they get the really big stars. As I walk past the box office, an elderly couple are surveying the posters of coming attractions. 'Ooh look, they've got *The Sooty Show* for one night.'

But enough of cultcha, I'm here to make some dosh and I head for the nearest bookie. Ever since Anna's freakishly accurate dream about our match against Everton, she's had the occasional recurrence with a disconcertingly high hit rate. Games against Man United, Coventry and Arsenal have all gone according to vision (although in our comeback against Arsenal at Highbury she had Phillips scoring the second goal, not the first). I'm normally far too cautious with my cash to risk betting on something as ephemeral as a football result, but I seem to have stumbled upon a loquacious and rather accurate horse. Today the whisper is 3–0 to us: Phillips after twenty-three minutes, then Hutchison and Rae in the second half. That might sound a bit optimistic, but last year we won 5–0. Naming all three scorers is perhaps pushing the prediction, so I settle for just terrifying the bookies with a fiver on us to win by the hat-trick.

Now I need to find the stadium. I don't normally bother researching directions to a ground. I don't have to. Just arrive at the station and follow the nearest group of men displaying an air of weary resignation. Here we go again. Did you see them last week? Bloody useless. Why do we bother? What's the point? I tell you, Reg, if they don't win today this is definitely the last time I'm coming.

In 1997, Derby moved from their long-time home at the Baseball Ground to a new stadium, Pride Park, on the outskirts of town and in the midst of a large industrial park. Access from the town centre takes me through a railway arch, whose gloomy interior and graffiti-spread walls hint of past troubles. It is classic Ambush Alley, but today's heavy police presence deters any trouble and I'm soon on the wide access road to the stadium. Although built the same year as the SOL, Pride Park seems to have lost its new-ground gleam, the once white exterior now rather grey and, well, looking like it could do with a good going over with the Hoover. Being in the middle of a sterile industrial zone does little for its ambience, and the ground has the flat-pack look of an anonymous US arena. Prominent sponsors' names add little to its character, although I do now know that Mansfield have been serving Smooth Creamy Ales Since 1855.

Inside, however, it's a different story. The continuous bowl of seating is reminiscent of Sunderland's own home, while the dramatic use of Derby's black and white colours gives a powerful example of what St James' could have been like, had the Newcastle Board plumped for something a little more adventurous than battleship grey.

The away fans' concourse is packed with some six thousand supporters, so I remain in the stadium and forgo the pleasures of the ubiquitous pie. Around the perimeter, Derby's mascot, Rammie the Ram, is trying to entertain the kids, but some of them look a bit uneasy and, frankly, I don't blame them. Faced with a creature half-man half-animal, nearly six feet tall and with a huge ram's head and curling horns, I'd be screaming for my mum too. It's like opening Beatrix Potter and finding Dennis Wheatley. Apparently Rammie's been toned down a bit for this very reason, but he'd still give me the heebie-jeebies.

Not that Derby's forbidding presence is limited just to their mascot. In skipper Daryl Powell they have a robust leader who bows to no one and shirks no challenge. During a recent home match against Man City, Powell spent the game suffering abuse from one particular Derby 'fan'. Having scored a vital equaliser, Powell sought out the fan on leaving the pitch in order to 'let him congratulate me'. In last year's match at the SOL, Powell viciously butted Alex Rae's elbow with his face, a no-doubt painful memory that may still be lingering.

Alongside Powell is Taribo West, a Nigerian international of consummate skill on loan from Milan. Described by Derby manager, Jim Smith, as 'a bit of a strange guy [who] likes going on planes too much', West's eccentricities have been accommodated in return for a talent that has transformed Derby from relegation certainties to likely survivors.

Sunderland are missing their own driving force with Quinn still sidelined through injury, so it's another chance for Dichio to prove his stuff. But up against West, I'm afraid he's struggling. Within minutes West easily robs Dichio of the ball before sending a glorious forty-yard pass that leaves striker Christie just inches from scoring. Then Derby's Carbonari smacks a screamer of a long-range free kick against the post. The lively opening continues when Powell repays a certain debt with a horror tackle on Rae, but any further retribution is cancelled when Dichio's awkward challenge leaves Powell with a broken nose and no further part in the game.

Our first significant chance comes after twenty-three minutes, when Phillips takes a pass from Gray on the edge of the box. In one sublime move, he turns and sends a curling effort that skims just wide. Was that Anna's predicted goal? Just as well I didn't take her complete forecast to heart. Next minute a flick from Dichio sees Phillips go close again. It's an open flowing game, but both sides are failing where it matters. Sunderland are missing Quinn and someone out wide, while Derby look promising but lack the final killer pass.

With five minutes to half-time, another Derby attack appears to break down, when a seemingly mis-hit pass skews off towards the corner flag and looks to be rolling out of play. The Sunderland defence relax, but suddenly Derby's Murray rescues the ball and whips in a powerful low cross, which Craig Burley hammers home under a diving Sorenson. It's another body blow after Wednesday's pounding and the Lads leave the field looking rather punch drunk. And I've just lost five quid.

Just after the restart, Phillips finds Hutchison unmarked in front of goal. It's our first real chance, but his first-time effort curls wide and betrays a lack of confidence that seems to have struck the whole team. When Dichio has a shot cleared off the line, you know it's just not our day.

Meanwhile, Derby are pushing us hard. Another superb pass from West puts Burley clear, but his well-struck shot hits the post and we breathe again. Their attacks come in waves but repeatedly fall victim to some dubious offside decisions by the linesman. In one bizarre two-minute period, three successive Derby players are deemed offside when seemingly safe. When the ref books all three for their aggrieved reactions, you have to wonder if he's getting air miles with each yellow card.

On seventy minutes, Phillips' spectacular volley is saved with ease, another effort of style but little impact. In the last ten minutes, Derby twice have chances to wrap it up when Burton and Morris race clear, but both shoot tamely wide.

In the ninetieth minute, a Hutchison free kick falls to our young sub, John Oster. He aims his side-foot volley wide of Oakes, but the debut keeper dives low and tips the ball on to the post for the last act of the match.

We had more than our share of the game but have nothing to show for it. Despite the odd spark from Phillips, a dearth of ideas beyond the high ball to Dichio left us ineffective and goalless. If this was a hangover from the

United game, then we'll need a quick pick-me-up for our next match, a home tie against an on-form Liverpool.

Saturday, 3 February 2001
DERBY COUNTY 1   SUNDERLAND 0
(Burley 42)

PLAYED	TRAVELLED	SPENT	POSITION	STATE OF MIND
34	12,833 miles	£1,833.04	4th	We need another striker

Liverpool (home) – Premier League

Have you got any hot snakes left?

The typical football supporter's diet flies in the face of any government directive on healthy eating. Low fat, low sugar, low salt? Bollocks, stick some more grease on, luv. Not that there's really much alternative. Around the stadiums, you don't see too many food stalls offering heart-friendly, organic tofu burgers. I've come to accept that on match day, I must abandon my usual pretensions towards pseudo-veggie culinary liberalism and indulge in a dose of dietary self-abuse: fish and chips, pies, ice cream, chocolate and thick pork sandwiches that ooze gravy and gunk – and I love it.

The *pièce de résistance* for the passionate patron is the pie. While burgers and kebabs have made their own in-roads into arterial blockage, the pie remains supreme. It is part of the football fan's Holy Trinity: *Nomine Padre*, a pie, a pint and a programme. Before the gentrification of football grounds, supporters would put up with just about anything: Black Hole crowding, hepatitis toilets, impossible sightlines. But take away the pies and the government would have fallen overnight. Sunderland used to offer an interesting range of their own: there was 'steak', 'beef' and, rather disturbingly, 'meat'. I've always hoped we'd be drawn away in the Cup to Norwich City, as apparently director Delia Smith has revamped the catering and their pies are Premier League (well, I guess you have to start somewhere).

Ah, but would she store them the right way up? On my last visit to Roker Fish and Chips, I noticed that all the pies in the warming cabinet were placed upside-down. Perhaps it was some novel means of keeping them hot, but no one in the shop seemed to know why. Eventually someone summoned the manager for an answer to this most burning of cookery queries. She thought for a moment. 'Because that's the way the previous owner did it.' So now you know. Or not.

But for all the conservatism of the average fan's fare, you occasionally get a glimpse of more esoteric tastes. On the train up for today's game, one of the London Branch notices a passenger with a small plastic sandwich box. Containing a live snake. 'If I were you, mate, I'd take that back to the buffet.'

A large crowd heading for a match involves elements both public and private. The sheer numbers force you into close proximity with complete strangers, so it becomes impossible not to eavesdrop (or if not exactly impossible, certainly a lot easier). There's the usual range of football talk:

'Dichio's brilliant if you need someone to smash up a piano . . .'

'Eeh, Ah wouldn't mind gettin' into Tommy's penalty box . . .'

'Aye, Maradona was magic, like, but Besty was more honest . . .'

Plus affairs of the heart:

'Since he finished with wor lass he's been snoggin' every fat bird in town.'

With the more relaxed atmosphere at matches, it's quite common to see both sets of supporters walking along together, although there'll still be the usual banter. As I approach the SOL, two groups of Liverpool and Sunderland fans are in full flow, the thick Mersey accents rising above the Mackem.

'Hey mate, I hear they're turning Sunderland's trophy room into a museum – Rare Finds and Ancient History.'

'Taak proper, y'Scouse wanker.'

But for all the bonhomie, this is another match with much at stake. Liverpool have edged into third, but if we win today we can leapfrog over them back into that all-important Champions League spot. Sunderland's preparations for this game were supposed to include a relaxing week away playing golf. Some teams take their players over to Spain, to let tired limbs soak up a bit of sun. Sunderland went up to Scotland. The local golf course was under three feet of snow.

So, revived and refreshed, they're back to face another of their bogey teams. We haven't beaten Liverpool at home since 1958, and well do I remember watching us play them in a relegation decider in 1970. We had to win to stay up, but with five minutes left there was no score. Then they sneaked one and we were down. Today promises to be no easier. We've got Arca back from international duty, but the suspensions and injuries are starting to mount up. It's time to see how good our squad really is.

Liverpool open the match with a run by Emile Heskey down the right wing. He belts the ball to the far post, where an unmarked Robbie Fowler is waiting to score. It's the kind of chance he has for breakfast. Yet, under no pressure, he heads wide. Perhaps he only bothers when it's difficult.

The next twenty minutes is all bish 'n' bosh, but to little effect. Then a Varga tackle on Heskey sees the Liverpool striker limp from the pitch after another brief appearance. The following minute, Liverpool's Henchoz repays the compliment with a crude challenge on Phillips. It looks like a possible penalty, but referee Graham Barber waves play on.

The stalemate continues and it's thirty-two minutes before there's a shot on target, when Phillips volleys a knock-down that Westerveld struggles to save. For the next attack, Kev skips away from defender Sam Hyypia and fires a shot that skims just wide. Throughout the rest of the half, neither side threatens much and half-time is a welcome relief.

The teams seem to return rather quickly, until I realise it's Sunderland's Under-10 Girls Squad, coming on for a half-time mini-match. With shorts reaching down to their ankles, there's initially the inevitable cute factor – until they start playing. I thought that girls were supposed to kick like, well, girls, but not this lot. Swift one-twos, powerful shots and Dervish-like tackles. Naah, forget the blokes, we'll watch the pros.

The second half starts with another penalty shout for Sunderland, when Hutchison is held back in the area, but again Mr Barber sees nothing. Then a third penalty claim is ignored when Hyypia brings down Phillips. But as the ref is dismissing the appeals, a deflected clearance falls to Hutchison, who blasts in a cracker to give us the lead.

Five minutes later, Arca nearly adds a second when he chips just over from twenty yards and we're into a good spell. Phillips has another shimmy and shot that scares the post, while Varga stifles any Liverpool attacks.

Then Owen comes on for Liverpool, Arca goes off for Sunderland and the balance begins to shift. Fowler shoots too close for comfort, then a Liverpool pass finds Owen in midfield. In one move, he turns and sends a ball through our back four to the sprinting Gary McAllister. He's away and clear, but Varga's after him. As the Liverpool man approaches the penalty area, Varga makes a desperate lunge that clips McAllister's heel. For a split-second McAllister continues on into the box, when suddenly a shot rings out from somewhere in the direction of the grassy knoll and the Scotsman crumples to the ground.

The Liverpool players vehemently claim a penalty, but given Barber's record there's no way he'll . . . he has. Sunderland surround the ref and persuade him to consult his linesman. While Barber was well behind the play, his assistant had an excellent view, yet still he upholds the award.

Litmanen calmly sends Tommy the wrong way for the equaliser. Amid all the chaos, the referee omits to book Varga for what should have been his second yellow card and a sending off. However, he does book Phillips for protesting and Kev will now face a two-match ban. All in all, it's a bit of a cock-up.

In their anger, Sunderland push forward and have their fourth penalty claim denied when Vignal pushes Hutchison down from behind. With five minutes left, Owen wriggles his way into the box and sends a low cross to the far post, where Fowler coolly puts the ball away for the winner. Except it's not. Even though he was level with Varga, Fowler's been given offside and the match ends all-square.

There is obviously some poetic justice in the disallowed Liverpool goal. But the abiding impression is that for the second successive home match, we have been denied by the referee. Perhaps it's because they're both called Graham and hail from Tring. But whatever the reason, a curse on both their houses.

Saturday, 10 February 2001
SUNDERLAND 1   LIVERPOOL 1
(Hutchison 51)   (Litmanen 77)

PLAYED	TRAVELLED	SPENT	POSITION	STATE OF MIND
35	13,397 miles	£1,889.59	4th	We Wuz Robbed II

West Ham United (home) – FA Cup Fifth Round

*Excuse me, your Majesty, could I have
a look at your programme?*

After three years back in England, I've just about come to terms with the notion that three o'clock on a Saturday afternoon is no longer sacrosanct. So with a midday kick-off, it's a 4:30 lie-in for the 6:15 train. King's Cross is full of West Ham fans all trying to out-geezer each other, but the majority have accepted the option of free coach travel, courtesy of a wealthy fellow supporter. A convoy of some sixty buses is heading north, complete with gasps of astonishment from the national media, as if they were setting out for the New World.

Unfortunately this laudable effort by six thousand Hammers fans is not matched by the home supporters, of whom only a paltry thirty thousand bother to turn up. That's about fifteen thousand below our average league gate. For the fifth round of the Cup. Against a Premiership side. With cheap tickets. Today you could stroll up five minutes before kick-off and have a choice of seats. Back in '73, getting a ticket was like scrambling aboard the last chopper out of Saigon.

It started with the fifth-round replay against Manchester City at Roker Park. The tickets went on sale at ten o'clock Sunday morning. I got there at six, but there was already a queue of about fifty yards. By ten, it was madness. On the night, over fifty-one thousand packed out the old ground and from then on, the roller-coaster to the final was all about tickets. The club hadn't a clue how to handle the demand. They'd become used to crowds of twelve thousand. After relegation in 1970, they gave up issuing season tickets for the standing ends and stopped printing 'loyalty tokens' in the programmes. Obviously no one could ever see us being in a big enough game to warrant them. Many of the die-hards, who'd spent years loyally watching crap and then seen their season tickets withdrawn, suddenly had to fight for cup tickets along with the tens of thousands of 'born-again' supporters who hadn't been to Roker for donkeys.

The club weren't slow to recognise a good thing. In a blatant move to boost league attendances, they started issuing vouchers at each home game. The vouchers were then drawn in a ballot for cup tickets. This new move was 'to ensure that our regular supporters have a chance of seeing the cup ties'. Huh. Suddenly they were getting nearly forty thousand to watch Sunderland play Second Division matches against Oxford and Carlisle. I was lucky in the ballots for the sixth round and semi-final, but come the final . . . I couldn't believe it. Six years of eating scraps, now finally the chance to dine in style and some overweight bastard's come along and nicked my table. I went from comparing universities to considering monasteries.

Then my father came up trumps. Somehow he got a ticket. But not just any ticket. For a start, it had a face value of six pounds. The most expensive on sale to the public was five pounds. Then I looked closer: 'North Stand. Reserved Area. Row B'.

I was sitting behind the Queen.

It was hopeless. I was used to the Fulwell End. I knew every song, every chant, I couldn't suddenly switch to decorous behaviour for the biggest game in the club's history. I'd be chucked out after five minutes. And there was another factor. For years, I'd been going to matches with a couple of lads from Blyth and, typically, they too had missed out on the ballot. But I knew that I held something of real value, certainly worth three normal standing tickets. If only I could find three people willing to swap their joint tickets for just one. Hmm. That was when it all started to get a bit strange.

My aunt, who had no interest in football, knew someone who knew someone who knew of a ticket tout working out of a grocer's in Gateshead. The store was small, run-down and in the middle of an anonymous council estate. I think it's safe to say I was a complete novice in the affairs of black-market ticket dealing. But, nothing ventured . . . I marched into the shop. Inside the gloomy interior, an elderly man behind the counter was talking to a twenty-something guy in a suit. I took a deep breath. 'I understand you have cup final tickets for sale.'

The old man exploded.

'What the bloody hell do y'think yer deein'? Gan on, get oot me shop,' and he ushered me swiftly out the door. Something told me that hadn't gone too well. Shocked, I hung around on the pavement, as the younger man rushed out looking very pleased with himself and drove off at some speed. The owner stuck his head out and gestured me back inside. 'Sorry aboot that, young un, but that was a reporter from *The Journal* lookin' for a story. Now, you want a ticket?'

He led me into the store-room and I explained my dilemma.

'Not a problem. Ah can swap you for three standin', but Ah need to get 'em from down south. Give us yours and Ah'll let y'knaa when they get here.'

Now, I may have been naive, but I wasn't stupid. He saw my concern.

'Divvent worry, man. Ah've got heaps o' them special tickets,' and with that he opened his wallet and produced a sheaf of about thirty six-pound tickets. Her Majesty was seemingly on a nice little earner. So, apparently both naive and stupid after all, *I gave him the ticket.*

The following week, nothing. Nor the week after. Perhaps handing my only chance of getting to Wembley over to a ticket tout hadn't been such a good idea. I kept phoning him. He was collecting the tickets right enough, but then selling them at pre-arranged stops on the drive back north. There was only one answer. I had to go with him. We drove down the A1 to a greasy spoon just outside Wetherby. He bought me a cup of tea, then plonked me at a table before joining his contact at another. When I glanced across, thick wads of notes and tickets were changing hands. And this was just one trip. In my complete innocence I'd stumbled into the main touting operation for channelling cup final tickets to the North-east. I suddenly felt rather nervous.

Back in the car, he duly handed me my three tickets. For the Leeds end. On the day, we somehow found three Leeds fans in the same dilemma, and, with the result, it all ended rather well, even though I'd apparently blown the lid on the whole affair. The day after my first visit to the shop, the front page of *The Journal* screamed, 'Cup Tickets For £11 At The Grocer's'.

The rash of bookings over previous matches has finally come home to roost, as today we are without three suspended key players: Hutchison, Rae and Gray. West Ham are at full strength, as are their fans who have taken over the whole of the South Stand and are giving an unusually subdued home crowd a lesson in vocal support. They arrive here after their shock win in the fourth round against Man United, when Barthez tried to kid Di Canio. He'd have been better off trying to con Ernie Bilko.

We start brightly enough, but Reid still seems bent on a high-risk offside strategy. The classic Arsenal back four of Adams and co. could pull it off, but we're some way from matching their synchronicity. Twice within the first ten minutes, Frederic Kanouté romps happily through our defence to collect a killer pass, only for each attempt to be denied at the last moment. But another eighty minutes of this?

Five minutes later and another Kanouté effort goes wide as Cole and Carrick start to control midfield. Sunderland look bereft of ideas, other than the high ball to Qui . . . I'm sorry, I nodded off for a moment. Phillips is scampering round Quinn like a sheepdog on speed, but Niall's clearly not one hundred per cent and is losing most of his battles with Croatian defender, Igor Blimey – sorry, Igor Stimac (very old Croatian joke).

The only bright spot for Sunderland is young winger, John Oster, signed two years ago from Everton and still to establish himself as a first-team regular. Today he's fast and full of trickery and keeps trying 'mazy dribbles'. It's as if he's been reading back issues of *Roy of the Rovers*.

'Young Oster's playing a blinder! The Eastburn defence don't know which way to turn.'

'He's beaten three of them – and what a great pass to Roy!'

Unfortunately it is often not a great pass to Roy or anyone else, and Oster's whirligig energies fail to dent the West Ham defence. Meanwhile Kanouté keeps adding more offside decisions to his collection, and the match is becoming a lively but ineffectual midfield struggle.

After half an hour, Oster shimmies his way through, but his weakish shot is turned round the post by keeper Hislop. At the other end, Sorenson makes two good saves from Lampard and Kanouté and the first half ends scoreless.

The second half opens with a sublime piece of skill by Joe Cole, but as he prepares to shoot, Di Canio nips in and blasts the ball into the side netting. The play remains in a state of energetic stalemate, although gradually Sunderland take the initiative. Phillips tests Hislop with a fine cross, then Quinny finally loses Stimac as Makin floats a superb pass to the big Irishman. As the ball comes down, Niall's unmarked in front of goal, but he fails to control the pass and the chance is gone.

With fifteen minutes left, Quinn shows his true skill in setting up a certain Phillips goal, but Stuart Pearce saves the day with a last ditch header from under the crossbar. In the next West Ham attack, our offside trap finally fails and Kanouté is off and clear. Sorenson races out of his area, realises he's come too soon, and Kanouté coolly passes the ball into the net.

The next minute Kanouté nearly adds another and with the cushion of the goal, West Ham look more confident. In the last ten minutes, Oster jinks his way into the box, but is denied by another superb tackle from Pearce. Stefan Schwarz tests Hislop with a powerful drive but we can't find the equaliser and the tie goes to the Hammers.

While we weren't outplayed, we struggled to exert any real influence on the match. The sad fact is that while we have a very good pool of perhaps thirteen or fourteen players, once outside that core we tend to struggle. Off the field, the home crowd were significant by their absence and we've been outsung at the SOL for the first time. The exodus of Sunderland fans before the final whistle perhaps summed up their feelings towards the match. After all, it's only the Cup.

Saturday, 17 February 2001

SUNDERLAND 0   WEST HAM UNITED 1
                              (Kanouté 76)

PLAYED	TRAVELLED	SPENT	POSITION	STATE OF MIND
36	13,961 miles	£1,953.14	Out!	I got up at 4:30 for this?

Leicester City (away) – Premier League

And after a sunbed session,
always use a good moisturiser

Any area that gave the world the pork pie, Walkers Crisps and Gary Lineker must have something going for it. On the other hand, Leicester City do have the worst toilets in the Premiership. The very act of visiting every Premier League ground invites comparison, and while one might debate the larger issues of capacities, sightlines and ticket prices, the bog-standard facilities also leave an impression. Admittedly I still have five grounds to visit, but I know The Dell and Highfield Road from last season and I can't imagine the new Stamford Bridge, Riverside Stadium or Goodison Park having loos anywhere near as bad as those in Leicester's East Stand.

Not that Filbert Street is all bad. The large modern Carling Stand is as good as any, and the proximity of the crowd to the pitch creates an atmosphere missing from larger stadiums, where the stands are often set back a few metres. But the East Stand is like being back at Blyth Spartans. Before the improvements. A wire cage separates the away fans from the home crowd and access is only via one narrow walkway along the back. To be fair, Leicester are planning to move to a new stadium in 2002, so understandably they are not minded to spend a penny on the old place – or in it.

Prominent are several notices warning against 'persistent standing', with the threat of possible closure of the stand if the practice continues. As threats go, it seems both redundant and appealing. But the whole issue of standing at games is becoming more topical, not that it ever really went away. The sudden imposition of all-seater stadiums after Hillsborough was always going to conflict with decades of ingrained tradition. For years fans stood through choice or economic necessity and the transition to sitting has never convinced. People still stand at exciting moments in the game, it's impossible not to, and there has been a persistent and growing campaign by some supporters to revive standing in Premiership grounds.

Overshadowing the debate is the sensitive issue of the Liverpool fans who died and their families, but proponents of standing claim that new approaches to the problem are worlds away from the cattle pens of old. In Germany, Borussia Dortmund have a standing section that can hold twenty-five thousand, yet have never had an accident. Indeed, virtually all German grounds have something similar, but no history of mishaps or significant crowd trouble. Ironically, the current all-seater stadiums in the Premiership are potentially more dangerous than the new standing terraces. When several thousand people suddenly rise to their feet, there is nothing to stop anyone lurching forward onto the person in front, particularly given the steep inclines at some grounds. With the new design of standing area, each step of the terrace has a waist-high bar that runs along its entire length, stopping anyone from falling. Everyone has their own safety barrier, which also prevents the old 'rolling wave' effect that was so overpowering.

The standing faction also point to benefits such as reduced prices, greater capacity and better atmosphere. The opposition, including those connected with the Hillsborough Family Support Group, argue that all-seater stadiums have improved the game's image and safety record, got rid of the troublemakers and attracted more women and kids to matches. The sport's authorities are equally divided. FIFA, UEFA, the Professional Footballers' Association and the Football Licensing Authority have all given varying degrees of approval to the idea, while the FA, the Premier League and the Football Foundation are firmly against. Even the relevant government officials can't agree. Sports Minister, Kate Hoey, has angered the Liverpool families with her willingness to consider the new designs, while her boss, Culture Secretary Chris Smith, is firmly opposed.

I like standing. It's a better atmosphere and less inhibiting. Yelling and singing while seated always feels slightly ridiculous, the anarchist on their best behaviour. But I also like being able to see and breathe. The old-style terraces, with their three-inch steps, were hopeless for seeing anything when packed, unless you were over six foot. And I never want to re-live that day on the Kop. If I could be guaranteed a good view and a secure spot, I'd give it a try. At present, the standers and sitters are lumped together, causing each other grief and aggravation. Segregating a stadium into seating and new standing areas would restore choice without compromising safety.

For all the reasoned arguments of both sides, I suspect each camp harbours an element with a hidden agenda. Among the pro-standing lobby will be some fans who seek a return to the bedlam, the liberation of 'having a bit of a larf wiv yer mates'. And while the anti-brigade present safety as their *raison d'être*, some authorities no doubt equate standing with troublemakers. They regard seating (and higher prices) as having been a key factor in defeating the yobs and are not about to give it up. It's become not so much 'sit down' as 'sit down and behave'.

If our team selection against West Ham was hindered by suspensions, today we're positively crippled. Still missing Hutchison, Rae and Gray, we are also denied the suspended Phillips and the injured Varga. I've brought my boots along just in case.

Unfortunately there is no equivalent affliction for the Leicester side. They all appear to be present and correct and in rude health, and none ruder than captain-in-spirit, Robbie Savage. The Leicester City website now contains a section on the thoughts of Robbie Savage, or 'Savisms', which presumably include 'My Top Ten Tanning Tips' and 'Bad Luck With Bleaching?'

Sunderland start brightly, passing the ball well and putting Leicester under pressure. With the memories of last year's 5–2 thrashing still vivid, we need to establish some authority from the start. After just ten minutes, a neat pass by Quinn presents Kevin Kilbane with an excellent chance just yards out, but his tame shot is easily saved and shows all the signs of a player lacking in confidence. Nevertheless we continue to dominate and it's twenty minutes before Leicester have a decent shot, a powerful drive by Akinbiyi that Sorenson does well to stop.

Quinn's looking good up front with no sign of the injury that has plagued him for weeks. He fires a long-range effort that tests Royce in the Leicester goal, while at the other end, Akinbiyi wins a rare battle with Thome to go close with another effort. It's a lively game which we seem to be controlling, when an innocuous-looking cross floats over into our penalty area. Leicester striker Dean Sturridge goes to challenge for it with our dependable centre-back, Jody Craddock, which hardly seems fair given Craddock's six-inch height advantage. So watching Sturridge loop a header into the net is something of a surprise.

Despite this setback, we continue pressing as both Kilbane and Makin try long-range efforts. Then Sturridge nearly grabs a second when he fires just past the post. Half-time arrives with no further score. We've had a couple of scares, but we're still in the game and could easily grab a draw – or maybe even the win.

So much for optimism. A few minutes into the second half, a lunging tackle by Kilbane misses defender Gerry Taggart by some inches, but the

Leicester man's exaggerated reaction convinces the ref of the foul. The bad temper from this soon erupts. John Oster steams in to challenge Savage for a loose ball. It's a clumsy effort and he clips the bronzed one on the calf. While it's certainly a foul, Savage collapses to the ground as if Oster's de-legged him with a chainsaw. As Savage lies motionless, the ref shows the young midfielder his second yellow card and he's off. Oster dutifully starts for the tunnel, but his sense of injustice at Savage's apparent playacting boils over. He rushes over to the still-prone figure, probably with the intention of finishing the job properly, but is dragged away by a team-mate. I'm sure he'll calm down when he starts shaving.

So, we're losing one–nil away from home, missing five regular players and we're down to ten men. Ten minutes later, Sturridge hustles Thome off the ball and sends in a low cross that bounces off Akinbiyi's knee into the net. And that's the end of that.

Or it should have been. Reid's team genuinely do not seem to know when they are beaten. Incredibly, we pressurise Leicester and start to come back into the game. Craddock heads just over, then Quinn controls a looping free kick on his chest but volleys straight at the keeper. Makin bustles his way through but shoots wide, Quinn has another good effort and Shwarz also has a go. Meanwhile, Leicester have two goals disallowed in the last fifteen minutes. We finish unbowed but very beaten.

From the heights of our win at West Ham, we've gained just two points from five games and scored only one league goal. Our post-Christmas slump seems to have arrived after all, albeit a touch later than last year. However, unlike last year, the level of play has remained generally high and once we get through this bout of suspensions, we should hopefully bounce back. We just need to sit tight (or stand firm).

Saturday, 24 February 2001

LEICESTER CITY 2   SUNDERLAND 0

(Sturridge 29, Akinbiyi 65)

PLAYED	TRAVELLED	SPENT	POSITION	STATE OF MIND
37	14,174 miles	£2,004.44	4th	Don't panic

Aston Villa (home) – Premier League

And this is for all the gang in Nether Poppleton

It's a Monday night match, which means another two-day trip and overnight stay. Originally tonight's game was going to be on the Saturday, but Sky want to televise it, so it's been shifted and never mind the supporters. Yes, it's an extra hassle for me because I choose to live in London, but there are many others in the same boat. Many fans live away from the North-east for work reasons, while Sunderland's idea of the community seems to extend for about a hundred miles north, south and west. It seems not unreasonable that the club might consider the consequences of re-scheduling matches for its more distant supporters. But ever since the 'strategic media alliance' between Sunderland and Sky in 1999, the broadcaster seems able to snap its fingers and change matches at will. This evening's clash with Villa is the second of four games that will be moved in just a two-month period.

Sky's money has brought enormous improvements to the game and it's difficult to imagine how else the recommendations of the Taylor Report could have been financed. Even the most conventional Sunderland fan now accepts the need for big money if we are to compete with the big boys. However, the alliance with Sky set alarm bells ringing for most supporters, fearing shades of Man United and a corporate makeover. The feelgood press release certainly echoed *The Sun*'s exaltations over Murdoch's bid for United in 1998, as if their club being valued at £623.4m was actually relevant to a traditional Manc supporter. The various safeguards in the Sunderland deal seemed designed to keep the media giant at arm's length, and Bob Murray is probably the only Premiership Chairman I would trust with my club. But Sky's apparent influence over the schedules sits uneasily with the average punter. Many fear this initial arrangement to be the thin edge of a commercial wedge where the mentality shifts from community to corporate. Next time you see a photo of a Man United player, take a closer look at the club badge on the shirt. No longer any mention of 'Football Club'.

The section of line between Doncaster and York is closed because of the Selby crash five days ago. Train travel always used to seem ludicrously safe: nothing coming the other way (theoretically), can't veer off the track (supposedly) and unaffected by other forms of transport (hypothetically). Now it's like flying with Aeroflot.

A replacement bus service has been provided, but I'm not sure how confident I feel with any company that dresses its drivers in bright purple sweaters. For the hour-long journey we are obliged to listen to Radio One. I was hoping there might be an alternative. Like being dragged behind the coach. At least it's a chance to hear what the station sounds like post-Travis, Bates, Freeman et al . . . Hmm, exactly the same: hype up the hysteria and roll out the sub-Kenny Everett characters. I thought the new breed of DJs were supposed to be cool, laid-back and radiating street cred. This lot have about as much street cred as Mr Blobby.

One advantage of coach travel is the degree of contact with the passing world. In a train it's fields and houses and the odd station, but little sense of where you actually are. On the road it's towns and villages and signposts to intriguing places. One thing Yorkshire is not short of is intriguing placenames. There's Sprotsborough, Bubwith and Houston Pagnall. Or how about Sherburn-in-Elmet, Gingley-on-the-Hill and Holme-on-Spalding-Moor? Fancy a climb up to Ackworth Moor Top? On the way down we could pop into the Poppletons (Upper and Nether) or have a chat in Askham Richard and Askham Bryan. For Chelsea fans, there's also Stamford Bridge, which was going to be the club's original name, but the Chairman didn't want the team associated with a village in Yorkshire.

To add to the chaos of recent months wrought by floods, fuel crisis and Railtrack, we now have foot and mouth. Apparently the plague of frogs has been delayed on the M6. As we enter York, the famed racecourse is eerily deserted on an afternoon when it might otherwise be teeming with serious horse flesh. Just to complete this portrait of misfortune, we arrive at the hub of English railways, otherwise known as the National Railway Museum.

If my match report appears more one-eyed than usual, it's because I cleverly mistook some contact lens cleaner for eyedrops. Thankfully it's a cold North-east night, so the biting wind is having something of a numbing effect as tears stream down one side of my face. No one seems to be taking much notice, but then at Sunderland it's not uncommon to see grown men cry.

Despite our disappointing results over the last few matches, we're still in with a shout of Europe thanks to some equally poor performances by the other top teams. We haven't slipped as dramatically down the table as we might, and a win tonight can lift us back to third. We're still missing Phillips and Rae, but Don Hutchison and Mickey Gray are back, while Reid has stayed faithful with John 'Badass' Oster after his indiscretions at Leicester.

A good goalkeeper can be like a rock in the heart of the defence. Villa have David James and right from the start he looks like he's crumbling. A mis-kicked clearance goes straight to Quinn who controls the ball well, but then shoots wide instead of passing to an unmarked Hutchison. Then James makes a hash of clearing a corner. For the first half-hour it's all Sunderland, but despite the goalkeeper's fumblings, we fail to score. In one bizarre episode, James drops a shot by McCann which falls to Arca. His attempted chip over the fallen sentinel skews across the face of the goal to Hutchison at the far post. With James stranded and the yawning net just begging for the ball, Hutch fires it back the same way into the arms of the scrambling and grateful keeper.

It is over forty minutes before Sorenson has a save to make. Dion Dublin puts Julian Joachim clean through and he blasts a shot that the Dane does well to stop. Otherwise Villa present no threat and, despite James' antics, the score remains 0–0 to half-time.

The second half seems set to continue in much the same vein, when a McCann drive goes close. Three minutes later and James is involved again, but this time at the opposite end. He boots a long clearance into the heart of our defence, but Thome and Craddock are both playing 'Yours' and the ball bounces between them. Villa's young striker, Lee Hendrie, takes advantage of the confusion and nods the down ball to Joachim who fires low beyond Sorenson for the first goal.

How the hell did that happen?

The shock jolts Sunderland into action and within minutes, Hutch hits the bar with a long free kick. But we're without Quinn who was replaced by Dichio in the first half. Our attacks are floundering around the big forward, who can't win a high ball or low ball or use any pass that comes to him. We still dominate the play, James is still faffing and it's all quite exciting, but we can't nail our chances. Then with fifteen minutes left, Dublin breaks clear. He's just got Tommy to beat and this is curtains – he's making to shoot – and he's shot wide.

With time running out, James flaps away another attack and the ball falls to Dichio. He shoots, but it's going wide of the far post and that's another chance blown. Then suddenly McCann appears and guides the miscued attempt into the net. Great pass by Danny.

The last few minutes and Sunderland attack like a cavalry charge. It's blood and thunder stuff, the crowd are on their feet and finally James comes good (or bad) when he saves brilliantly from Hutchison and Dichio.

Injury time and a corner to us. It floats high to the far post, where Craddock is waiting. As James comes out, he collides with one of his defenders, leaving Craddock to head the ball back into the goalmouth. In a flash, Dichio hooks the ball in for a last-gasp winner!

But no. Referee Steve Lodge has given a free kick for an infringement on James. The only person who had any contact with him was his own defender. The match ends and for the third home game running, we've been denied by a clear mistake on the part of the ref.

The crowd outside are full of conspiracy theories about the recent rash of poor decisions: the Mags have bribed the FA, the refs don't want to be seen to give in to a noisy crowd, Sky have arranged for only the 'big' clubs to get into Europe. All perfectly feasible, of course, but less so than the truth – we didn't create enough chances and those we did, we largely failed to take. End of story.

Monday, 5 March 2001

SUNDERLAND 1   ASTON VILLA 1

(McCann 83)   (Joachim 51)

PLAYED	TRAVELLED	SPENT	POSITION	STATE OF MIND
38	14,738 miles	£2,071.77	5th	Reality bites

Chelsea (away) – Premier League

*That can't be right – an art gallery next to a football
ground?*
– SUNDERLAND FAN

It's the night before the Chelsea game and the London Supporters' Branch
have organised their annual social with players and staff from the club.
Generally these are held after the match with the whole squad attending,
but following tomorrow's game the team fly straight back to the North-east.
So tonight it's just a few of the younger reserve players and Assistant
Manager, Bobby Saxton. Everybody's waiting around like Westlife fans and
when the players arrive they certainly look the part of young popstars.
Close-up, professional footballers exude an aura of good health completely
alien to the normal person, yet these kids also seem impossibly thin and in
need of a good meal. John Oster is here, suspended for tomorrow's match
after his sending off at Leicester. Although twenty-two, he looks about
sixteen, and with his slight frame, the idea of his having flattened Robbie
Savage seems ludicrous.

For a while, the atmosphere is like that of a school disco, the players as
the best-looking girls all huddled together, and us the spotty lads too shy
to approach them. Gradually the ice breaks, largely thanks to Bobby
Saxton acting as teacher/chaperone. In contrast to his fearsome reputation,
Saxton comes across as a genial father figure, more likely to place a
comforting arm around the shoulder of an out-of-form player than to give
him a kick up the backside. With his vast experience in the game, he offers
an insight into a world that supporters can only dream of, and handles a
question and answer session with humour and easy charm. Afterwards in
the bar, he hears about a member of the Branch football team who has
recently suffered a broken leg. He offers to get a copy of tomorrow's
programme signed by all the players as a get-well card, which somehow I
am delegated to collect. As a parting shot, I ask him for a prediction for
tomorrow's game.

He replies with some confidence: '1–1'. Given Chelsea's formidable home form and our recent run of results, I think he's being a touch optimistic.

After travelling some fourteen thousand miles to matches, it makes a pleasant change to just hop on a local bus. Once home to Wilde, Twain and Whistler, Chelsea has to be the trendiest locale of any English football ground. You can't move for chi-chi shops, wine bars and antique dealers called Guinevere, Rupert Cavendish and Edwards Charles. It's all a world away from Sunderland and Frank's Factory Floorings, whose big and bold illuminated yellow sign proclaims, 'I Luv Carpets, Me!' But who would you rather do business with, Guinevere or Frank?

Complementing the fashionable area is Chelsea Village, the impressive shopping and hotel complex that adjoins the football ground. There was a time when any major stadium development seemed to incorporate a shopping and leisure complex, sketches of which would show smartly dressed football fans engaged in a spot of pre-match consumerism in a bright, airy, atrium-like mall. Yet for all of Man United's wealth and pompous stature, Chelsea are still the only club to have even approached this ambitious vision, with two hotels and a selection of bars and restaurants.

In the heart of the Village is the smart, wood-panelled Shed Sports Bar, named after Chelsea's famous stand that was once as notorious for trouble as the Stretford End. With the development of Stamford Bridge, the old Shed terrace has gone, but posterity has preserved the entire back wall. It now stands outside the new stadium and stretches unbroken for about a hundred yards. At some thirty feet high, it's still impressive, and oddly reminiscent of the Berlin Wall, both structures now tamed by more enlightened times. The Shed wall is festooned with ivy and old-style lanterns, dignified in its retirement, yet its fearsome reputation lingers. I remember Chelsea's old pop song, 'Blue Is The Colour', perhaps the first club anthem to have any success, which contained the ominous line, 'Come to the Shed, we will welcome you'. Yeah, with a hail of bricks. While Chelsea Village has gone some way to improving the club's image, the recent *MacIntyre Undercover* programme on football violence showed that the spirit of the old Shed is still alive and very much kicking.

Consistent with the upmarket style of the complex, Chelsea's Megastore is a cut above your average club shop. Spanning three floors, they have space enough for more than the usual range of items. There's Chelsea cutlery, grass wallpaper and, most impressively, a royal blue, Chelseacrested Vespa scooter. At two thousand pounds, it must represent the supporter's ultimate impulse buy. 'I'll have a programme and a scarf and, er, oh yeah, I'll take one of those scooters.' The store is also unique in displaying the club's trophy cabinet. Oddly, the smallest trophies are the most prestigious. While there are four miniature replica FA Cups, each perhaps only nine inches tall, these are dwarfed by the Zenith Data Systems Cup, one of several former artificial competitions that failed to grab the public imagination. But pride of place in the cabinet goes to the huge Football League South Cup of 1945. Well, I suppose if you've just helped rescue the free world from the threat of Nazi tyranny, you can afford to celebrate with a bloody big cup.

My favourite item in the store looks suspiciously like an in-joke. Proudly clad in a Chelsea strip is the Home Gnome, a cheerful little chap resplendent with white hair and beard. It has to be Ken Bates. Meanwhile the real Chelsea Chairman is featured on the inside cover of the store's brochure, unfortunately still posing with former manager Gianluca Vialli. Ken's hand is resting ominously on Vialli's shoulder. 'We need to have a little chat, Luca.'

Back outside the store, the crowds are gathering for the match. Everyone seems to be in designer gear, still geezer territory but definitely upmarket. Everything about Chelsea oozes money and expensive style. In the programme, several supporters' evenings are advertised, usually offering dinner and a chance to meet former players. For most clubs the tickets for these kinds of events are about twenty pounds. For Chelsea, the going rate is around fifty pounds (or '£250 per couple, including overnight stay and full English breakfast'). One particular bash concludes with dinner at Paul Getty's house.

Inside the stadium, the re-development that began in 1994 is almost complete, as the finishing touches are put to the new West Stand. This will increase the capacity to forty-three thousand, making Stamford Bridge the biggest ground in London, until Arsenal steal their thunder in 2004. Chelsea's high-octane commercial approach is clearly visible with the largest number of advertising hoardings I've ever seen at a football venue. There must be some one hundred and forty signs, and all major companies. Sony, Nestlé, McDonalds, Sky, Sanyo and Carling all jostle for space, but most prominent is a huge banner for Claims Direct ('Sidelined by Injury? We're On Your Side'), which must be reassuring for any player entering a crunching tackle.

In a swift and surprising move, Sunderland full-back Chris Makin, has been transferred to Ipswich. The club have remained significantly tight-lipped about why they've transferred one of our most consistent and popular players, particularly to a team who are challenging us for a place in Europe. In Makin's stead has come Frenchman, Patrice Carteron for a baptism of fire against a Chelsea side that at home have averaged nearly three goals a game.

Sunderland begin strongly, Phillips' initial clash with Desailly leaving the big defender sprawling on the ground. Clearly the Lads are not going to be overawed by the occasion, and in the opening ten minutes we force four corners against a nervous and struggling defence.

But it's Chelsea who strike first when our dangerous offside ploy fails again and Hasselbaink sprints clear with only Tommy to beat. At the last second, instead of shooting he passes to a clearly offside Gronkjaer, whose subsequent conversion is disallowed. With Hasselbaink poised as the first Chelsea player in over ten years to score twenty goals, you'd expect him to be Scrooge-like with his chances.

Despite the scare, we continue positively, Kilbane in particular playing with restored confidence on the left. Don Hutchison, standing in for an injured Quinn, is relishing his role as striker and sends one effort just a whisker past the post.

After fifteen minutes, Chelsea win their first corner. It's played short to our near post and our defence seem to dither in moving out to attack the ball. Suddenly Gudjohnsen's flicked it over Sorenson for Desailly to head into the net, a sloppy goal to give away. We keep pressing and win a free kick thirty yards out. Arca curls in a low fast cross, Hutch is in the box with his back to goal, but in one sublime move he turns and volleys past keeper Cudicini. He's made a difficult strike look like a simple flick and left World Cup defender, Frank Leboeuf, for dead.

Unfortunately for Chelsea, Hasselbaink is not in similar form, and skies a good chance when under no pressure (other than scoring that twentieth goal). But we are still playing the offside trap, and with half-time approaching, Gudjohnsen races through before coolly firing in Chelsea's second. I've lost count of how many times we've been caught like that over the season and no one can understand Reid's persistence with the ploy.

Two minutes later Chelsea go close again, when good interplay ends in a cross which Gudjohnsen fails to convert from just three yards out. Although we've played well, we're lucky to make the interval just 2–1 down when they could have had five.

When Chelsea manager Claudio Ranieri gave his first post-match interview, his lengthy analysis of the game was famously summed up by his interpreter as 'a game of two halves'. Although Claudio's now progressed to writing his own column in the programme ('Now I see the mentality of our players!'), Sunderland have consistently proved themselves the epitome of that most basic football truth.

Like a boxer getting his second wind, the Lads come out doing what they do best: hustling, fighting, running and tackling. More crucially, they abandon the offside tactics of the first half. Suddenly the defence is tight and secure, while Hutch and Phillips finally start to connect up front. Seven minutes in and Phillips scampers away to the right before lofting over a high cross. Hutch is there but the ball drops a couple of yards beyond the far post, almost on the byline. All Hutch can do is head it back towards . . . bloody hell, it's in! Somehow his header has sneaked inside the post past a flapping Cudicini. It may have been luck, it may have been keeper error, but it's a goal and we're back in this.

Next attack and Gavin McCann fires a screamer from twenty-five yards that has Cudicini at full stretch. This is more like it. McCann and Schwarz are running the middle, Kilbane keeps bursting down the left while Arca's doing his magic on the right. And Hutch is terrifying the Blues defence. Another assault and he chips forward into the box for McCann to chase. Desailly and Le Saux both fail to clear and McCann nips in to roll the ball past a flat-footed Cudicini. Two goals in five games, and now three in one match. For the away fans this has been some time coming and we sear the air with a roar of celebration.

Chelsea are punch-drunk. Hasselbaink keeps firing, but he's way off target and having a miserable afternoon. They bring on the magical Zola and start to click as the match winds up towards a lung-bursting climax. A Sunderland attack appears to break down and a Chelsea defender makes a simple backpass to Cudicini, but the keeper fails to control it and McCann rushes in for the tackle. The ball flies up from the clash and loops towards the goal, and Phillips barges past Desailly to bundle it home and give us three points.

It's been one of the matches of the season. OK, their keeper had a nightmare game, but our lads all played well and Hutchison was a star. But significantly, it showed that we have more to our game than just the high ball to a big forward.

I go round to the players' entrance to collect the programme from Bobby Saxton, although with the euphoria of the win I'm not really expecting him to remember about it. But he's there, and waves in recognition with the signed memento, a real collector's item given the result. I remind him of his forecast. 'I thought you said it would be 1–1.'

He gives me a sly wink. 'Aye, well, you have to say that.'

Saturday, 17 March 2001

CHELSEA 2   SUNDERLAND 4

(Desailly 15, Gudjohnsen 38)   (Hutchison 28, 52, McCann 59, Phillips 78)

PLAYED	TRAVELLED	SPENT	POSITION	STATE OF MIND
39	14,750 miles	£2,103.17	4th	Oh happy day!

Leeds United (home) – Premier League

You can have Jaffa Cakes when we get into Europe

Look, I know I keep banging on about how special the SOL is, but *Total Football* magazine have just voted it one of the ten best stadiums *in the world*! It's up there with Stade de France, Nou Camp, San Siro, Bernabeu, Maracana and, of course, Estadio Da Luz, our namesake in Lisbon. The SOL is the only UK stadium to be listed – no Old Trafford, no Ibrox, no Millennium Stadium, and certainly no Sid James' Park.

It wasn't until I took the backstage tour that I realised why the SOL makes such an impact when you emerge from the concourse into the stadium itself. It is one huge optical illusion. From the outside, the building is certainly impressive, but not overpoweringly so. Yet inside it appears much larger, the Tardis of football grounds. It's all due to a brilliant piece of lateral thinking. As it's cheaper to build down than to build up, the pitch has been sunk almost thirty feet below street level. What is visible from outside is perhaps only three-quarters of the stadium's true height.

Statistics first. Present capacity 48,300 for a bill of £28,000,000. The new Wembley will seat 70,000 and cost £650,000,000. I think a stray nought must have crept in there somewhere. The SOL has a component structure that allows the capacity to be increased in stages when demand justifies. In 2002 another extension will take the limit to fifty-five thousand, with a maximum potential of sixty-three thousand, although I think Sunderland may need to actually win something before even the Mackems start turning up in those kind of numbers.

If you visit the SOL you'll need to be on your best behaviour. There are plenty of stewards, but the real surveillance is largely unseen. There are sixty-seven CCTV cameras, all linked to one control centre. Any individual can be picked out in close-up, their image scanned and then checked against a database of known troublemakers. The five police cells are significantly all at the away end.

Down at pitchside, the impact of the soaring terraces is extraordinary. At the London Branch social, Bobby Saxton mentioned how difficult it was to communicate with the players because of the noise that reverberates around the huge bowl. Even empty, the ground is intimidating.

Standing in front of the home team dugout, I notice several discarded pieces of gum on the perimeter track. Whenever you see Peter Reid during a match, he is invariably chewing and reportedly gets through six packs a game. I've always wondered why Orbit never used him for their advertising campaign. 'I'm no ***** dentist, but after each ***** meal I chew ***** Orbit ***** sugar-free gum.'

Apparently the club don't bother cleaning up the pieces, because the visiting schoolchildren take them away as souvenirs ('Look Mum!').

The pitch itself conceals a mass of technology. Seventeen sprinklers pop up to do the watering, while fifteen miles of hot water pipes ensure a frost-free surface. Should the temperature drop to the critical level, sensors automatically switch on the heating, while a computer rings the groundsman at home to let him know the system has been activated. I can't get a reliable alarm clock. But there's more than just technical wizardry beneath the grass. When the club moved from Roker, a half-metre wide strip of turf from the perimeter of the pitch was transplanted around the edge of the new playing area. The old turf contained the ashes of past supporters and this tradition has been maintained, if slightly updated. Now the club have a custom-designed machine that digs two holes just large enough for the contents of an average urn.

The dressing-rooms are the hallowed inner sanctum of the temple. I have more chance of becoming Prime Minister than of getting in here on merit. I'm surprised at how small they are, not much more spacious than the changing-rooms I remember from school. And each player has just one hook for their clothes (apparently nobody likes using lockers). While the home and away areas are identical in size, they differ in significant, and not very subtle, aspects. After consulting a sports psychologist, the club designed the home dressing-room in bright, strong, positive colours, but gave the visitors a more oppressive atmosphere, with a heavy red floor and a band of deep blue tiles about head height to give the impression of a lower ceiling. Unlike Sunderland's dressing-room, there is no warm-up area and, as a final irritant, the clothes hooks are much smaller than those for the home team. I just love the idea of Beckham not being able to hang up his clothes properly.

With all the importance placed on diet, you would imagine the half-time snacks to be the epitome of sports food science, but it's all reassuringly rather park football. While some teams do nibble bananas, others seem to revert to childhood treats. Apparently Manchester United really do eat Jaffa Cakes, while Leicester City prepare for battle with Jelly Babies (just take a second to visualise Mr Savage eating Jelly Babies). Sunderland used to eat Jelly Tots, but presumably Reidy decided this wasn't tough enough, so they too have moved on to Jelly Babies. And I bet if Peter Reid wants all the red ones, Peter Reid gets all the red ones. Chelsea bring their own Canadian mineral water, which seems a little ungracious as Sunderland always provide the visiting team with a nice range of fizzy drinks.

Today's match marks Peter Reid's sixth year in charge of Sunderland. When he arrived, the team were heading for the Second Division with an antiquated ground and crowds of just eighteen thousand. Now it's forty-eight thousand, one of the best stadiums in the world and a chance of Europe. The guy is magic (but I still wish he'd change his offside ploy).

With just eight games left, Leeds provide perhaps the best test for judging our continental credentials. They play a similar style of fast, physical football and sit just one place and one point behind us. The outcome of today's six-pointer could determine who'll be playing in Europe.

For the first twenty minutes, it's all Sunderland but no goals. Leeds survive the opening onslaught, then Bowyer suddenly breaks through our defence. He's clean away, but scuffs his shot wide to the relief and delight of the crowd. Phillips has a similar chance when he beats Ferdinand to a long high ball from Carteron. As Ferdinand tries to recover, he brings Phillips down in what is not only a clear foul, but also a sending-off offence, as the last defender. So naturally the ref waves play on. Leeds take the ball upfield, get a corner and an unmarked Alan Smith heads in with Sunderland still reeling from the decision.

The goal knocks Sunderland back. Emerson Thome has a header cleared off the line, but for the remainder of the half, Leeds contain our efforts with a depressing confidence.

The second half begins with a replica of the Phillips foul, but by Jody Craddock on Smith. Again the ref ignores it. While one can argue that this cancels out the first decision, the earlier incident would have set the game on an entirely different course. As Sunderland push up for the equaliser, Kewell breaks through our defence and only a brilliant save by Sorenson stops Leeds from going two up.

As the tempo rises, so do the tempers. Smith is not renowned for his calm demeanour, and when he lashes out at Carteron, he receives his second yellow card and is sent off. With the extra man advantage, it's all Sunderland for the last twenty minutes. Arca controls the midfield with his twists and turns and nearly equalises with a low shot but for an excellent save from Nigel Martyn. Then Schwarz blasts just over from twenty-five yards, Arca goes close again and with Leeds on the ropes, a goal has to come. And it does, in the final minute, when Robbie Keane races clear of our back four, beats Thome and passes to Viduka, who pokes home from close range.

Although we had most of the game, they had all the goals. Again the game turned on a decision with the referee some way behind the play, but it's perhaps unrealistic to expect middle-aged part-timers to keep up with the current pace of the game. I don't see video replay as the answer; a ref may be wrong, but if he believes he's right then he's not going to consult the replay. Players would also end up hassling the ref to review every decision against them. I'd prefer to see two refs, one for each half of the pitch. If the ball is suddenly cleared upfield and an incident occurs, an official would already be well-positioned to make a decision. American football requires seven officials, so five is not that radical. But ultimately Leeds' blend of guile, style, strength and skill was too much for us and no video replay or extra ref can change that.

Saturday, 31 March 2001
SUNDERLAND 0   LEEDS UNITED 2
                    (Smith 32, Viduka 90)

PLAYED	TRAVELLED	SPENT	POSITION	STATE OF MIND
40	15 ,314 miles	£2,160.97	6th	Ciao, au revoir, auf Wiedersehen

Middlesbrough (away) – Premier League

I'm never ever coming back here ever again – probably

If you remember my attempts to get to Villa (tardily early, punctually late) and Crystal Palace III (just when you thought it was safe to go back to Croydon), you'll have deduced that I'm perhaps not the best person to tackle a nine-month odyssey of times, travel and trains. I arrive at King's Cross with just a couple of minutes to spare for the Newcastle train and start walking down the platform. Some people are sitting at one of the tables in First Class, but otherwise the train seems quiet. Well, it's the 11.30 a.m., not a popular time to travel. Further down the platform, I enter a coach in the standard section. Good, lots of empty seats – a chance to spread out. I'm just about to sit down when a voice calls out behind me. 'Can I help you?'

I turn to see a woman holding a rubbish bag. She's wearing a cleaner's outfit. In an otherwise deserted train.

'The train about to depart from Platform Five . . .'

Back down the platform, past the cleaners having their tea break in First Class.

'. . . is the 11.30 to Newcastle, calling at York, Doncaster . . .'

Off Platform Two, sprinting, past Three, Four . . .

'. . . Durham and Newcastle . . .'

Skid the turn onto Five, heels smoking.

'. . . unlike the train on Platform Two . . .'

Come on, come on!

'. . . which is going absolutely nowhere.'

Thirty yards, twenty . . .

'Please stand clear of the automatic doors, as they are about to slam shut . . .'

Ten . . .

'. . . and guillotine your goolies.'

I hurl myself through the first available door. Thunk. Quick check: arms, one, two; legs, one, two; miscellaneous body parts . . .

'Do you have a First Class ticket, sir?'

'Huurrr . . . huurr . . .' I think he probably knew that people holding First Class tickets tend to arrive with a little more style.

Over the past few years there has been growing concern about the risk of a large meteorite slamming into the planet. And rightly so, for the consequences would be pretty unpleasant. Tectonic plates would split like crazy paving, causing earthquakes and volcanic eruptions to ravage the globe. Mega tidal waves, hundreds of feet high, would race across oceans, surging far inland in a deluge of total destruction. Ash and dust from the impact would be thrown miles into the atmosphere, forming a dense cloud that would block out the sun for several years. Meanwhile, back on Teeside . . .

'Turned out nice again.'

With its sprawl of chemical and industrial plants, Teeside has the unenviable reputation of being one of the unlovliest parts of Britain. It's an award that's richly deserved. You don't achieve that kind of ugliness just by chance. It's become a sort of showhome for the industry. 'And as you can see, lots of storage space for all your old chemicals.'

Although Middlesbrough is some twenty-five miles south of Sunderland, this is going to be the longest trip of the season. As with Newcastle, it's a clash with a record of trouble between the supporters, so Sunderland have laid on the same convoy of buses to get us in and out safely. That means my first going up to Newcastle, then back down to Sunderland, then south again for the match. Or I could just make my own way to Middlesbrough, but with it being an evening game and no trains back, I'd have to spend the night there.

'I say, Landlord, what's that strange-looking castle on top of the hillside?'

'Oh, you don't wanna be a-goin' up there, zir, not after dark. Not with your young bride.'

'But it looks so fascinating – fancy a walk after dinner, darling?'

When I arrive at the SOL, the clans are gathering as for the Newcastle match, but there's not the same energy, passion and excitement. For Boro, we are their nearest neighbours and so by rights, their derby nemesis. They hate us and want the enmity to be reciprocated, but for us it's just a minor local skirmish, which of course annoys them even more. They just want to be loathed, bless 'em, but frankly my dears, we don't give a damn. While Newcastle are the school bully who tries to nick our dinner money, Boro are just his irritating kid brother. The atmosphere is less the stuff of Agincourt, more the annual trip to the relatives. In deference to the area, we've at least dubbed them 'The Smog Monsters', and many Sunderland fans are wearing pollution masks. Some have gone the whole hog and donned full chemical protection suits. Makes a change from Elvis and the sheikhs.

The BT Cellnet Riverside Stadium was the first of the new breed of stadiums to be built following the Taylor Report. It was also the first winner of 'Most Ridiculous Name For A Football Ground'. It looks like a scaled-down version of the SOL but without the grandeur and it's, well, just rather dull, as if they'd bought the whole lot at IKEA. As a finishing touch, they've built it next to a chemical plant.

I get chatting to one of the stewards. He's been with the club ten years, during which time they've lost four cup finals and been relegated twice. He says the stadium was built in 1995 and can't quite believe it was almost six years ago. 'Mind you,' he adds, 'time passes when you're having fun.'

Under Terry Venables' stewardship, Boro have pulled themselves together, but still hover dangerously close to the relegation zone. Points are vital for them, as they are for our own fading chances of Europe, and with the added spice of the game's 'derby' tag, it promises to be a lively evening.

Within minutes, Boro's new striker, Dean Windass, delivers on the promise with a crunching late challenge on Sorenson that leaves the keeper with a ripped jersey. Windass has the looks and build of a rugby league player and is a recent signing from Bradford. As both Bradford City AFC and Bradford Bulls RLFC share the same ground, I think there may have been a slight mix-up somewhere. This enthusiastic opening sets the tone, and in the first fifteen minutes three players are booked and one is stretchered off. As Boro skipper, Paul Ince, says in his programme column, 'It's a man's game' (and, of course, you have to be butch to come onto the pitch bare-chested).

Gradually sporadic bouts of football start to break out as Sunderland take command. Hutchison bends a free kick just round the post, then Arca weaves his way into the penalty area, only to be floored by Vickers. Penalty? We aren't allowed penalties. Phillips hits the post after rounding the keeper, Schwarz and Hutch fire free kicks just inches wide and a clever Phillips chip lands on the roof of the net. The pressure is unrelenting but still we don't score. With half-time approaching, Phillips hits the post again with a header and Kilbane scuffs the rebound to crank up the agony. Typically, in the last minute of the half, Boro almost snatch the lead. A corner sees chaos in the Sunderland defence, which only ends with a brilliant save by Sorenson.

To have dominated so thoroughly without scoring does not bode well and, sure enough, Boro come out for the second half as men reprieved from the gallows. They take charge of the game and in the first twenty minutes hit the side netting twice, fire just over the bar and go inches wide of the post. The Boro crowd finally wake up, with chants of 'Boro' and 'We Hate Sunderland'. Oh, alright then: 'We Hate Boro', which is greeted with an ironic cheer.

On the pitch, Sunderland also respond and nearly grab the lead when their keeper just beats Thome to a Phillips header. Then Boro miss from an indirect free kick only seven yards out. In the closing minutes Karembeu is sent off for wrestling with Sunderland's Williams and Quinn nearly snatches the game when his header flashes just wide of the post.

Although any away draw is a reasonable result, we could, and should, have won the match in the first half. To complete a frustrating evening, the police take our convoy back to Sunderland via Moscow, and it's after midnight before we finally arrive at the SOL, cold, tired and very pissed off. I think it's safe to say that I hate Boro. I do, I really, really do.

Monday, 9 April 2001
MIDDLESBROUGH 0   SUNDERLAND 0

PLAYED	TRAVELLED	SPENT	POSITION	STATE OF MIND
41	15,934 miles	£2,234.83	6th	Get me outa here

Tottenham Hotspur (home) – Premier League

It was like Billy Smart's Circus out there
– PETER REID

Six months after the Hatfield train crash, some semblance of normality is finally returning to the railways. Throughout the chaos (which was largely of Railtrack's making) and the battle to keep open the London–Newcastle line, GNER staff maintained a surprising degree of good cheer. In contrast to many large UK companies, who seem to have their telesales centres in Guatemala, GNER work out of Newcastle, using Geordies who appreciate the local culture. When I phoned to re-arrange my train ticket at the height of the delays and confusion, the woman in the Sales Centre handled it all with efficient charm, adding, 'Oh, it's no bother, pet – w'knaa y'like to get there early for a pint.'

Most of my calls seem to end up with us having a bit of a chat. Even when I was living in the North-east, my accent was fairly mild and having been away for almost thirty years, it is now well hidden, only emerging at moments of extreme stress (Sunderland's offside game usually does the trick). So the ticket sales staff assume I'm a native Southerner coming up from London. On one occasion when I was booking the add-on ticket for the local Newcastle–Sunderland train, I was cheerfully advised, 'Oh, y'divvent wanna gan there, man – you wanna stay ower here with the Geordies.'

Sometimes my lack of accent is a distinct advantage. For today's match with Spurs, I'd just completed buying the £30 Day Return when the guy handling the booking declared, 'It's just as well you're a Tottenham fan – if you were a Mackem I'd have charged you the full £149.'

After eighteen rail trips north this season, I know Newcastle Central Station like my local tube. Built in 1850, it is one of the great Victorian termini from an age of architecture that celebrated style on a grandiose scale. An element of that style has just been restored, with the opening of a bar/restaurant in what was once hailed as the finest First Class railway lounge in the world. The original station architect, John Dobson, had intended to open the lounge as part of the new building, but so ambitious were his plans that the project ran out of money, and it was forty years before the work was completed. Surpassing its role as a mere waiting-room for the wealthy, from 1920 to 1940 the lounge flourished as a stylish restaurant and the place to be seen for the rich and famous visiting Newcastle. But by the '50s its heyday was past and British Rail converted it into cafeteria, ripping out many of the original fittings. Further ignominy befell in 1963, when the café closed and the space was turned into an engineering workshop. Finally it was abandoned and left to rot.

Last year a Herculean restoration project began, removing fifty years of paint and several layers of plastic floor tiles. The original doorframes were re-cast, as were hundreds of ceramic wall tiles. Now the Centurion bar is a beautiful Grade I Listed Building. A golden glow emits from the caramel-coloured walls as they stretch up to the high glass ceiling, while potted plants and heavy armchairs complete the image of old-time wealth and privilege.

Meanwhile, over in Sunderland, another great dining tradition is enjoying a second lease of life. Joan's Café, opposite the SOL, was an institution with the miners of Wearmouth Colliery until the pit closed in 1994. The stadium has brought a new wave of customers and now on match days, Joan's is similarly the place to be seen. Always bustling and loud, it offers a warm and cheerful venue for a pre-match pie or belt-busting breakfast. A production line of four teapots ensures a perfect cup of tea, and you can tell it's a classy caff because they keep their Mars Bars in the fridge. Photos of the Lads adorn the walls and in the days before footballers became superstars, it's the kind of homely place where players would gather after training. Four women control the chaos with humour and efficiency, although I've yet to work out which one is actually Joan. Perhaps they all are.

If ever there was a chance to jolt us back into winning, it should be today. Tottenham have just fired manager George Graham, so they'll still be in a state of flux, and they have the second-worst away record in the Premiership after Bradford (although it's perhaps best not to recall how we performed at home against Bradford).

At the start of the game, my hopes seem to be confirmed when we storm into the attack and send Spurs reeling. After just two minutes, Carteron bends in a cross that manages to beat everyone and appears to be heading out past the far post. Suddenly Kilbane flies in to volley past an astonished Neil Sullivan in goal and we're one up virtually from the kick-off.

With Quinn finally back from injury to link up with Phillips, it is the first time they've started together in six weeks. Quinn looks eager and hungry again, and is a constant source of worry to the Spurs defence. From another attack, Stefan Schwarz hammers a free kick which Sullivan can only deflect into Quinn's path. The Irishman reacts instantly and, from a narrow angle, guides the ball home for our second goal.

Well, that's it, two up after twelve minutes, Tottenham are nowhere and we are playing superbly. Our defence is snuffing out any attack, the midfield is passing well and our strikers are a constant threat. Now it's just a question of how many. Quinn nods a ball down for Phillips to blast narrowly over from twenty yards, and should have scored himself when he powers a close-range header directly into Sullivan's arms.

For the rest of the half, we are strolling and I'm sure I can see some Tottenham fans starting to leave. The break arrives with no further score, but with a shots-on-goal statistic of nine-zero to us, it's been the most one-sided first half at the SOL all season.

The second half doesn't continue in quite the same vein. After seven minutes, Spurs perform a series of keepy-up passes that you can normally only get away with in training, as the Sunderland defenders almost stand back and applaud. With the final delivery, Davies loops a pass to Clemence who is unmarked in our penalty area. Without breaking stride, he volleys into the top corner. Oh.

Spurred on (I'm sorry), Tottenham look much sharper and I think we'd better start paying attention. Phillips does his best, first with a near header and then with a good run and lay-off to Arca, whose shot is well saved by Sullivan. Quinn narrowly misses and then Arca has another chance after rounding the keeper, but stumbles at the vital moment. But we're starting to look nervous and with twenty minutes left, Spurs go close with a header at the far post. A few minutes later, Sorenson has to pull off a great stop to deny Korsten. Come on, lads, what happened to the first-half display?

After seventy-five minutes, a defensive error sees Spurs striker Doherty suddenly race onto a loose ball. He's forty yards out, but has a clear run at goal. Only Thome is anywhere near him, but the big defender is struggling to get back. As Doherty reaches our penalty box, he stabs a shot that bobbles into the net for the equaliser. I don't believe this.

If the Lads were nervous before, now they're desperate and push forward to grab a goal and save the game. Phillips has a chance just yards out, but his touch fails him and Sullivan saves again.

With two minutes to go, Korsten beats our offside trap and again our defenders are caught square and chasing. A desperate tackle by Thome only sends the ball to Doherty, who has supported Korsten's run. From inside the penalty box, Doherty fluffs his shot and the ball screws away to Mickey Gray. At least he'll belt it clear. But no – the ball bounces farcically through Gray's legs and back to Doherty. Grateful for the second chance, he sidefoots it past Sorenson from just six yards.

And that's it. We've lost at home after being two up and in total control. For the first time all season, the Lads leave the field to the sound of booing. Somewhere in Zurich, a Swiss banker must have his eyes on Peter Reid's swear box.

On the train back to London, everyone in the Branch is understandably depressed. You can accept losing, but not like that. One win in the last ten league games, and we've got the Mags next Saturday. Then out of nowhere, a lone voice strikes up.

'We'll win again . . .'

Suddenly the whole carriage is joining in.

'. . . don't know where, don't know when,

But I know we'll win again some sunny day.'

I've never heard that sung before, but it's a heartfelt release of how we all feel. Somehow it helps.

Saturday, 14 April 2001

SUNDERLAND 2   TOTTENHAM HOTSPUR 3

(Kilbane 2, Quinn 12)   (Clemence 52, Doherty 75, 88)

PLAYED	TRAVELLED	SPENT	POSITION	STATE OF MIND
42	16,498 miles	£2,299.83	7th	Shock

Coventry City (away) – Premier League

What theatre, what drama, what entertainment!
– *JIMMY HILL*

I don't like Coventry.

It's a boring city, the ground's a half-hour hike from the station and there's something from the *X-Files* in this butty. I don't like Coventry. My first serious girlfriend dumped me there and it's where I once spent my worst-ever Christmas. But the main reason I don't like Coventry is their football team.

Since being promoted to the top division in 1967, Coventry City have been a largely nondescript and generally poor side, who have faffed around near the bottom of the table, only narrowly avoiding the drop on many occasions. Basically they are Sunderland in the late '60s. But at least when Sunderland were crap, they had the decency to get relegated, not hang around like the vicar at the wedding reception. Apart from a Cup win in 1987, City have achieved little since promotion except survival. As such, their record far surpasses that of Sunderland, who over the same period have been promoted or relegated a staggering twelve times – but at least it's never been boring. Coventry have turned avoiding relegation into an art form. On ten occasions since '67, survival has come down to the last game of the season. And in '77, their escape caused Sunderland's relegation in contentious circumstances that still rankle today.

The events surrounding Thursday, 19 May 1977 have become something of an urban myth. With one game left, Sunderland, Coventry City and Bristol City were all candidates for the last relegation spot. Each team had thirty-four points and, just to make it interesting, Coventry were at home to Bristol, while Sunderland had to visit Everton. Essentially, if Sunderland won or drew, they would survive. They could even survive if they lost, but only if the Coventry–Bristol game didn't end in a draw. The only certain means of escape for any of the teams was a win. Still with me? Good, then I'll begin.

While Sunderland's game kicked off on time, crowd congestion at Coventry saw the police advise the referee to delay the start of the match. The extent of that delay has become shrouded in controversy. Sunderland lost 2–0, but with Coventry and Bristol still playing, there remained a glimmer of hope – as long as they didn't draw. The score at that point was indeed 2–2. If it remained that way, both clubs would survive. Enter Coventry Managing Director and *Match Of The Day* stalwart, Jimmy Hill. Hill ordered the Sunderland result to be displayed on the stadium's giant electronic scoreboard. The effect was extraordinary. Aware of the consequences if the match remained a draw, both teams effectively declared a truce and stopped playing. For the remaining minutes, the Bristol City defenders passed the ball among themselves, while the Coventry forwards stood back and watched. The game ended with both clubs avoiding relegation and Sunderland were down.

But for exactly how long did this farce play out? According to *Sunderland AFC: The Official History*, the Coventry match was delayed by fifteen minutes, and this is the version that is always quoted by Sunderland supporters. If this was the case, the match truly was a travesty, for in a game where victory was the only sure means of survival, anything could have happened in that last quarter-hour. The facts, however, suggest otherwise. Bristol equalised to make the score 2–2 after *eighty* minutes, i.e. a full five minutes after the players had supposedly stopped trying. Several national newspaper of the time, plus *Rothman's Official Yearbook* and even the North-east papers, record the kick-off as being delayed by only three to five minutes. So the match might well have ended in a draw anyway.

But that's not the point.

The broadcasting of the Sunderland result transformed what had been a desperate relegation battle into a meaningless kickabout, albeit if only for the last few minutes of the game. Yet there are many cases of teams scoring a winning goal in the dying seconds. In the aftermath, Coventry were reprimanded by the Football League for their actions, but on appeal this was withdrawn and the matter dropped.

But that's not the point.

Had it been Leeds playing and Don Revie who had revealed the scoreline, you would have expected it, hell, almost grudgingly admired him for his ruthless professionalism. But it's the fact that it was Jimmy Hill, Mr 'Play-Up-Play-The-Game-Chaps-Now-That's-Not-Very-Nice-Is-It?', who'd spent years on *Match of the Day* going on about the need for ethics and sportsmanship and doing the right thing, *that's* what really angered the Mackems. Hill claims that shouts from some spectators had alerted the players to the Sunderland result minutes before his action, and that they were already just 'going through the motions'. All Hill was doing was letting the rest of the stadium know, so that 'relief and joy would be felt'.

Which is all a little odd.

Bristol player Don Gillies said after the match, 'When the Sunderland score flashed up on the board, both sides knew just what it meant. Nobody spoke about it but we knew we would both be safe.' Ten national and local newspapers all reported the scoreboard display as being the cue for the players to stop trying. Even Bristol manager, Alan Dicks, said 'It was good psychology on Jimmy Hill's part to go rushing out of the directors' box to get the Sunderland result flashed on the scoreboard.' Not a single mention of shouts from the crowd. Not a single mention of the play even slowing down before the score was broadcast. Clearly, whatever Hill may have thought was going on, it was his action and his action alone that turned the game into a farce.

Twenty-four years later, does any of it still matter? It certainly does to the Mackems, who still chant anti-Hill slogans. And it mattered enough for Hill to justify his decision in his recent memoirs. So I think he might look again at the evidence. Not too much to ask of someone whose autobiography proclaims him as 'a passionate campaigner for justice, improvement and fair play'.

From the above, you may have gleaned that, much though I admire Gordon Strachan as both a canny manager and rare wit, I won't be shedding too many tears if Coventry finally do capitulate this season. Yet from a seemingly doomed position, they appear to be pulling off another Houdini stunt. In signing John Hartson (and his hair transplant), they have acquired their battling totem who has given them self-belief. His five goals in seven matches have at least dragged City to the surface of the relegation swamp, but they are still some way off solid ground.

Big John makes his presence felt immediately, with a swift elbow to the face of Emerson Thome. That's the thanks you get for suggesting a good trichologist in Rio. Coventry look lively and are clearly going to battle for every ball. After twenty minutes, Sorenson sends Mackem hearts all a-flutter when he comes out of his area to meet a long clearance, only for the ball to bounce over his head. Fortunately Thome clears before Hartson can pounce.

The next City attack sees a lob into the penalty area which Bothroyd chests down to Carlsey. He chips it neatly into the centre for Hartson to dive away from his marker, Darren Williams, and head powerfully into the net. It's an excellent goal, the culmination of eight passes and a six-man move, but Williams could have made it more difficult for Hartson. That's now six in eight for the Welshman, and even paying him fifteen thousand pounds a game, he could be priceless for Coventry.

It's half an hour before we have our first chance, when Kirkland, Coventry's keeper, deflects a Hutchison cross that was heading straight for Phillips. But we're just not in the game. Our passes are going astray and Coventry clearly want this victory more than we do. Just before half-time, Varga beats the offside trap and is suddenly alone in front of goal with only Kirkland to beat. Come on, Stan! But at the last second, his touch fails him and the chance is gone. It's not a good sign when our only real scoring opportunity of the half falls to our centre-back.

At soon as the second half begins, Varga's back in the action, but for the wrong reason. A mistimed tackle sees him booked for the second time and he's off. Looks like we've got another struggle on our hands. Inspired, Coventry pile forward and Hartson almost grabs a second goal when he outleaps Thome and heads onto the bar. The near miss signals a rash of Coventry attacks, which are only thwarted by some phenomenal saves from Sorenson. He is keeping an otherwise crumbling Sunderland still in the match. Our defence is a disaster, as Thome and young George McCartney crash into each other, while Darren Williams is displaying impeccable manners with his 'after you' approach to marking.

With twenty minutes left, Quinny comes off the bench and his presence starts to lift the team. Phillips finally hits one on target, which Kirkland saves, but at least we're getting back in the match. As full-time approaches, it's Coventry on the back foot and looking nervous, as our ten men try to grab at least a point.

Into stoppage time and another of our young players, Paul Thirlwell, gathers a Quinny knock-down in the box only to be bundled off the ball at the vital moment. Then Kilbane finds Quinn with a hopeful cross and big Niall's unmarked in front of goal. Just blast it, Quinny! But he ignores me and instead attempts a lob that Kirkland gathers easily. Finally Williams is upended by Kirkland as he chases his own throw-in into the box, but the ref never even looks like giving it.

Unless something miraculous happens over the last four games (like four wins), we can kiss goodbye to Europe. But next up is the derby, and if we can do the double over the Mags, many supporters will settle for that as a good end to the season.

Monday, 16 April 2001

COVENTRY CITY 1   SUNDERLAND 0

(Hartson 20)

PLAYED	TRAVELLED	SPENT	POSITION	STATE OF MIND
43	16,702 miles	£2,384.63	7th	The sky is falling

Newcastle United (home) – Premier League

I think you've waited long enough.

So, why 'Mackem'? (If you're 'local' you probably know all this, so now might be a good time to nip out and put the kettle on). Twenty-five years ago, I hadn't even heard the term. It was never on the radio, television or in any newspaper. Anybody from the North-east was simply a Geordie. Sunderland supporters had red-and-white car stickers that declared, 'Divvent dunsh us – we're Geordies!' ('dunsh' – to crash into). Yet 'Mackem' has been around for decades.

It derives from a combination of the area's shipbuilding past, the Wearside dialect and a dose of local rivalry. Although the River Wear shipyards were the most prolific in the world, the River Tyne yards were better equipped for finishing the job once a ship's basic hull had been completed. Vessels launched on the Wear were often towed round to the Tyne to be fitted out. This work was held in higher regard than the initial construction and the Geordies lauded their skills over their neighbours. In the two local but distinct dialects, 'make' and 'take' are pronounced 'myek' and 'tyek' in Geordie, but 'mack' and 'tack' on Wearside. So in a double jibe at their Sunderland counterparts, the Tynesiders would say, 'Ye mack 'em and we'll tack 'em.'

There are several apocryphal variations on this theme, but all revolve around the local rivalry. Sunderland workers who came over to the Tyne yards would 'mack' the ships but 'tack' the jobs from the Newcastle men. In response, the Geordies would deride the Wearsiders' skills – and their dialect. 'Them Sun'lund lads are bloody useless, man – y've gorra mack 'em dae this and mack 'em dae that.'

However it arose, Mackem was only ever used in a derogatory sense and remained dormant among the Wearsiders. Then came the Geordie renaissance. In 1992 Sir John Hall took control of the Mags, brought in Keegan and the roller-coaster took off. The Toon became the place to be and the team to watch, party city of the UK and contenders for the Premiership. In the eyes of the country, the North-east was the Geordie Nation and Newcastle United. Heartily fed up at being hijacked onto the black-and-white bandwagon, Sunderland supporters sought an emblem of identity. With typical humour, they took the one-time insult and transformed it into a badge of pride. They were no longer Geordies. They were Mackems.

To dismiss all this as immature posturing between football fans is to fail to appreciate the history of the two communities. The Newcastle–Sunderland clash is unique in English football as the only big derby between teams from different towns. Arsenal–Spurs, City–United and Everton–Liverpool are all local affairs from within the same city, where allegiances can split across areas, streets and families. But in the North-east it's tribal, us lot against them lot from ower the water, the essence of conflicts down the ages. Football has simply become the expression of a divide that stretches back hundreds of years.

In the early seventeenth century, the Sunderland and Newcastle ports competed fiercely to transport coal from the North-east to London and Europe. But Tyneside had the edge, a Charter from the King that restricted the coal trade from the River Wear. When the Civil War began in 1642, Sunderland understandably backed Cromwell United, while Newcastle went for Royal and the Rovers ('Eeh, Ah really fancy mesel in one o' them feathery hats.') When Newcastle stopped supplying coal to Parliamentarian London, the Wearsiders maintained the vital supplies, thus preventing a civil uprising from lack of fuel that could have seen the return of the King. In essence, had Sunderland supported King Charles, we might not have a Parliament today.

The rivalry between the two towns continued unabated thereafter. As one conflict faded, another replaced it. Issues such as coal transportation and shipyard jobs may be no more, but resentment for one reason or another still thrives. During the last thirty years, Sunderland ratepayers have begrudgingly subsidised various schemes that have largely benefited Newcastle: Eldon Square shopping centre, Newcastle Airport and the Tyne-Wear Metro.

Even the two dialects are used in the fight for supremacy. Over recent years, the Geordies have started baiting the Mackems with the phrase 'wheez is theez keez?' (whose are these keys?) and jangling sets of keys. This, incredibly, is because of a slight difference in the Sunderland dialect that pronounces the phrase as 'wheeyz is theeyz keeyz'. What?! The Mags are claiming superiority over the Mackems because of the way they *speak*! Discrepancies between the two dialects are subtle but distinctive, enough to give yourself away if you venture into the wrong pub. Geordies say 'mate', Mackems say 'matey', they say 'divvent ye' and we say 'd'ayn't ye', 'beefborga/beefburger', 'anotha/another' – let's call the whole thing off.

When football arrived with the first derby match of 1898, it polarised the mutual antipathy. Within three years, a game at St James' was abandoned when seventy thousand people tried to enter a ground designed for only twenty thousand. Over the years the animosity has only intensified. When Sunderland were leading in a vital First Division play-off game in 1990, hundreds of Newcastle fans invaded the pitch and tore down the goals in an attempt to get the match abandoned. Before last year's derby at the SOL, the police intercepted a large furniture removal van containing dozens of Mags intent on creating trouble at the stadium.

While I enjoy the rivalry, I don't hate either Newcastle or their fans, yet the mutual loathing appears disturbingly genuine. Perhaps Newcastle's hatred is born of frustration from having gone so close to becoming champions under Keegan, only to see it all crumble away and Sunderland rise above them. I find it impossible to exchange good-natured banter with a Newcastle supporter. They transform into Gothalla The Terrible.

'FuckinwannafuckinfightfuckinMackembastard?'

Which is not really what you expect to hear from a British prime minister.

After Metro FM's Simon Crabtree made his spoof broadcast at last year's derby, he received over a dozen death threats from enraged Newcastle fans who didn't appreciate his send-up of the Norwegian commentator from 1981 when Norway defeated England. That's how seriously the games are taken.

Yet if you find all this enmity depressing, take heart, dear reader, from The Legend Of Angie And Arty. Angie, a staunch member of the London Sunderland Supporters' Branch, is married to Arty, another staunch member of the London Branch – of Newcastle supporters. A match made in Hell you may think, but forces are at play here beyond the ken of man. They met at work, Angie's red-and-white-covered desk initially creating tension with Mag-mad Arty. Nevertheless, a friendship developed, until one day Angie discovered Arty pretending to set fire to her beloved shrine. From that moment on the flames of love were ignited and she knew he was the man for her. Who said Geordies are unromantic? At their wedding three years ago, invitations to the respective camps requested, 'No colours to be worn, no songs to be sung'. Since then, marital bliss has blossomed under strict house rules. The two spare rooms have become the Mackem and Geordie suites, but otherwise their home is bare of favours. If one team loses and the other wins, the winner will always wait for the loser to call first. No songs, chanting or wearing of colours are allowed within the house. On the one occasion when Angie transgressed, returning in triumphant mood after an important Sunderland win, Arty wagged a stern finger: 'Rules are rules.' He then guided a still-singing Angie gently but firmly into the bathroom and shut the door.

If anyone queries Angie's alliance with a Mag, she counters, 'But how could I marry someone who doesn't understand how I feel about my team?' They can empathise and, when necessary, provide emotional support. After last week's losses by both sides, Arty expressed his sympathy with a cellphone call after the game. 'Why do we bother, pet? Why don't we just gather up the thousands of pounds we spend every season, put it in a big heap and set fire to it?'

Now that's passion.

With two hours to kick-off, the streets around the SOL are eerily quiet, as if war has just been declared and everyone's indoors listening to Mr Chamberlain. By the time the first bus of the Newcastle convoy arrives, a healthy crowd is waiting to 'greet' them. As each coach passes, the Mags jangle their keys and the Mackems react accordingly. The police, in full riot gear, are standing for little nonsense. When some Sunderland lads get too close to a passing bus, the police shove them back unceremoniously. Suddenly it starts, just a couple of voices.

'The miners, united, will never be defeated.'

It spreads like wildfire, forty or fifty voices, angry, resentful.

'The miners! United! Will never be defeated!'

It dies as quickly as it began, but the police look momentarily shocked, a sudden time warp. This is an area that still remembers the Civil War.

Inside the stadium, the tension is palpable – there's too much at stake. We won at their place, but that magnificent victory could be cancelled out if we lose today. The club have supplied large coloured cards for each fan to hold aloft, so that as the teams enter, the stadium will be transformed into a mass of giant red-and-white stripes, save for an appropriate section of black and white.

Prokofiev blasts out and as one, the stadium erupts in a burst of noise and colour, the huge stripes sweeping right round the stadium. Unfortunately, the three thousand Newcastle fans decline to take part, which shows rather a lack of wit. By mixing their cards up to produce a chequerboard effect, they could have presented rebellious support, rather than a mass sulk.

While we are at full strength, the visitors are missing Shearer and Dyer, both hugely influential. Yet even without their inspirational captain, Newcastle blaze forward and Gary Speed almost repeats his early goal from the first match when he blasts an effort just over the bar. Like many derby matches, there are lots of tackles but little football and the opening fifteen minutes are tense and scrappy.

Gradually the match settles down and Phillips and Arca both test goalkeeper Shay Given. Then a Quinn header forces a brilliant save from the ex-Sunderland keeper and it's starting to warm up. Newcastle are nowhere as Sunderland charge forward. Our French full-back, Carteron, interlinks well with Quinn before firing a shot that Given again saves well. With half-time looming, Julio Arca, playing a gem of a game, crosses to Thome. The big Brazilian powers a header and this time Given's beaten . . . but it hits the post.

The next minute Arca sends over another cross that Newcastle centre-back O'Brien miscues and slices just past his own post. Our pressure has been unrelenting, but with a minute to go, visiting striker Cort has a great chance but fires straight at Sorenson. We've completely dominated the first half, but after our last home match against Spurs, I'm still wary and nervous of what is to come.

The game restarts in the same manner, with Given saving twice from Phillips in the first fifteen minutes. There's no sign of any half-time breakdown or, significantly, of any improvement by Newcastle, who are still playing as individuals and not connecting at all.

After twenty minutes, Hutchison makes a break down the right with Carteron overlapping. The Newcastle defenders close in but don't commit themselves. As Hutch holds, he indicates to Carteron, the defenders, in fact the entire stadium, where he's going to pass the ball, but the Frenchman doesn't seem to understand. Finally he clicks, sprinting past the last black and white shirt as Hutch cuts the ball through with surgical precision.

Carteron collects the pass, storms into the penalty box and smashes a low drive that flies past Given into the net.

The home crowd celebrate in an explosion of relief. It's a goal that's been due us and now we can relax and start to play. But the Mags fight back and in their next attack, Sorenson tips a shot over the bar with an incredible one-handed save. Then Phillips responds with a curling effort past the post and the game is living up to all expectations.

With twelve minutes left and Newcastle going nowhere, Robson takes a huge gamble with a triple substitution. It risks disrupting a disjointed team even further. Griffen, one of the subs, crosses the ball to Cort just outside our penalty area. He shoots but scuffs it and the ball skims awkwardly across goal to O'Brien. Unmarked and six yards out, he can't miss. And he doesn't. It's a lucky goal from a mis-hit pass, but they all count.

Inspired, the Mags finally start to play and in the last minute almost snatch a winner. It's ends all square – no double victory for us this season, but of the last four derbies, we've won two and drawn two. That'll do.

Saturday, 21 April 2001
SUNDERLAND 1   NEWCASTLE UNITED 1

(Carteron 66)   (O'Brien 77)

PLAYED	TRAVELLED	SPENT	POSITION	STATE OF MIND
44	17,254 miles	£2,475.83	8th	Ho-hum – but still Cock o' the North

Southampton (away) – Premier League

Dear Supporter,
I am writing to inform you that your ticket application for
the Southampton away game has been unsuccessful . . .

Oh bugger.

Oh buggery, buggery bugger. After 44 games, 17,254 miles and £2,475.83, I'm just three matches from completing my quest. It's Just Not Fair. But I've only myself to blame. Having acquired a reasonable tally of loyalty points during the season, I'd become rather blasé about getting tickets for away fixtures. I certainly didn't see a problem for Southampton. We've essentially blown our chances of Europe, so this is just an end-of-season match against one of the Premiership's smaller teams who are about a thousand miles from Wearside. No one in their right mind is going to trek down for that.

Sunderland receive 8,000 applications – for 1,200 tickets. The cut-off for loyalty points is actually higher than for the Newcastle game. I hadn't reckoned on Southampton's tiny ground (15,000) and this being our last ever game there before they move to a new stadium. I should have applied a fortnight ago to the Branch or contacted Deep Stottie, but now it's too late. Time to press the Panic Button.

I phone everyone, but it's the same story. Getting to this match has become Mission Impossible. But there's a thought. At last year's game, I met a Saints fan on the train down. Andy is now in his late twenties, but when he was nineteen he applied for the job as manager of Southampton. Surprisingly, he didn't get it, but here was a guy who clearly relished a challenge. I email him and whadya know? With just two days to go, he snags one for the sold-out fixture. OK, it's among the home crowd but it's a ticket. I'd sat among 20,000 Charlton fans at the play-off final. This would be a doddle.

Then it starts getting silly. The next day, a ticket arrives from the Branch.

A phone call offers me another. When I arrive at the station, a Branch member has a spare. For a completely sold-out, sell-your-grandmother match, I've ended up with two tickets and could have had four. It took two weeks of pleading, panic, persistence and phone calls to get one ticket, but two days of nothing to get three more. It's always the same. For the games at Man United, Liverpool and even Newcastle, the seat next to me was mysteriously vacant. I'm now convinced there is no such thing as 'completely sold out'.

Southampton is bright, clean and easy going. The long, broad High Street is dominated at one end by Bargate, the gateway in the medieval city wall. There are more parks per square mile here than any city in the UK, and large areas of green greet you at every turn.

In East Park stands the grandiose Titanic Engineers' Memorial, a huge granite carving with a bronze frieze. The legend reads: 'To the memory of the Engineer Officers of the RMS Titanic who showed their high conception of duty and their heroism by remaining at their posts', At the Titanic Musicians' Memorial, the plaque proclaims: 'They died at their posts like men.' While one can criticise the ethos of the period, with its rigid class structure and culture of unquestioning obedience, it also fostered the kind of heroism displayed on 15 April 1912. Dying at one's post should never have been part of the engineers' rota or the musician's repertoire, but they saw it as such and it still brings a lump to the throat.

By 1912, Southampton FC were settled into their new ground, The Dell, having moved from their birthplace at St Mary's, near the docks. Formed by St Mary's Church Young Men's Association in 1885, Southampton St Mary's became plain Southampton in 1897, but retained 'Saint' for their nickname, hence the halo in the club's badge. It can't be easy having God as Supreme Chairman, but they probably get better decisions from the ref. Now the Saints are going home, with a new stadium due to open in 2002. 'The Friends Provident St Mary's Stadium' is a bit of a mouthful, but hopefully it will just become St Mary's. As Andy proudly gives me the tour, it seems uncannily like the SOL, if a little smaller. The architect probably offered them the same set of plans: 'Now here's a lovely stadium, very popular with our customers in the North-east.'

After 103 years at The Dell, Southampton are making sure they say goodbye properly, with more farewells than Frank Sinatra. There's the final Premiership match, the final testimonial, the last official tour, umpteen commemorative events and then the Final Game Ever . . . followed by Honestly The Positively Last Ever Final Farewell Event Ever – a Farewell

Dinner on the pitch. I just hope they don't change their minds. Within the new stadium, various stands, bars and suites all have to be named. To their credit, Southampton have invited the fans to submit suggestions, but the democratic process has gone a bit haywire. With additional nominations for the Hall Of Fame and Player Of The Year, there are four separate polls and a multiple-transfer voting system. It's sufficiently complex that one of the new stands will probably end up being called George W. Bush.

Outside The Dell, there's a good end-of-term feel to the place, and players are signing autographs with none of the aloofness evident at Leeds. Andy gets me into the Saints Supporters' Club where I'm able to pass on my spare home ticket. The bar is loud and friendly, with a good mix of fans from both sides. This is how it should be, but rarely is.

The Dell is the smallest ground in the Premiership, but with an atmosphere that has intimidated the mightiest of visitors – and we are far from that, with our New Year slump now just one win in twelve. Southampton have their own problems, having failed even to score in the four games since Hoddle's departure to Spurs, but at least they are now mathematically safe from relegation.

The match starts amid high winds, hindering any chance of flowing football. In a huff 'n' puff opening, Southampton striker James Beattie races from his own half and past our last defender to collect a through ball from El Khalej. The linesman raises his flag for offside, causing everyone to pause, but then he suddenly lowers it, and Beattie is off again. As Sorenson advances, Beattie chips the ball over him from 30 yards in a repeat of his wonder goal at the SOL. It look a perfectly good strike, but the ref's called it back and given the original offside decision. Perhaps God's taken the afternoon off.

We can't get into the match and have to resort to some desperate defending. When Craddock lets in Tessem, Sorenson has to produce one of his miraculous saves. After twenty minutes, Quinn has our first shot, but it's a tame effort and for the rest of the half we make little impact up front. It's all Southampton and we only hang on thanks to more saves by Sorenson. As the teams leave the pitch, there's a collective sigh of relief from the Mackems.

During half-time, Southampton commemorate the twenty-fifth anniversary of winning the FA Cup, with a parade of the trophy and an appearance by the team of '76. As the tannoy introduces each player, there's a touch of The Grey, The Bald and The Hobbling, but heroes all. Their manager, Lawrie McMenemy, is noticeably absent, which probably wouldn't be the case if we weren't today's visitors. As his brief but highly lucrative tenure at Sunderland sent us plunging towards the old Third Division in 1987, he's not exactly Messiah material. Not for nothing is he known on Wearside as Lawrie Mackem-Enemy.

As we start the second half, you can tell Mr Reid's had one of his little chats. There's more urgency to our play and within minutes, Quinny almost rounds the keeper, but is forced wide at the last second. We push up and win a free kick about forty yards out. McCann sends an optimistic punt towards the box, where Kilbane is waiting on the edge of the area with his back to goal. As the free kick flies towards him, Kilbane flicks out a hopeful boot. The ball seems to bounce off the top of his foot and lobs gracefully over the keeper into the net. It is a bizarrely spectacular strike, either Goal Of The Month or Fluke Of The Month.

Southampton respond by bringing on Saints favourite, Matthew Le Tissier. One of the most gifted footballers of his generation, Le Tissier's full potential has perhaps never been realised due to his 'struggles with fitness'. I'm trying to be tactful here, but it has been alleged that no pie has ever got the better of Sir Matthew. His arrival is greeted by the Sunderland fans with chants of 'Belly's gonna get yer!' from the recent Reebok advertisement. Ah, the rapier wit of the terraces.

Inspired by Le Tiss, Southampton push up and a Beattie strike beats Sorenson, only for Carteron to clear off the line. Minutes later, Beattie is clear with enough time to pull up a chair, light his pipe and read a good book, but still he shoots hopelessly wide. In the final stages, the Saints miss two more easy chances and we hold out for the victory. It wasn't a match that justified my efforts to get here, but I've seen us win, I've seen our last ever game at The Dell, and with just two games to go, I think I'm going to make it.

Saturday, 28 April 2001
SOUTHAMPTON 0   SUNDERLAND 1
(Kilbane 54)

PLAYED	TRAVELLED	SPENT	POSITION	STATE OF MIND
45	17,424 miles	£2,531.23	7th	So that's what it feels like to win

Charlton Athletic (home) – Premier League

To say these men paid their shillings to watch twenty-two hirelings kick a ball is merely to say that a violin is wood and catgut, that Hamlet is so much paper and ink.
– FROM THE GOOD COMPANIONS BY J.B. PRIESTLEY

The former Labour leader Michael Foot has discovered the secret of eternal life. He has declared that he will not die until Plymouth Argyle win the Premiership.

That's certainly one reason to support a football team, but generally if you ask someone 'Why do you support Grimsdale United?' the reply may offer little more than Mallory's 'Because it's there'. Why did fifteen hundred Sunderland fans travel six hundred miles, despite floods and rail chaos, to watch the Lads play Bristol Rovers in the rain on a cold Tuesday night? Why do thousands continue to watch lower-division teams whose past suggests the future will offer little more than struggle, both on and off the pitch? Why did the supporters of Palace, Charlton, Bournemouth, Brighton and the world's most famous small team, Accrington Stanley, mount passionate campaigns to save their clubs? Why, in the words of Arty, do we bother, pet?

The great questions of philosophy have rarely yielded simple answers. What is the meaning of life? Why are we here? What was all that Cantona stuff about seagulls and trawlers? One thing is clear: people don't support a team for its success. In fact, quite the reverse. Manchester United fans are generally dismissed by the rest of the football community precisely because watching the Reds involves little pain. Any fool can follow success. Failure is a higher calling.

Hope, romance, glory? Glory is scarce and fleeting. While every team has its moment in the sun, for many it comes as frequently as Halley's Comet, too rare a day to spend years awaiting its arrival. The FA Cup can still offer romance, but again only for a few whose brief affair inevitably ends in heartbreak. And hope? While hope is universal at the start of a season, it is soon dashed as reality takes hold. Indeed, as the Sunderland fanzine declared, 'It's the hope I can't stand.' Yet still they come.

There must be something stronger, more constant, not dependent upon triumph or fame, something that appeals on a deeper emotional level. For J.B. Priestley, to go to a match was to become 'a member of a new community, all brothers together for an hour and a half'. Supporting a football team offers identity, comradeship and social acceptance, a chance to join a cause, help shape its destiny and create its tradition. It's your tribe, united, regardless of all else. Victory and defeat are shared alike, each high and low another family tie.

Football is all about emotion. Women who complain that men are unable to show commitment or express emotion should go to a game. You can't be a fan without commitment. Stress, angst, despair and disappointment – see you next match. Emotions? Take your pick: passion, anger, laughter, the occasional tears but more often unadulterated joy. I've been lucky in both my professional and personal life but for simple joy, nothing, absolutely nothing, comes even close to that explosion of sheer happiness when my team scores. I know the old chestnut about scoring being like sex. My experience of one is only vicarious, but George Best and Kevin Phillips maintain they are different and that's good enough for me. Ecstasy and joy are not mutually exclusive, but different mountains in the same range. At the SOL, you see archetypal blokes hugging each other when we score, but I don't think it's sexual (they're just really good friends).

A match is perhaps the only public arena where you can truly let rip with your emotions. It's almost a regression to childhood. You might not be able to run around, but you can make as much noise as you like. The worst excesses of drudgery and hardship in the mines, shipyards and factories may be no more, but there are still many jobs where emotion has no release. Telesales centres, production lines and service industries all restrict the display of true feelings. A week of dealing politely with pain-in-the-bum customers requires a little expression. Basil Fawlty should have spent more time watching Torquay United.

Ultimately, there is only one sensation that can do justice to how a true fan feels about their team, why they carry on supporting them through the bad times. At Sunderland it is a recurring theme, reflected in the fanzine, songs and chants. 'I can't help falling in love with you, it's a love supreme, so stand up if you love Sunderland, because we love you, Sunderland, we do.' Most crucially, it is a love that will never be spurned, one based on mutual need and the only constant in life from childhood to death.

Beyond this surging wave of emotions, the game can appeal as sublime entertainment. Priestley spoke of football offering both Conflict and Art and at its height, it is perfect theatre, part of Brecht's 'ultimate theatre' of sport. The two acts unfold with scenes of comedy, tragedy and impossible drama, a tale played out by heroes and villains that you, the audience, can both critique and help shape. Our victory at Newcastle will persist above many other derby games as an adventure of classic dimensions. The small band of warriors, setting out on a perilous journey against overwhelming odds, suffering an early setback but finally triumphant, despite almost having victory snatched away at the death. You couldn't write it.

Or you can dismiss all the above as a load of pretentious waffle. It's really very simple. When a stunned Alex Ferguson was interviewed just seconds after Man United had snatched the European Cup with two last-minute goals, he perfectly encapsulated everything I've been trying to say.

'Football – bloody hell!'

It is twenty-eight years to the day since Sunderland gave me my life moment by winning the Cup, and as a perfect tribute, the team is lead out by eight-year old James Kerr, son of skipper Bobby. Me? No, no, I'm fine, just something in my eye.

Charlton, of course, complete the Wembley connection, as the opponents from our other final that acquired legendary status. Today they too are clinging to the finest of threads from which hang their chances of qualifying for Europe, so this is going to be no end-of-season stroller.

For the first ten minutes Sunderland are passing and running well, with both Phillips and Kilbane looking lively. Then Kilbane picks up a Quinn header inside his own half and, like a racehorse given his head, he's off. Over the half-way line, past one, two Charlton players. He cuts inside and makes for goal. This is a brilliant run and the crowd's on its feet. Up into top, he's past another defender and is now approaching the penalty area. As he reaches the box, he clips a swerving left-foot shot with the outside of his boot that curves gracefully into the top corner. Get in, Killa! It's a brilliant solo effort and the stadium rises to applaud a player who seems to be coming through the bad times. The next minute, Mickey Gray sends over a trademark cross and Quinny's header squeaks just past the post.

Well, quite an opening. Unlike our lacklustre display at Coventry, we clearly want this and the crowd are up. Charlton are also in there battling, and Johansson pounces on a rare error by Craddock to force another save from our Miracle Man.

Next Charlton attack, a cross bends over into our box. Craddock and Thome both miss it, Johansson heads back across goal and it looks to be going out past the far post. But Powell just manages to hook it back in again, we still fail to clear and Svensson scissor-kicks a spectacular volley for the equaliser.

Right, if that's the way you want it. A minute later, Stefan Schwarz sends over a measured cross to the far post, where Quinn rises above two defenders and loops a classic header into the far corner. So there.

Yet here they come again. A good Charlton move ends with a shot just over the bar and this is turning into one hell of a match. Kilbane's playing like a man inspired, Charlton have another rasping drive, then a Sunderland corner is scrambled off the line. When Johansson breaks through, he looks certain to equalise until McCann robs him with a tackle as clean and sharp as a scalpel. Taking us up to half-time, Phillips has two more efforts before we can all finally take a breather.

During the interval, Rupert Prokofiev, the sixteen-year-old grandson of composer Serge Prokofiev, comes onto the pitch to a huge welcome. Russian composers always seem shrouded in mystery. You don't really expect their offspring to be living over here and supporting Charlton Athletic.

Ready for the second half? OK, hold on, here we go.

Phillips instantly picks up the game with a shot to test Charlton keeper, Sasa Ilic. Then from a corner, Hutchison swings in a cross and Phillips breaks through a line of four defenders to volley home his first goal in six games. It's much deserved after all his efforts and the stadium cheers in delight to salute its favourite son.

Well, that should just about do . . . I don't believe it. Within two minutes of Phillips' goal, Charlton break down the left, and from the cross, Jensen drives past fellow Dane, Sorenson. In our first home match with Charlton since Wembley, we're re-creating the final. To quote '50s baseball legend, Yogi Berra, 'It's déjà-vu all over again'.

Another two minutes and a deflected Charlton shot nearly grabs the equaliser. It's like watching two perfectly-matched boxers. Young Kevin Kyle comes on for Quinn and nearly scores with his first touch, then a Phillips header is cleared off the line. Into the last fifteen minutes and Charlton hit us with everything. From a corner, Todd hits the post and Fish blasts over from just seven yards. In the last minute, another Charlton cross swings in. Substitute striker Kevin Lisbie beats everyone to send his header a whisker past the post. The whole stadium groans in relief or pain, and we scrape our first home win since New Year's Day.

Football – bloody hell!

Saturday, 5 May 2001

SUNDERLAND 3   CHARLTON ATHLETIC 2

(Kilbane 11, Quinn 20, Phillips 50)   (Svensson 18, Jensen 59)

PLAYED	TRAVELLED	SPENT	POSITION	STATE OF MIND
46	17,988 miles	£2,593.53	7th	Have you got my nerve pills, dear?

Everton (away) – Premier League

*It was like Frank Sinatra. I thought he
was doing encores out there.*
— PETER REID

I arrive at Euston for the train to Liverpool to be greeted with the following notice from Virgin Rail: 'Due to a system fault the train reporting system is not working. All trains will be displayed as operating on time.' Or to paraphrase a current terrace chant, 'We're crap and we know we are.'

Sunderland's seasons, as I said at the outset, usually end in do-or-die struggles of promotion or relegation and, incredibly, it's the same this year. Although I thought we had bid adieu to any chance of the UEFA Cup, we now do have a slender chance of promotion to Europe but, as always, it depends on other results. If Chelsea lose at relegated Manchester City and we win at Everton, then we're in, but only that combination will suffice. Actually we can also do it if Chelsea draw, but we'd need to beat Everton by eighteen goals.

So, in a spirit of *c'est la vie* the Mackems descend on Merseyside, the carnival atmosphere enhanced by fancy dress, most of which seems to have been inspired by *Star Wars*. Although the fans are mixing in good humour, the force is certainly with us, as the police are much in evidence. One constabulary group loiters suitably beneath a Tory Party poster proclaiming, 'You've paid the taxes, so where are the police?'

Although Goodison Park dates back to 1892, it was not Everton's first home. Many Victorian teams had only a tenuous hold on their early pitches, and after a financial dispute with the owner of their ground, Everton moved to Goodison. Left with a pitch but no players, their former landlord created a new team. If Everton had just kept paying the rent, Liverpool might never have been born.

Over one hundred years later, Goodison now seems an organic part of the surrounding narrow streets. One corner of the ground is formed by St Luke's church, whose accompanying hall serves tea and snacks on match days. Inside, the scene resembles a BBC drama set in the '50s, as cheery church ladies dispense tea in gilt-edged cups with non-matching saucers. Uplifting posters proclaim, 'We can refresh your body but the Lord can refresh your soul' and 'I will take the Cup of Salvation' (unless AXA get it first). In addition to rock cakes, you can also buy badges to help support former Everton players.

As a founder member of the Football League in 1888, Everton are one of the guardians of the game's soul. With a style of play that saw them dubbed 'The School of Science', they achieved sufficient success to be eternally regarded as a 'big' club, even in the years of struggle. In the club shop, a small museum contains a few tantalising remnants of that tradition: a season ticket for 1886–87, no larger than a book of matches. A pair of Alan Ball's white boots from the early '70s (I used to have a pair of those, but I was still useless). Pride of place is a thick woollen football jersey worn by '20s legend, William 'Dixie' Dean. His incredible tally of sixty goals in season 1927–28 assured both Everton of the title and Dean of immortality, and his status as Goodison deity has just been officially recognised with a large bronze statue outside the ground. It's never easy to appreciate players from another era. Facts and figures offer only their deeds, not how they played or stirred the soul. When I remember Best, it is not how many goals he scored, but how he scored them. But Dean was obviously a bit special, and clearly impressed a young Bill Shankly: 'The only way to stop him scoring was to hold his legs, and when he headed the ball it frightened the life out of people.'

Of late, Everton could do with another legend. For a club whose motto is *Nil Satis Nisi Optimum* (Only The Best Is Good Enough), they've had to accept significantly less. This season is the fifth consecutive year when the team have finished in the bottom third of the table, and the main fanzine, *Satis?* (Good Enough?) simmers with injured pride. Many Blues fans see the proposed move to a new stadium by the docks as the ideal opportunity to rejuvenate the club, but initial optimism has turned to suspicion and scepticism. Fans hand out leaflets claiming conspiracy connections between the owners of the docklands and Everton's main rivals for the site.

While Goodison Park is not exactly falling down, it certainly looks a bit weary. There is only one modern stand, although the huge three-tiered Main Stand is still impressive. But what it doesn't lack is atmosphere and you've no doubt as to what colour the home team play in. Everything is blue: the seats, the stands, even the perimeter track. And a club so steeped in tradition and identity is not going to change its tune. As Everton run out of the tunnel, it's still to the theme of *Z-Cars*, the old BBC series. This was also Sunderland's tune up to their last match at Roker Park – which just happened to be against Everton.

Although the match is potentially important for us, the opening ten minutes are just midfield hustle and bustle. Then Everton get a free kick on the edge of our area. Idan Tal's blasted shot hits our defensive wall and deflects past a wrong-footed Sorenson. Last year we lost here 0–5. This is not a good start.

However the goal spurs us on and we have a penalty shout when Thome's header appears to be handled in the box, but you know our luck with penalties. Someone nearby with a radio: 'Chelsea are one up.' So, it's all looking peachy.

Our first real chance comes when McCann cleverly works his way down the right and crosses for Quinn to head just over. Then Phillips hits a twenty-yard drive and we're starting to click. After twenty minutes, Arca chips a ball into the box to apparently no one, but suddenly Phillips is there on his own. With his back to goal, he kills the ball on his chest and in one sublime move, spins, controls and shoots past keeper Gerrard to equalise. It's a difficult goal made easy by a piece of superb skill.

Now we take charge, with McCann brilliant in midfield. Following his superb goal against Charlton, Kilbane has another glory run into the area, but this time his shot is parried away. Arca nearly grabs our second with a curling free kick, and right up to half-time we dominate the game. Everton's only effort comes in injury time when Pembridge fires a low drive that Sorenson tips onto the post.

At half-time, my remarks about Goodison not actually falling down seem premature. A water pipe in our stand has fallen away and is flooding the seats and concourse. First one steward arrives. Then another. Then a policeman and finally a maintenance man with spanner and some tape. None of them know what to do, so a Mackem plumber helps fix the problem. I think the sooner Everton move the better.

Manchester City are now level with Chelsea. All we have to do is win 19–1.

For the second half, Don Hutchison comes on as sub to a standing ovation from the home crowd. Along with Gavin McCann, Hutch is one of several Sunderland players with Everton connections, Reid himself being from their glory side of the mid-'80s when they twice came close to winning the Double.

The Blues begin again in livelier fashion, but it's Phillips who has the first chance. Running onto a Quinn flick, he's clear of the defence with just Gerrard to beat, but blasts straight at the keeper's legs. Everton respond with a free kick that smacks against the bar.

Manchester City 1 Chelsea 2.

Buoyed by the near miss, Everton press again. Unsworth runs onto a pass into our penalty area. He's beaten the back four and only Hutch is anywhere near him. With a desperate tackle, Hutch brings him down and it's a penalty. Being the last man, the Sunderland midfielder is also sent off, but as he leaves the pitch he receives another ovation from the home crowd. He must have scored against Liverpool.

Unsworth lines up the penalty. After his save against Shearer, you'd back Tommy to stop anything. And he does! Diving low and right he palms it away to a roar from the Mackems.

The incident lifts the game and tackles start flying in everywhere. Carteron is tripped by Weir in the area, but naturally we don't get the decision. Then Craddock brings down Naysmith in the box with a rather innocuous challenge, so of course it's another penalty for Everton. None of us really expect even Tommy to save a second – and he doesn't. For the fourth time this season, we are a goal down with just ten men. With ten minutes left and Chelsea still winning, I think it's time to put away the passports.

Yet Sunderland keep pushing. With eight minutes left, Phillips nips onto a flick by substitute Kyle, squeezes past the last defender and from a tight angle, blasts a shot high into the net. We might not make Europe, but we're not out of this match.

Injury time. A pass back to the Everton keeper gives us an indirect free kick in the box. The Everton players complain, so the ref moves it forward ten yards. The ball is now just seven yards out, with Everton players crowding the goal line. It's a chance not only to win the game but for Phillips to end the season on a hat-trick and silence his critics. Kev blasts the kick. It beats Gerrard, but full-back Watson jumps instinctively, and the ball flashes off his head and over the bar. Three inches either way and it would have been in.

With Chelsea's win, our result was meaningless, but we didn't lose and nearly snatched it after another great fightback. We applaud the players and they respond likewise. Sorenson throws his gloves into the crowd, Phillips his boots (now there's a souvenir). As Thome attempts the same, a steward tries to stop him, but with Brazilian flamboyance, Emerson hurls the boots over the protesting official into the crowd. The players turn and leave the pitch to our farewell chants.

I've done it.

Saturday, 19 May 2001

EVERTON 2　　　　　　SUNDERLAND 2

(Tal 10, Ball 77)　　　　(Phillips 21, 82)

PLAYED	TRAVELLED	SPENT	POSITION	STATE OF MIND
47	18,426 miles	£2,651.68	7th	Mission Accomplished

Extra Time

Phew. It's over. Expensive, time-consuming, nerve-wracking, exhausting. Hundreds of hours and thousands of miles. And I wouldn't have missed it for the world, a lifetime's ambition and a unique season. There were defeats and downfalls, fiascos and flops, inevitable potholes on the road to famous victories. It was precisely the lows of Middlesbrough and Derby, Man City and Leicester, Coventry and Palace that heightened the highs of Arsenal, Chelsea and Newcastle. You have to suffer to enjoy it.

Any review of a season is about what might have been. It's easy to claim that the errors of officials in our home games against Man United, Liverpool, Leeds and Villa cost us a place in Europe. But we also benefited from questionable decisions in our favour: the disallowed goals of Coventry, Boro, Liverpool and Southampton; the penalty at Arsenal; Hutchison's quick free kicks against Man City and West Ham, that in other matches had to be re-taken. If inconsistent and poor refereeing cost us vital points, it also saved us a few. We've probably ended up roughly where we deserve to be, which ultimately is rather disappointing. After lying second in January, to have missed out on Europe is hard to accept, although I suspect we would struggle with our present squad. The turning point for me was the home match against Bradford in January. A win would have maintained our momentum, even though we probably wouldn't have caught United, but the draw knocked our confidence for the next three months.

We finished seventh with fifty-seven points after a twelve-match New Year slump. Last year we finished seventh with fifty-seven points after a twelve-match New Year slump. I've travelled 18,426 miles to watch Sunderland end up right back where they started. My team have become football's answer to *Groundhog Day*.

Next season? A couple more strikers, some cover for the full-backs, but what is crucial is a killer instinct. Aside from Man United and Leeds, we did relatively well against the top teams, but failed to punish the lower clubs. Next year is all about Europe. If we fail to qualify, the knives will be out for Reid, but I think he's safe with Murray. My prediction? Fifth.

Would I do it all again? My journey certainly wasn't unique. There are many for whom seeing every game is an annual quest of devotion and sacrifice. Holidays vanish in mid-week trips, while savings dwindle on tickets and train fares, programmes and pints, fanzines and fish cakes. But I can't see me repeating my trek. For the last nine months my life has been on hold. I've battled floods, fuel protests, train timetables, ticket offices, National Express, Railtrack, Sky, the railway companies, car-hire firms, and navigationally-impaired coach drivers. To continue that indefinitely is simply not possible. Of course, with a season ticket, I'll still go to all the home matches. And naturally I won't miss our London games. Ipswich and Southampton are just an hour away, as are all the Midlands teams. Obviously, I can't miss the derbies at Newcastle and Boro, or the big games at Man United, Liverpool and Leeds. Then there are the two promoted sides, Bolton and Blackburn, I have to see their grounds, and . . . oh well, here we go again . . .

Bibliography

Television

Dick Clement and Ian la Frenais, *Whatever Happened To The Likely Lads*, BBC, 1973

Books and articles

Norman Baker, *Have They Forgotten Bolton?*, The Sports Historian, The British Society of Sports History, May 1998

Joan C. Beal, *From Geordie Ridley to Viz: popular literature in Tyneside in English*, Language and Literature, 9 (4), 2000

Joan C. Beal, *'Geordie Nation': Language and Regional Identity in the North-east of England*, Lore and Language 16, 2001

Paul Callaghan and John Hudson, *Sunderland AFC: The Official History 1879–2000*, Sunderland AFC Press, 2000

Denis Campbell, 'Football chiefs in plea for stand on terraces', *The Observer*, 25 February 2001

Garth Dykes and Doug Lamming, *All The Lads – A Complete Who's Who of Sunderland AFC*, Sunderland AFC Press, 2000

Simon Hattenstone, 'Stan Collymore – All Played Out', *The Guardian*, 16 April 2001

Jimmy Hill, *The Jimmy Hill Story – My Autobiography*, Hodder & Stoughton, 1998

Paul Joannou, *Newcastle United 1882–1992: The First One Hundred Years – And More*, Polar Publishing, 2000

Simon Kuper, 'Safe Standing – Stuff your Sitzplatzhorrors', *The Observer*, 25 February 2001

Simon Lee, *Bringing The Game into Disrepute? The BSkyB Bid for Manchester United PLC*, Dept of Politics and Asian Studies, Hull University, 3 February 1999

Stanley Matthews, *The Way It Was – My Autobiography*, Headline, 2000

David Powter and Michael Robinson, *Sunderland FC The 25 Year Record 1971–1996*, Soccer Book Publishing Limited, 1996

J.B. Priestley, *The Good Companions*, 1929

William Shakespeare, *Henry V*

Robert S. Shiels, *Fatalities At The Ibrox Disaster of 1902*, UMIST

Colin Shindler, *Manchester United Ruined My Life*, Headline 1996

Hugh Tisdale and Marcus Tate, *Chelsea 2000: The Official Graphic History*, Sportsdays 2001

'The Hatfield Crash – Special Report', *The Guardian*, October 2000

Newspapers, magazines, fanzines

5573, SAFCSA (London & Southern England Branch)

A Love Supreme, ALS Publications, Sunderland

The Birmingham Post

City Gent, David Pendleton, Bradford

The Coventry Evening Telegraph

The Daily Express

The Daily Mail

The Evening Chronicle

The Journal

Legion Of Light, Sunderland AFC Press

The Observer

Satis, Phil Pellow, Everton

Sex & Chocolate aren't as good as football, ALS Publications, Sunderland

The Sunday Times

The Sunderland Echo

The Times

The Wearside Roar, Northeast Press

Matchday Programmes 2000–01

Arsenal

Boro (Middlesbrough)

Chelsea

City (Manchester City)

Claret & Amber (Bradford City)

Coventry City

Crystal Palace

Everton

Hammers (West Ham United)
Ipswich Town
Leeds United
Leicester City
Liverpool
Luton Town
Newcastle United
Red'N'White Review (Sunderland)
Spurs (Tottenham Hotspur)
The Ram (Derby County)
The Saints (Southampton)
The Pirate (Bristol Rovers)
United Review (Manchester United)
Valley Review (Charlton Athletic)
Villa (Aston Villa)

Websites

www.anvil.clara.net/cockney
www.arsenal.co.uk
www.arsenal-world.net
www.astonvilla-fc.co.uk
www.bradfordcityfc.co.uk
www.bristolrovers.co.uk
www.cafc.co.uk
www.ccfc.co.uk
www.chelseafc.co.uk
www.contrast.org/hillsborough
www.cpfc.co.uk
www.cpst.org.uk
www.dcfc.co.uk
www.derbyuk.net
www.dmm.org.uk/colliery
www.evertonfc.com
www.footballgroundguide.co.uk
www.itfc.co.uk
www.lcfc.co.uk
www.liverpoolfc.net
www.lufc.co.uk
www.mcfc.co.uk

www.mfc.co.uk
www.nufc.co.uk
www.pbs.org/wgbh/nova
www.readytogo.net
www.rsssf.com
www.safc.com
www.saintsfc.co.uk
www.san.beck.org/AB21-Europe13thCentury.html
www.soccer-fanzine.co.uk
www.spurs.co.uk
www.standupifyouhatemanu.com/fanzineworld
www.stateliners.freeserve.co.uk
www.sunderland.com/localhist
www.the-afs.com
www.thenortheast.fsnet.co.uk/Sunder.htm
www.umist.ac.uk/sport
www.whufc.co.uk